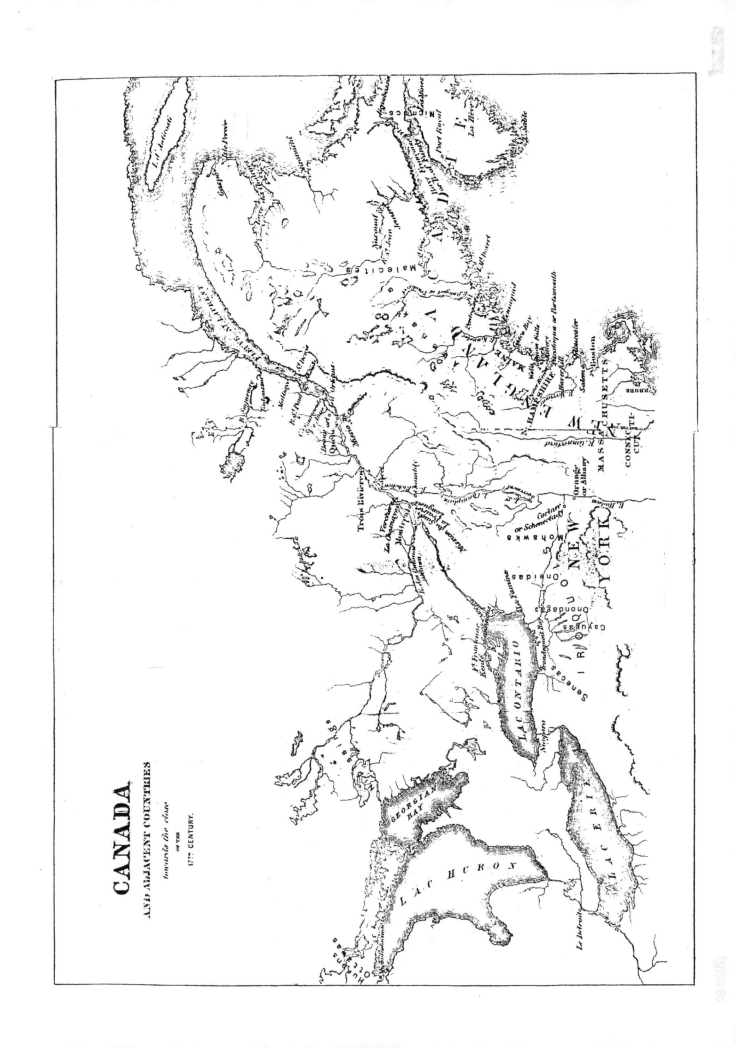

Richard Shute

of
Boston, Massachusetts,
1631-1703,
and
Selected Progeny

WITH A BRIEF DISCUSSION OF HIS BROTHER,
WILLIAM SHUTE, ALSO OF BOSTON

Alan H. Shute
AND
Clark H. Flint

HERITAGE BOOKS
2017

HERITAGE BOOKS
AN IMPRINT OF HERITAGE BOOKS, INC.

Books, CDs, and more—Worldwide

For our listing of thousands of titles see our website
at
www.HeritageBooks.com

Published 2017 by
HERITAGE BOOKS, INC.
Publishing Division
5810 Ruatan Street
Berwyn Heights, Md. 20740

International Standard Book Number
Paperbound: 978-0-7884-0348-4

Richard Shute

of
Boston
Massachusetts
1631-1703
&
Selected Progeny

With a Brief Discussion of His Brother, William Shute, also of Boston.

---

by

Alan H. Shute & Clark H. Flint

HERITAGE BOOKS, INC.

Published 1995 by

Heritage Books, Inc.
1540-E Pointer Ridge Pl.
Bowie, MD 20716
1-800-398-7709

ISBN 0-7884-0348-6

A Complete Catalog Listing Hundreds of Titles on
History, Genealogy and Americana
Available Upon Request.

Table of Contents

*****

*****

Preface

"...good Puritan blood of the stanchest strain"

In her history of Malden, Massachusetts, published in 1899, the author, Ms. Deloraine Pendre Corey, noted that the Reverend "Daniel Shute, son of John and Mary (Waite) Shute ... inherited good Puritan blood of the stanchest [sic] strain; for his father was a grandson of Deacon John Greenland, and his mother a granddaughter of Captain John Waite." This work is concerned with his <u>other</u> than Puritan strain, the Shutes, and commences with a discussion of his great-grandfather, Richard Shute (1631-1703), mariner, sometimes of Boston, in the province of Massachusetts Bay.

I am reminded of a conversation overheard in the historic Bruton Parish Church in Williamsburg, Virginia, not so long ago, in which the volunteer docent, in a strained Chesapeake accent, explained to an innocent tourist: "Dear, this isn't New England. We didn't come here for religion. Virginians came here to make money." I venture to say the same holds true for the Shutes of 17th-century New England and the Caribbean.

Mariner, trader, merchant, and privateer -- all are appropriate in describing the immigrant, Richard Shute, and indeed, his sons, Captains Michael and Richard Shute, or his sons-in-law, Captains Nathaniel Nichols and Joseph Buckley, for that matter. That the distinction between these professions and those of smuggler, illegal arms-dealer, rum-runner and pirate may have occasionally overlapped, is something of an enigma to many soon to be, 21st-century descendants, but from a 17th-century perspective, life held no such contradictions. Suffice it to say, that whatever the endeavor, a true Shute never shirked from opportunity, nor from what history might call it.

They also ate, drank, smoked, brawled, enjoyed sex, gave birth, prayed, and cared for one another. They erred, forgave, and were forgiven. They were, and remain, our people. From them came noted ministers, doctors, lawyers, scientists, military officers and teachers. And then there were still others, like you and me.

The following is an attempt to document the descendants of Richard Shute (1631-1703) of Boston, mariner, and to a lesser degree, those of his brother, William Shute, mariner, also of Boston. It is an incomplete and ongoing work. It is a beginning, rather than an end. Continued study of Suffolk and Middlesex deed, court and probate records will undoubtedly shed still further light on these early colonists, as will further research of English and West Indies primary sources. The compilers wish to thank all that contributed to this project, and would hope to hear from those families not included for simple want of data. Correspondence may be addressed to Alan H. Shute, 7948 Harwood Place, Springfield, Virginia 22152.

Clark H. Flint
Evanston, Illinois

Acknowledgements

The compilers wish to thank the following individuals and institutions. Without their help, support and contributions, this work could never have been attempted. Thanks are due too, to our parents and relations for instilling an interest in our family's past, and providing the impetus to preserve it.

Of old friends and new-found family, thanks go to Bob Merchant of Danvers, MA (deceased), Mildred Shute Smith of Annisquam, MA, Lillian Shute of Markville, MN, Doris Shute of Sebastion, FL, Ginny Woodman Cordes of Glen Mills, PA, Margery Brooke of Newfields, NH (deceased), Barbara Shute Friberg of Gloucester, MA, Edith Shute Tirone of Amesbury, MA, Nan Rice Shute of Washington, DC (deceased), Emma Fredericks of Everett, MA, Jessie Richmond Hooper of Ft. Myers, FL, Araba G. Clark of Springfield, MA, Wayne L. Plummer of Moorhead, MN, Mabel Moyer of Jacksonville, FL, Richard R. Johnson of Seattle, WA, John D. Burton of Evanston, IL, Darrell T. Shute of Kettle Falls, WA, Margaret L. Wright Shute of Rochester, WA, Patricia Earl Shute of San Francisco, CA, Philip K. Shute of Ft. Myers, FL, and Kenneth E. Shute of Concord, NH.

Of the nation's archives and research institutions, our special thanks go to the Massachusetts Historical Society of Boston, MA, the Archives & Records Preservation Department of the Supreme Judicial Court in Boston, MA, the Massachusetts Archives in Boston, MA, the New England Historic Genealogical Society of Boston, MA, the National Genealogical Society of Arlington, VA, the National Archives of Washington, DC, the DAR Library of Washington, DC, the Library of Congress, the Smithsonian Institution, the Mormon Family Research Centers of Annandale, VA, and Wilmette, IL, the Newberry Library of Chicago, IL, the Everett Historical Society of Everett, MA, and the Public Libraries of Portland, ME, and Winnetka, IL.

Introduction

The following is a record of facts. They are the facts as we know them of the immigrant brothers, Richard Shute (1631-1703) and William Shute (c1633?-c1668) of Boston, Massachusetts, as well as of their progeny. Facts, however, when few and far between, as often is the case in 17th-century New England, require a bit of "glue." That "glue," is educated conjecture, and as such, is in high demand in explaining the world in which these Shutes, immigrant mariners, and their children, lived and thrived.

Even pairing Richard and William Shute as brothers has required a good bit of conjecture based, primarily, on circumstantial evidence that places the two Shutes within doors of one another in Boston's North End, and presumes that the "kinsman" mentioned in Richard Shute's will of 1703, is that of his nephew, William Shute, Jr., son of William Shute, Sr., and son-in-law of Edward Budd, a Boston ship's carver. Further credence to this assumption is found in Boston's deed record: William Shute, Sr.'s lot and house on Battery Alley is identified as belonging to Richard Shute, Sr. in two deeds recorded after William Shute, Sr.'s death and before William Shute, Jr.'s coming of legal age. Thereafter, the property is described as the land of William Shute, Jr.

As so little is known of William Shute, this work focuses on his brother, Richard Shute, Sr. To understand how the immigrant, Richard Shute, interacted with Boston or Massachusetts, or the fur-trading regions of Maine, or the fishing villages of Acadia in French Canada (now Nova Scotia) in the late 17th century -- as he obviously did -- it is important to remember who and what Richard Shute was, as well as what he wasn't.

To begin with, Richard Shute was not a Pilgrim. They arrived over 35 years prior, and decamped on a craggy rock in an altogether different province (Plymouth). By Richard Shute's time, those Separatist English immigrants were long integrated into a far more secular world.

Further, Richard Shute was not a Puritan. He did not arrive in Winthrop's Fleet, nor as part of the Great Migration of settlers and planters that followed. From what we can surmise, he wasn't even married when he reached these shores, prior to 1659. He brought with him no fame or fortune to sustain him, no farming skills or city trade to employ him. He was a mariner and an Englishman, plain and simple. With hard work, a bit of luck, and the right connections, the New World might provide a better life than he or his brother, William, had known in Bristol, or London, or wherever they were from.

As such, Richard and William Shute's initial voyage(s) to New England could have landed them anywhere. Further, they could have been sailing from virtually any port. Up from Barbadoes or Nevis, working as seamen aboard a trading vessel? Or across from England, to join the fishing fleets off Newfoundland? We may never know.

Did Richard and William Shute already have relatives here? Possibly. There were too many Shutes in 17th-century North America and too few extant records to prove or disprove familial relationships. What can and should be clarified, however, is the fact that the immigrant, Richard Shute of Boston (1631-1703) cannot be one in the same as either the Richard Shute of Milford (1642), the Richard Shute of Pemaquid (1651), or the

Richard Shute of East Chester, NY (1665), although there is speculation that all of these last three were, indeed, the same person. And further, that William Shute of Boston (c1633?-c1668) cannot be one in the same as the 29-year old, William Shute who provided a deposition to the Boston court on 9-Aug-1672, although there is speculation that the latter William Shute was one and the same with the William Shute of Jamaica who married Joseph Deacons' widow, Rachel Allen, daughter of Hope and Rachel Allen of Boston, prior to 1671.

Of Richard Shute, the man, or even his wives, Elizabeth and Katherine, we know very little. At his best, he could be described as a member of the lesser merchant-trader class. From what we can reconstruct from existing records, it would seem that Richard Shute was a law-abiding, tax-paying English citizen, who had risen from the ranks of mariner and seaman, to trader and merchant, by exchanging trade goods procured in Boston with the pro-French Indians in Maine and Acadia for furs. The demand for beaver, muskrat and moose pelts, by the mercantile houses of Boston made these long and arduous trading voyages comfortably profitable. With his profits, he bought more goods and returned to trade, again and again. He knew the waters of Pemaquid, like the back of his hand -- knowledge undoubtedly shared with his son, Richard, who was to later pilot the Royal Frigate "Rose" to Pemaquid in 1688.

From trade goods, Richard Shute diversified into buying "shares" of vessels -- much as one would invest in shares of mutual funds today -- and in real estate. If one's ship came in, as it were, laden with Barbadian sugar and lime juice, or fine Madeira and Canary wines, or, possibly African slaves, the profits were substantial. As for property, Richard Shute not only purchased a home in the North End of Boston, but provided a home across the river, in Charlestown, for his daughter, Joanna, and her second husband, Joseph Buckley. He also invested wisely in a working farm in Malden, complete with house, barn and out buildings.

For his sons, Richard Shute provided contacts, if not entry, to the merchant-trader class of pre-1689 Boston. That date is a significant one, for it speaks of Boston under the rule of Governor Edmund Andros, and the reign of James II. After that date, the Glorious Revolution swept James II from the throne and installed the Dutch-speaking William of Orange with James' daughter, Mary, as co-regents. In Boston, a street-riot mob imprisoned Andros and as many members of Boston's Anglican church as could be caught. The latter was readily pertinent to Richard Shute and his family.

By necessity, if not definition, the Boston merchant-trader class was closely bound to the power of the King in colonial New England. For it was the power of the king that regulated commerce -- be it through the Lords of Trade, the royal-appointed Governor, or the equally-powerful Customs Collector. How well one benefited from those in power was determined by how well one got along with those in power. While officially tolerant of the Puritans, the Catholic James II resented their autonomy in matters of self-rule and commerce, and perhaps had not forgotten that many New Englanders had returned to fight with Cromwell's forces in overthrowing and beheading his father, Charles I. Eventually James II did away with Massachusetts' charter altogether, and created, under Andros, the Dominion of New England as a political reality, encompassing present-day Massachusetts, New Hampshire, Vermont, Maine, Rhode Island, Connecticut and New York.

Andros' mission was to centralize power throughout New England, in part, to better protect it from Indian or foreign invasions, but also to better regulate trade. That is, to keep the king's thumb in as many pies as possible. Naturally, Andros turned to those he thought he could trust for support, people like him -- mainstream Church of England Englishmen -- rather than the radical Puritan elite of Boston. The merchant class of Boston provided that support. That's not to say that all Boston merchants were Anglicans; Samuel Sewall was a notable, Puritan, exception. Nor is it to say that Boston's Anglican merchants weren't just as happy to see Andros leave, once deposed. However, Puritans did not command a majority among Boston merchant-traders. Anglicans like merchant Charles Lidget, and Anglican-sympathizers like Colonel Samuel Shrimpton, did.

To be an Anglican in 17th Century Puritan Massachusetts was not without its drawbacks. Church and "state" were not so clearly divided in the province in the late seventeenth and early eighteenth centuries, as they would be afterwards. Anglican births and marriages could only be "officially" recorded within the Congregationalist Church. As a result, many marriages and births were not recorded, in defiance of the Puritan church, by equally stubborn Anglicans. In addition, "freeman" status was granted by the General Court only to members in good standing of the Congregationalist Church, or to those endorsed by the Congregationalist Church.

It is most probable that Richard Shute and his children were members of the Anglican Church of England, prior to 1689. Of "evidence," one need only note that neither Richard Shute, nor his brother, William, nor their sons were made "freemen" by the general court; the absence of marriage records for either of Richard Shute's marriages, as well as the absence of birth records for his first two children; the fact that his daughter, Joanna, married the Anglican Joseph Buckley; the fact that his son, Michael, married into the Anglican Rainsford family; the fact that his granddaughter, Hannah Nichols, married into the Anglican Mountfort family; and the fact, that though his son, Richard, married the native-born daughter of a Puritan deacon (Greenland), there is no record of the marriage. Further, the likelihood of Governor Andros entrusting his life and his only frigate of the Royal Navy to the hands of a Puritan pilot in 1688, is somewhat doubtful.

When the Boston mob took to the streets on 18-Apr-1689, their anger was directed not only against Governor Andros, but to those they saw as abetting Andros, namely, the Anglicans of King's Chapel. Though none of Richard Shute's family was recorded as detained, the anti-Anglican sentiments aroused, lingered in Boston for some time.

In point, the Anglican advantage, enjoyed by many of Boston's merchant class under Andros, virtually disappeared after 1689. One rather telling sign of all this, among Shutes, was the sudden increase in records: In 1696, Richard Shute, Sr. became a member of the Second Church; in 1702, his daughter-in-law, Lydia (Greenland) Shute was received into the convenant at the Second Church, and subsequently had most of her children baptized there; in 1707, his son, Richard, was also received into the covenant and baptized at the Second; and starting in 1701, each of the elder Richard Shute's granddaughters by son, Michael, were married within the Congregationalist faith. Alas, the Shutes had become "Puritans." Or at least, Congregationalists.

Perhaps no one weathered the transition from Dominion to Glorious Revolution better, than Samuel Shrimpton. A one-time councilor for Andros, and Anglican sympathizer, he signed the petition demanding Andros' surrender, and served on the Committee of Safety that assumed power in 1689. The richest merchant in Boston in the 1680s, Shrimpton issued a power of attorney to Richard Shute's former partner, Thaddeus Maccarty, in 1681, to collect an outstanding debt, and most probably owned at least one of the vessels commanded by Richard Shute's sons. What one could no longer achieve through the Governor's patronage, it seemed, was obtainable through important merchants like Shrimpton, or Shrimpton's brother-in-law, Eliakim Hutchinson.

Samuel Shrimpton died in February, 1697/98; the elder Shute died in October, 1703. Shute was older; Shrimpton was richer. Shute's son, Michael, died in 1706. For the surviving son, Richard (1666-c1742), the world, i.e. Boston, had become a much different place. Shrimpton was gone, but another successful merchant, a Barbadian by the name of Hugh Hall, Jr. seemed supportive of his services. And after that, Hall's partner, Enoch Freeman, remained a friend and carried his account. It was Freeman, after all, not a Shute, that served as executor of the younger Richard Shute's estate in 1742/43.

Therein lies many questions and answers. Each of the younger Richard Shute's sons turned their backs to the sea. One became a Malden deacon, town clerk and farmer; another a Chelsea housewright, the other a Newbury shipbuilder. The age and the prospects of the English merchant-trader were coming to an end. The Shutes would become Americans.

Descendants of Richard & Elizabeth Shute

The following register report was generated utilizing Brothers Keeper 5.1 software, designed and developed by John Steed. Brothers Keeper software is available through him at 6907 Childsdale Road, Rockford, MI 49341.

Footnote citations, as well as an index to this report, follow immediately.

Each person in the direct family line is numbered in the order of their appearance in the register report (example: 1 - Richard, 2 - Joanna, 3 - Michael, etc.). Lowercase roman numerals are used to indicate the number of children and birth order in the family. When the record of a given person is expanded on a subsequent page (or pages) a plus sign will appear to the left of their cardinal number (example: + 3, + 223, +397), and that additional information will be found by turning ahead to that same cardinal number. If no further information is available on an individual, no plus sign appears to the left of their cardinal number.

Descendants of Richard & Elizabeth Shute

1. **Richard Shute** b. 1631, England?,[1] Occupation: Mariner, m. (1)
bef 1659, in Boston, Suffolk Co., MA?, **Elizabeth** -----, b. 1628, d.
8-Sep-1691, Boston, Suffolk Co., MA,[2] Buried: Copp's Hill Burial
Ground, Boston, MA, m. (2) bef Oct-1694, in Boston, Suffolk Co., MA,
Katherine -----, d. aft 1703, Boston, Suffolk Co., MA. Richard died
2-Oct-1703, Boston, Suffolk Co., MA,[3] Buried: 1703, Copp's Hill,
Boston, MA.

Richard Shute, Sr. was born in 1631 (according to his grave
stone), and reached Boston sometime prior to 1659. It is not known
whether his presumed brother, William Shute, sailed with him, or
arrived at an earlier or later date. William Shute is first documented
in Boston on 1-Jul-1659, the date of his marriage to Hopestill Viall.

The births of Richard and Elizabeth Shute's first two children,
Michael (b. cir 1659) and Joanna (b. cir 1661) were not recorded. The
remaining children, Elizabeth (27- Jan-1665), Richard (b.
31-Aug-1666), Elizabeth (b. 1-Jan- 1668) and William (b. 1-Oct-1670),
were born in Boston, Suffolk Co., MA.

It would seem that Richard Shute, Sr., was often away on trading
trips to "the Eastward," or Maine and Acadia. On 21-Mar-1671, Richard
Shute was "East," at "Muspeeky" (now Moosepeak or Mooosabec Reach, in
eastern Maine -- then considered French territory) with partners,
Edward Naylor and Thaddeus Maccarty, on a "trading voiadge" with the
Indians along the St. John's River.

Of Shute's partners, little is known of Thaddeus Maccarty, save
that he was commissioned by Governor Andros on 24-Mar-1688 to receive
contributions towards building an Anglican church (King's Chapel) in
Boston, and that he died in 1705, aged 65, having had at least eight
children by his wife, Elizabeth Johnson. One son, Thomas Maccarty,
graduated from Harvard in 1691.

Edward Naylor, on the other hand, was no stranger to the Boston
courts, wherein he was once described as a "frequenter of widow Alice
Thomas's baudy house," and most often appeared as a defendant for
failing to pay his creditors. Samuel Eliot Morison in his
introduction to "The Records of the Suffolk County Courts 1671-1680,"
refers to Naylor as "a well-known reprobate." Edward Naylor died
sometime after 1679.

In April, 1671, Richard Shute was at "Muskquash Cove" in Maine,
where, according to his sworn deposition of 15-Jan- 1672, given before
Edward Atkinson, Shute remembered "that being to the Eastward in a
barque in the Company of George Manning, Master of another barque in
Muskquash Cove, about the beginning of April last past, at which time
we did receive of Severall goods of John Perkins, which hee saide were
the Estate of Oliver Duncomb, William Waldren & Christopher Smith in
partnership, a good quantity of Beaver, Moose & other goods..."

Later that summer, in August, 1671, in what was then called
"Kabunkidle," Maine, Richard Shute, master of a barque, was recorded
as intervening in a dispute between a crewman and the same Christopher
Smith, master of a trading sloop. In return, Capt. Smith "sent off
his vessel ... by one Richard Shute three trading gunns, as tokens to
his wife at Boston." [Suffolk Co. Court Recs., Waldron v. Smith]

Richard's first wife, Elizabeth, was born in 1628. In Boston, on
7-Sep-1672, Elizabeth Shute was called to serve as a witness against

Edward Naylor (her husband's partner) at divorce proceedings brought by his wife, Catherine (Wheelright) Nanney Naylor, tried before the Courts of Assistants in Boston. Elizabeth Shute, however, was apparently excused from appearing, as the constable found her ill in bed. She later did give a deposition (5-Oct- 1671) regarding Edward Naylor's unmarried mistress, Mary Reed (aka Mary Moore or Mary Kimball), a prostitute who worked from widow Alice Thomas' bawdy house, by whom Naylor had an illegitimate daughter, Deborah, born 4-Sep-1668 in Hampton, NH.

In her deposition, Elizabeth Shute, "aged about 41 years," related problems she had with her lodger, William Browne, described as the "boatswain of Mr. Jones," and undoubtedly a member of the Royal Navy billeted with the Shutes for his stay in Boston. Browne, it seems, also procured the favors of Mary Reed, known to him as Mary More, and was caught leaving the Shute's house at 3:00 a.m. on at least one occasion to rendezvous with Ms. More at widow Thomas' house, by the "trumpeter of Mr. Jones," who had previously lent him three shillings. The trumpeter, however, did not blow the whistle on Mr. Browne. Rather it was Browne's dirty laundry that did him in.

Mrs. Shute had hired Mrs. Elizabeth Watts, "aged about 40 years," to wash the household's linens. Mrs. Watts shared certain information about Mr. Browne's "shift", or undergarment, which led the two ladies "to suspect he had bene foule of some woman." Prior to confronting Mr. Browne, Mrs. Shute shared the dirt, as it were, with her neighborhood friend, Mrs. Brookings -- Elizabeth Brookings, wife of John Brookings, the proprietor of The Salutation Tavern -- who, in turn, confirmed that Browne and More had been something of an item for weeks, according to the local grapevine. Once accused, Mr. Browne responded by informing Mrs. Shute that, "he would lye with any woman ye would let him." Elizabeth Shute's answer was that "he could lodge no more at my house." Richard Shute, incidentally, did not have a role in this domestic drama; the events unfolded "a month or a few weeks" after he had again put to sea.

Richard Shute first appears on the Boston tax rolls in 1674, and was included on the tax list of 1687. "Richard Shoot" and "Michael Shoot" were enumerated in a list of Boston inhabitants in 1695. On 8-Nov-1696, Richard Shute became a full member of the Second Church of Boston.

Published Suffolk County deeds show that Richard Shute bought parcels of land in Boston's North End as early as June 1670 through the Spring of 1682/83. According to these records, Richard Shute, Sr. owned all of these properties through 1697. He most likely transferred these properties to his three surviving children prior to his death in 1703, as none of these lots are listed in his estate inventory.

The first two, adjoining parcels were purchased from Daniel Henchman, and located on the southeast side of Henchman's Alley between present-day Charter and Commercial Streets. The three remaining parcels were located within the triangle formed by present-day Hanover, Battery and Commercial Streets. The first of the latter three parcels, was purchased from Robert Thornton. It was an interior lot, accessed via two alleys from Commercial Street. Richard purchased an adjoining lot to the southwest from John Howlet two years later. By 1682, Richard Shute purchased yet another lot, this one to the northeast and adjoining the Thornton purchase of 1678. This final parcel, bought from Thornton's son-in-law, Edward Page, fronted on Lyn (now Commercial) Street. The Henchman Alley properties measured approximately 3,700 square feet; the three parcels northeast of Battery Alley and connecting to Lyn Street totalled approximately 8,500 square feet [see Suffolk Deeds, Lib. VII, 272-273; Lib. X, 243-244; Lib. XI, 220-221, 222-223; and Lib. XII, 366-367]. None of these purchases included mention of a dwelling house.

On 28-Aug-1679, Richard Shute appeared before the Suffolk County Courts and accused Jonathan Turner of stealing his furs. Shute received a favorable ruling against the defendant; Turner was found guilty of stealing seven beaver skins (valued at four pounds) and was sentenced to be whipped ten stripes and to pay Shute eight pounds in money.

In October 1680, Richard Shute filed both civil and criminal suits against a Richard Loft (also Lift and Left in court records) for what was described only as "abuse of the complainant's wife." Both suits were heard before the Inferior Court of Pleas held at Boston. Shute was forced to withdraw his civil suit for lack of evidence (both in October, and again in April 1681), but in the matter of the criminal suit, the court found against the defendant, and Loft was fined 40 shillings and bound over on 20 pounds for good behavior. [See the WPA's Historical Records Survey's Abstract and Index of the Records of the Inferiour Court of Pleas Held at Boston 1680-1698 (1940).]

Richard's wife, Elizabeth, died in Boston on 8-Sep-1691. Her stone in Boston's Copp's Hill Burial Ground reads: "Elizabeth Shute / late wife to / Richard Shute / Aged 63 years & 1/2 / dec'd September ye / 8th 1691."

Shortly thereafter, Richard married Katherine Gutteridge, widow of the Boston mariner, Thomas Gutteridge (aka Goodridge) who died in 1691. As part of her dower, the aging Richard Shute provided that upon his death, his new bride was to receive 10 pounds per annum during her life, and that his farm in Malden was to serve as collateral. In his will of 1703, Shute altered this arrangement by increasing his wife's per annum legacy to 12 pounds, if she relinquished her right to the Malden farm, which was then left to his children. The farm, and his shares in vessels, however, were not to be dispersed until after the death of his wife.

In March, 1694/95, Richard Shute was one of 74 "proprietors and freeholders" who shared in the final land allotments of the Malden (2,000 acre) commons. As Shute was a resident of Boston, it may be assumed that his farm in Malden was of sufficient size to give him a freehold, thus entitling him to a share in the allotments. It is not clear when Richard Shute bought the farm in Malden.

Richard and Katherine Shute, "both of Boston," appeared before the 2-Oct-1694 sitting of the Suffolk County Court of Common Pleas, as defendants in an action regarding the administration of the estate of Thomas Guttsridge [sic], brought by the plaintiff, Jarvis Ballard. Ballard, a Boston merchant and constable, claimed that the estate still owed him six pounds, 16 shillings, for "114 yds. of fine Ozonbrigs" and "26 yds. of Blew Linning," which Thomas Gutteridge

purchased on 9-Jun-1688. The court found for the plaintiff and
ordered that Shute pay the amount due, plus court costs..

On 27-Sep-1695, the Sheriff of Suffolk County was instructed to
deliver a writ, binding Richard Shute to appear before the Inferior
Court of Common Pleas on the first Tuesday of January, 1695/96, in an
action brought by Walter Merry, Jr., son and heir of Walter Merry,
Sr., on behalf of his estate. [n.b. --Walter Merry, Sr., was a
shipwright in Boston's North End, who drowned in Boston's harbor on
28-Aug-1657. His house, wharf and warehouse were located at what was
called Merry's Point, later the North Battery.] James Amsden, Deputy
Sheriff, attempted to deliver the writ the next day, but found that
Richard Shute, Sr. was not home. Surety that Shute would appear in
court, however, was offered by his wife, Katherine, who produced a
chafing dish to serve as his bond. The court found for the defendant,
and Walter Merry was instructed to pay court costs.

The suit brought against Richard Shute by Walter Merry, Jr., in
1695, claimed that Shute (as well as two other neighbors, who Merry
sued separately) was illegally occupying a parcel of land which
belonged to his father's estate, at Merry's Point. The writ, in part,
read that Shute was to answer to Merry in an action "of the case for
that the said Richard Shute doth withhold & refuse to deliver by
pet[tioner] the possession of a certain piece or parcel of land
situate lying & being in Boston aforesaid at the northerly end of
saide towne near the North Battery bounded on the southerly side by
the building yards formerly of Alexander Adams late of Boston,
shipwright, dec'd, northerly by ye way going by ye Battery [now
Commercial St.], which land was sometime the land of Walter Merry
aforesaid, dec'd, & of which he had seized and now duly appertain of
right unto the pet[itioner], son of said Walter Merry..." Walter
Merry, Jr., claimed not only the land, but 150 pounds in damages, from
Richard Shute.

The writs issued to Shute's neighbors, Timothy Thornton,
shopkeeper, and Thomas Hunt, smith, are identical in their
descriptions of the properties. No decisions in either of these
latter cases has been found, but it would seem that Walter Merry,
Jr.'s claims were again unsubstantiated, as Capt. John Bonner's 1722
map of Boston clearly shows "Thornton's Ship Yard" and "Hunt's Wharfe"
due north of the Battery.

The North Battery was connected to North Street by what was at
one time known as "Shute's Lane," later Battery Alley. One of the
earlier inhabitants, aside from Walter Merry, Sr., was John Viall,
owner of the "Noah's Ark" tavern, and father-in-law to William Shute,
who in 1658, sold part of his holdings to Alexander Adams. The Adams'
property was inherited by William Parkman and his wife, Elizabeth
(Adams), and subsequently sold, on 11-Jan-1699 for 140 pounds, to
Deacon John Greenland Jr., and given to Richard Shute, Jr., and his
wife, Lydia (Greenland) Shute, prior to 1702. Clearly, both William
and Richard Shute, and their children, lived in a very finite
neighborhood.

Richard Shute continued trading along the Maine coast well into
his late sixties. His son-in-law, Joseph Buckley, a Charlestown
merchant, provided trade goods to him as late as February, 1699/1700.
In January, 1700/01, Richard Shute, Sr., leased a wharf and the land

above in Charlestown, from Nathaniel Adams, presumably to continue or expand his base of operations.

Richard Shute, Sr., died 2-Oct-1703, aged 73, presumably in Boston. Although described as a "mariner," Richard Shute attained a certain level of financial comfort as his will, drawn 11-Sep-1703 and proved 6-Oct-1703, lists legacies including his silver tankard, beaker and porringer; shares in ocean-going vessels; the farm in Malden (now Everett, MA) with house and barn, valued at 250 pounds; and cash disbursements to his wife, children, 12 grandchildren, and "kinsman" William Shute (most likely his nephew, the Boston ship's carver). As Richard Shute's will makes no mention of his daughter, Elizabeth, nor son, William (or spouses or children), it may be assumed that Elizabeth Shute (b. 1666/67) and William Shute (b. 1670) died prior to their father's death and without issue.

The "inventory of the goods & Estate of Richard Shute, late of Boston, mariner," was taken on 6-Oct-1703. The estate was valued at 495 pounds, 14 shillings. It was not a humble household. In addition to the silver pieces cited in his will, the estate also included a sterling salt cellar, eight silver spoons, six gold rings and, what would seem to have been his most esteemed material possession (other than real estate, bonds and shares in vessels), a four-poster bed complete with feather bed, bolster and pillows, imported Dutch bed linens as well as domestic "homespun," all drawn tight at night with serge, valanced curtains, trimmed with imported silk fringe. Another, less impressive bedstead sported calico bedhangings, but even the lowly trundlebed came complete with feather bed and linens. His home boasted a well-equipped kitchen for its day, complete with iron pots, brass and bell metal kettles, warming pans, chafing dishes, drip pans, mortar and pestle, even six knives in a case, six eathernware dishes, five tablecloths with 10 imported, damask napkins, and what looks to be over 40 pounds of pewter plate. The front room(s) would have held his "great Chair," and six "turkeyworked" chairs. The latter's seats were upholstered in oriental or "Turkey" carpet material, hence "turkeyworked." In addition, there were another six chairs covered with serge, two small tables, a "looking glass," brass candlesticks, a cupboard, and fireplace complete with brass andirons and fender, brass tongs and shovel, and a pair of bellows. The home arsenal comprised two guns, four pistols, one flint-lock rifle, a powderhorn and a sword, as well as a ready supply of powder, bullets, and flints. The inventory was accepted, and the estate of Richard Shute was closed on 22-Feb-1703/04.

Richard Shute, Sr., was buried at Copp's Hill Burial Ground in Boston next to his first wife, Elizabeth (d. 1691), and their infant daughter, Elizabeth Shute (d. 1665). The inscription on his stone was recorded in 1936/37 by the Old North Chapter, DAR, as reading: "Her Lyes Buried Ye Body of Richard Shut / Aged 72 Years / Died October Ye 2d 1703." The stone still stands and is quite legible (July 1995). Katherine Gutteridge Shute, Richard's widow, survived her husband, but her exact death date is unknown.

Children by Elizabeth -----:
+   2.   i **Michael Shute** b. cir 1659.
+   3.   ii **Joanna Shute** b. cir 1661.
     4.   iii **Elizabeth Shute** b. 27-Jan-1665, Boston, MA, d.

2-Feb-1665, Boston, MA,[4] Buried: Copp's Hill Burial Ground, Boston, MA.[5]

+ 5.   iv **Richard Shute** b. 31-Aug-1666.
6.   v **Elizabeth Shute** b. 1-Jan-1667/68, Boston, Suffolk Co., MA,[6] d. bef 11-Feb-1703.
7.   vi **William Shute** b. 1-Oct-1670, Boston, Suffolk Co., MA,[6] d. bef 1703.

Second Generation

2. **Michael Shute** b. cir 1659, Boston, Suffolk Co., MA?,[7]
Occupation: Capt./mariner/privateer, m. bef 23-Dec-1681, in Boston,
Suffolk Co., MA, **Mary Rainsford**, b. 10-Jan-1662/63, Boston, Suffolk
Co., MA,[8] (daughter of **John Rainsford** and **Susanna Vergoose**) d.
16-Sep-1709, Boston, Suffolk Co., MA,[9] Buried: 18-Sep-1709, Copp's
Hill Burial Ground, Boston, MA.[10] Michael died bef 23-Oct-1706,
Jamaica,[11] Buried: 1706, Jamaica.

Michael Shute took the Oath of Allegiance in Boston on
11-Nov-1678, administered by the Hon. John Leverett, Esq., Governor.
Two years later, in 1680, Michael Shute, aged 18, if not employed by,
was certainly well acquainted with, Col. Samuel Shrimpton, a Boston
merchant trader, described by the historian Richard R. Johnson as a
"rich merchant (and adept political chameleon) ... accused on several
occasions during the 1680s of using his island to outfit pirates and
engage in illegal trade." For in 1680, and again in 1684, Michael
Shute served as a witness to both a promissory note and a receipt
which benefitted Mr. Shrimpton. The former, dated 2- Dec-1680, and
signed by Thomas Jarvis, promised "to pay Mr. Samuel Shrimpton on his
order in Boston the full sum of three thousand pounds of good
merchantable tobacco in caske," by the 20th of May following. The
latter, dated 27- May-1684, again witnessed by Michael Shute, was a
receipt, signed by Perez Savage, acknowledging he had "Rec'd. of
Samuel Shrimpton One quarter Caske of Canary, which if Mr. Matthew
Middleton doe not pay for in Six months after the date hereof, then I
doe promiss to pay for the Same." Photostats of both notes are held by
the Massachusetts Historical Society. [n.b. -- "Canary" was a wine
made on the Canary Islands, similar in general character to the
competing madeira.]

A mariner, like his father and brother, Michael Shute, was one of
three men selected to appraise the ketch "Friendship," of Boston, for
the Courts of Assistants on 19- May-1686.

By 1687, aged 25, Michael Shute was Master of the "Returne," a
Boston-based, 40-ton pink with four guns, engaged in transatlantic, as
well as West Indian trade. Massachusetts shipping records reveal that
on 15-Jun-1687, Michael Shute "entered out [of Boston harbor] bound
for Madera [sic], carrying fish and lumber." On 25-Nov-1687, the
"Returne" of Boston [...] came from Jamaica [...] carrying 20 bales of
canvas and two boxes of English goods signed by Reginald Wilson that
they were lawfully imported."

Not all of Michael Shute's cargoes were necessarily "lawfully
imported." He was probably the unspecified "Shute," reported by
Edward Randolph, the admittedly corrupt Customs Collector for New
England, to the Lords of Trade in London, in April, 1689, for engaging
in "irregular trade" (i.e. smuggling). Massachusetts' agents, then in
London, were called to answer Randolph's charges. The testimony of
Samuel Turell assured the Lords of Trade that "Shute carried Fish but
we know not of any tobacco." Among the Massachusetts agents present
was Epaphras Shrimpton, nephew of Col. Samuel Shrimpton. [n.b. -- See
Andros Tracts, Vol. 2, p. 131]

It may never be known whether it was Captain Michael Shute or his
brother, Captain Richard Shute, who, in the summer of 1690, was

impressed with his vessel to ferry Massachusetts militia and
pro-British Plymouth Indians to Canada in Sir William Phips failed
expedition against Quebec. But as Captain Michael Shute already
commanded his own vessels by 1690, whereas his younger brother,
Richard, had only served as a pilot as late as 1688, the evidence
would seem to indicate that Michael Shute was far the more likely
candidate for Quebec.

     Both Samuel Seward in his diary, and Major John Walley in his
"Journal in the Expedition against Canada," simply refer to this
captain as "Shute." [Note: Given the later corroboration of Sewall's
"Shute" as Wait Winthrop's "Michael Shute" in April, 1699 (see below),
it seems certain that Michael Shute was the captain in question before
Quebec.] Shute's vessel in 1690 is not named, but Walley, the
commander of the land forces, mentioned "Shute and others of the the
larger vessels that were not men of warr." Sewall's notes also
credited Shute with a larger ship.

     The amassed fleet of 32 trading and fishing vessels, along with
tenders, set sail from Hull, MA, near Boston, on 9-Aug-1690. Admiral
Sir William Phips' flagship, the "Six Friends," with 44 guns and 200
men was, in fact, a West Indies trader owned by a group of Barbadoes
merchants. No regular British Navy or land forces took part in the
expedition which ended in defeat before the cliffs of Quebec on
8-Oct-1690.

     In the general retreat back to Boston in October and early
November, 1690, smallpox broke out aboard Shute's vessel. Sewall
notes in his diary of 8-Nov-1690: "... News of Canada came from
Salem. Shute comes into Boston that night or next morning, hath
thrown over aboard more than Sixty persons since his going hence, most
Indians of Plimouth." And the next day, Saturday, Sewall wrote:
"Council meets. Send away Major Hutchinson, Capt. Townsend and others
to Wells to treat with the Indians, and commit the care of the sick on
board Shute, to the Select-Men. Two lie dead on board at this time,
the Small Pocks and Cold kills them."

     Another participant in Phips' expedition to Canada was that of
Michael Shute's brother-in-law, Captain John Rainsford. As commander
of the new, 60-ton brigantine "Mary" of Boston, Rainsford, too, had
been impressed to transport men to Quebec. In the retreat of
8-Oct-1690, Rainsford's ship ran aground, stranding he and his men on
Antecosta Island in the mouth of the St. Lawrence River. They were
stranded for six months before five of his men built a small craft and
sailed for Boston. The tiny craft was picked up by a shallop off Cape
Ann in May, 1691. Over half of Rainsford's 60 men perished before
relief from Boston arrived.

     On 28-Oct-1695, the Boston merchant and Major General, Wait
Winthrop (youngest son of John Winthrop, Jr., Governor of
Connecticut), entrusted a letter to his brother, Fitz- John Winthrop,
then in England, to Captain Micaell [sic] Shute, commander of the "St.
Joseph." With his correspondence, Winthrop also forwarded "two halfe
barrills of cramberryes" with Shute to England. [n.b. -- see Letters
of Wait Winthrop, Mass. His. Soc. Cols., vol. 8, 5th series, pp. 509,
511]

     This 1695 voyage of the "St. Joseph" was also recorded in a
letter, five years later, from Governor, Earl of Bellomont to the

Council of Trade and Plantations in London, dated from New York, 28-Nov-1700 [n.b. -- See Calendar of State Papers, Colonial, 1700, item no. 953]. Bellomont informed the Council that "In the year '95 the marchands [merchants] of Boston were incourage'd to send over a ship- load of severall sorts of ship-timber for an experiment. [...] The ship, St. Joseph, of 300 tons was loaded, but met with all the rubs and stops that could well have happen'd. First she lay three moneths [sic] loaden wayting for a convoy; then she had a very tedious passage and was forc'd by contrary weather into Milford Haven, where she waited five or six weeks for a wind. At last getting into the river as far up as Deptford or Woolwich, she lay five weeks there, before care was taken to unload her. [...] I have a copie of the master of the ship's journal, and of the invoice of the timber and the owners told me there was all the contrivance that could be by the officers of the [King's ship-] yard, which received the timber at last, to disparage it and discourage any further undertaking of that kind."

It is not known how Captain Michael Shute came to be Master of the "St. Joseph" by October, 1695. The ship may very well have been the "St. Joseph" which was brought to Boston by a "privateer of the Leeward-islands" as a prize in 1694, and recorded in Hutchinson's History of the Colony of Massachusetts Bay (Vol. 2, p. 76). Prize ships were generally awarded to their captors. Michael Shute may have been the "privateer of the Leeward-islands" who captured the "St. Joseph," but it is more likely that the prize was sold and purchased in large part by Samuel Shrimpton. For on 2- Jul-1700, an Ebenezer Pearmeter presented "An acompt of work don for the ship Sant Joseph, Cap. Michell Shut, Commander," for pumps, pump boxes, pump brackets and clocks, totalling over five pounds. The original document is in the Massachusetts Historical Society's D. Greenough Collection. The bill is marked as being paid in full by Madam Shrimpton. Clearly the "St. Joseph" was a Shrimpton concern.

Michael Shute commanded the "St. Joseph" for at least eight years, if not until his death in 1706. It was not all smooth sailing. In the Spring of 1699, Shute was boarded by pirates. The incident was recorded by Wait Winthrop in yet another letter to his brother, Fitz-John Winthrop, in London, dated 17-Apr-1699: "A brigantine with 80 men came on bord Shute at Salterteodase, but his ship was not for their turn. Thay took his carpenter away; would haue enticed his men. Thay are English, Duch, and French, and looke for a sutable ship, and intend to make up 200 men, and then will goe where thay shall get money enough, thay say. Thay take what thay want from every body."

Of this affair, Samuel Sewall merely noted in his diary of the same date, 17-Apr-1699: "Shute arrives from Salt- Tarbooda [Tortuga]."

And on 5-Oct-1703, Captain Michael Shute, plaintiff, found himself in the Suffolk County Court of Common Pleas, demanding restitution from his former Second Mate, Joseph White, for damages accrued from the latter's mutiny aboard his ship, the "St. Joseph," bound for Barbadoes, as the ship lay in Boston Harbor, on 8-Sep-1703. A writ had been issued as early as 21-Sep-1703, commanding the Suffolk County Sheriff to "attach the goods or estate of Joseph White [...] to the value of Sixty pounds and for the want thereof to take the Body of the said Joseph White (if he may be found in your precinct) and safely keep, so that you have him before our Justices of our Inferiour Court of Common Please next, to be holden at Boston, within and for our said County of Suffolk, on the first Tuesday of October next." But while the jury found for the plaintiff , Captain Michael Shute, they must have had some misgivings over the affair, as they reduced his damages from the 40 pounds claimed, to an award of only 25 pounds plus court costs due from the defendant, Joseph White.

A year earlier, Michael Shute served as a witness to the signing of Giles Fifield's will. Fifield was Michael Shute's wife's sister's husband.

An exact date or place of death is not known for Michael Shute. We know only that he was buried in Jamaica prior to his widow, Mary, being granted Letters of Administration on 23-Oct-1706. At that time, Mary Shute was joined by Jonathan Farnam, cordwainer, and William Shute, carver (her husband's first cousin), in signing a 600 pound surety to the probate judge, pledging a complete inventory and account of the estate, prior to 24-Jan-1706/07.

The estate was inventoried and valued at just over 635 pounds on 20-Nov-1706 [n.b. -- See Suffolk Co. Probate rec. no. 2998]. Included in the inventory taken by John Goodwin, Arthur Smith and Jonathan Farnum were Michael Shute's father's six "Turkey Chairs," 58 lbs. of pewterware, 51 lbs. of brassware, 92 oz. of plate (silver), one part of his father's farm in Malden (valued at 60 pounds), one fishing shallop (valued at six pounds), and an unnamed "Negro Woman" (valued at 30 pounds). The inventory also reveals that at the time of Capt. Michael Shute's death, he was owed over 48 pounds by his son-in-law, John Blew, and over 10 pounds by son-in-law Charles Hawes. Distributions were made on 29-Oct- 1707, including 98 pounds and dower right of one-third in the house and land for life to his widow; two pounds to his daughter, Elizabeth, wife of John Blew; four pounds to daughter Susannah Holton; and 51 pounds each, to daughters Mary Payne, Hannah Shute and Joanna Shute.

On 20-Oct-1708, Michael Shute's son-in-law, Captain John Blew, called upon Timothy Thornton, Thomas Hunt and Samuel Greenwood to attest to the dimensions of the house and land formerly belonging to Captain Michael Shute. As Thornton and Hunt were named as neighbors in a suit brought against Michael Shute's father, Richard Shute, Sr., in 1696, one might suggest that the house and land were, in fact, Richard Shute, Sr.'s, and had been signed over to his son, Michael, prior to the elder Shute's death in 1703. The lot may have boasted two other structures ("Two Small Tenements"); the adjoining garden measured approximately 156 ft. in length, by 20 ft. at the end of the house and 18 ft. at the upper end of the property.

Michael Shute's widow, Mary, survived him by only three years. The inscription on her stone at Copp's Hill Burying Ground in Boston reads: Here lyes ye Body of / Mrs Mary Shutt / the Wife of / Capt Michael Shutt / aged / 45 years and eight months / who deceased / September the 16th / 1709.

Children:
+ 8.   i **Elizabeth Shute** b. 19-Dec-1682.
9.   ii **Susanna Shute** b. 1685/86, m. (1) 30-Mar-1704, in Boston, Suffolk Co., MA,[12] **Charles Hawes**, m. (2)

3-Jan-1705, in Boston, Suffolk Co., MA,[13] **Joseph Holton**, m. (3) 29-Feb-1720, in Boston, Suffolk Co., MA,[14] **Derick Carver**.

10.   iii **Mary Shute** b. 17-Aug-1689, Boston, Suffolk Co., MA,[15] m. 20-Oct-1707, in Boston, Suffolk Co., MA,[16] **Ebenezer Payne**.

11.   iv **Hannah Shute** b. 31-Aug-1691, d. 29-Apr-1709, Boston, Suffolk Co., MA,[9] Buried: Copp's Hill Burial Ground, Boston, MA.

+ 12.   v **Joanna Shute** b. cir 1694.

3. **Joanna Shute** b. cir 1661, Boston, Suffolk Co., MA?, m. (1) bef 1682, in Charlestown, MA, **Nathaniel Nichols**, b. 10-Nov-1655, Charlestown, MA,[17] (son of **Randall Nichols** and **Elizabeth Pierce**) Occupation: Mariner, d. 29-Apr-1687, Charlestown, MA,[17] m. (2) cir 1688, in Charlestown, MA,[18] **Joseph Buckley**, b. Jun-1659, Occupation: Mariner, d. 1-Jan-1701/02, Boston, Suffolk Co., MA,[19] Buried: Copp's Hill Burial Ground, Boston, MA. Joanna died 4-Mar-1716/17,[2] Buried: Copp's Hill Burial Ground, Boston, MA. Nathaniel:

Nathaniel Nichols' [indentured] servant, Hugh Williams, died in Charlestown, MA, 13-Jun-1687. Joseph:

Mariner Joseph Buckley of Charlestown, MA, was also involved in transatlantic, as well as West Indian trade. Massachusetts shipping records reveal that as master of the 45-ton, plantation-built, ketch "Gabriel," Buckley entered Boston harbor on 7-Nov-1687, having sailed from Fiall, "carrying 60 pipes and 7 quarter casks of Fiall wine, and 2 pipes of vinegar." On 21-Jan-1688 he gave bond in London, "on clearing for the plantations." [n.b. -- See Calendar of State Papers, Colonial, vol. 12, item #1,599] In 1689, the "Gabriell" of Charles Towne, returned from Dover and "entered [Boston harbor] on 25th August, carrying sundry parcels of Dutch goods as per cockets produced." Buckley's certificate of bond was given on the 4th of June, and signed by the commissioners in London. [n.b. -- A "cocket" was a seal or document from the king's customhouse, given to the shipper, as a warrant that his goods had been duly entered and had paid duty.]

In 1689, Buckley was pressed into service by Governor Sir Edmund Andros, "for Six months Service, on board ye Katch Gabriel being by him [Andros] Prest in An Expedition Against ye Indians to ye Eastward," as he later recalled in his account book. For his time, Buckley continued to bill the Governor 54 pounds, 10 shillings, 3 pence. In 1700, Buckley settled for half that amount, which Andros, then the former Governor of Virginia and Maryland, paid in paper script.

Joseph Buckley and his family were members of the Anglican, King's Chapel in Boston.

Samuel Sewall's diary mentions Joseph Buckley in an entry of 1-Dec-1690, in which it was noted that the pink "Eagle," of 80 tuns (Joseph Buckley, master), loaded for Jamaica, burned in Boston harbor with "very little sav'd besides a new Cable, came by Carelessness."

In the Minutes of Council of Massachusetts, 19-Dec- 1695, it was noted that "permission [was] granted to Benjamin Emons to erect a small wooden edifice adjoining his house, and the like to Joseph Buckley."

One of Joseph Buckley's account books is in the manuscript holdings of the Massachusetts Historical Society in Boston. It starts on 15-May-1693, and runs through 26- Feb-1693/94, while Buckley was in St. Johns, Newfoundland. It resumes, after a three year lag, on 19-Jul-1696, in Boston, and continues until 31-Oct-1701, just two months prior to Buckley's death. Joseph Buckley was apparently a partner with, or an agent for, fellow Boston merchants Eliakim Hutchinson and Adam Winthrop in what was known as The Newfoundland Company. In St. Johns, Buckley operated both as a merchant and as a broker to over half a dozen "company" ships that would sail from Newfoundland for Barbadoes, laden with salted or dried Atlantic fish, and return with molasses, lime juice and rum. Other ships were directed to Boston, where fish was exchanged for the tools, cloth, sails, foodstuffs, cable, etc., needed to constantly outfit The Newfoundland Company's ships at St. Johns. Profits were relayed to Boston via bills of exchange. It is not clear when Buckley left St. Johns, but as the French retook Newfoundland in 1695, it's fairly safe to say that he didn't linger long.

Back in Boston, the account book resumes in 1696 and, indeed, The Newfoundland Company is still paying dividends to its share-holders. Buckley's interests in each vessel ranged from 1/8th, 1/6th, 1/4th, or more, as in the case of the brigantine "Joanna," built and named after Buckley's wife, Joanna Shute, in 1699, or the sloop "Swallow," which Buckley had built in 1699/1700. However, The Newfoundland Company was only one account in Buckley's Boston books. He also owned shares in any number of other ships and ventures, as well. He also operated as an independent merchant in Boston, selling everything from cables, anchors and trade goods, to bolts of calico, damask and linen, to pewter buttons and firearms. Buckley's clients included fellow Boston and Charlestown merchants, as well as private citizens and family members.

"Father Richard Shute" or "Richard Shute, Sr." was how Buckley referred to his father-in-law with whom, it would seem, he had only infrequent dealings. In 1696, Buckley was still paying five pounds annual rent to his father-in-law for his home in Charlestown. On 2-Mar-1697/98, Richard Shute, Sr. purchased a small anchor that had been a part of the ship "Three Friends" cargo from Newfoundland, as well as a compass. Shute returned later that month to buy 22 yards of "broad Lining" and "one groce of haire buttons." Buckley noted of Shute's purchase that "halfe of which I have sent by him as an Adventure." In February, 1699/1700, Richard Shute was back to purchase 16 yards of "duffills," whereof Buckley noted: "If he Sells it this Voyage to ye eastward but if he cannot Sell it then to return it ." Other entries include separate purchases, by Shute, of a bushel of wheat, a bushel of salt, and a "jarr of oyle." On the debit side, Buckley's father-in-law received two sizable loans (with interest), one in 1698 for 50 pounds, and the other on 15- Jan-1700/01, for 17 pounds, which Buckley described as "money Lent him to pay to Nathaniel Addams of Charlestowne for which he ye said Addams gave a mortgage."

Of his brothers-in-law, Buckley seemingly had no business dealings with Michael Shute, and Richard Shute, Jr. appears in his account only once, dated 19-Jul-1696, for owing Buckley nine pounds, four shillings, 6 pence for a "bill of exchange and other Small nessessareys."

Another, more distant relation with whom Buckley had dealings was William Shute, carver, who was paid for work on Buckley's sloop, built by John Taylor in January, 1699/1700. William Shute was Buckley's wife's first cousin, and son-in- law of Edward Budd, another Boston ship carver.

Yet one other family relation appears in Buckley's account book of 19-Jul-1696, and that is of his wife's former brother-in-law, Randall Nichols, to whom Buckley credits 11 pounds, 10 shillings, "for his part of Rent in England." What exactly Buckley or Nichols' dealings in England were, is not known, however Buckley's father was still living in England as late as 1700, when he paid a debt for his son to the London merchant, William Crouch. Nichols on the other hand, like Buckley's wife's children by her first marriage to Nathaniel Nichols, had inherited lands in Uxbridge, Co. Middlesex, England, upon the death of Randall Nichols, Sr., in 1681, which had belonged to the elder Nichols' father, William, and uncle, Robert Nichols, both of Uxbridge.

In his will of 24-Nov-1700 (proved 19-Mar-1702), Joseph Buckley provided that his wife, Joanna, should have the use of their dwelling house which had been given to him by his father-in-law, Richard Shute, for the rest of her life. To his sons Joseph, Richard, and Thomas, he bequeathed 300 pounds to each upon turning 21 years of age.

Joseph Buckley was buried at Copp's Hill Burial Ground in Boston. The inscription on his stone as recorded by Thomas Bridgman in 1852 read: "Here lyeth buried ye Body of / Mr. Joseph Buckley / Aged / 42 years and 6 mounthes / Died Jan ye 1 / 1701."

Children by Nathaniel Nichols:

+ 13.   i **Elizabeth Nichols** b. 14-Apr-1682.
+ 14.   ii **Hannah Nichols**.

Children by Joseph Buckley:

  15. iii **Joseph Buckley** Baptized: 1691, Charlestown, MA.
+ 16.   iv **Richard Buckley** b. 9-Oct-1695.
  17.   v **Thomas Buckley** b. 7-Oct-1700, Boston, Suffolk Co., MA.[8]

5. **Richard Shute** b. 31-Aug-1666, Boston, Suffolk Co., MA,[20] Occupation: Capt./mariner/trader, m. (1) 1692, **Lydia Greenland**, b. 02-Feb-1672/73, Malden, Middlesex Co., MA,[21] (daughter of **John Greenland Jr.** and **Lydia Sprague**) d. 3-Oct-1721, Boston, Suffolk Co., MA,[2] Buried: Copp's Hill Burial Ground, Boston, MA, m. (2) 29-Nov-1723, in Boston, MA,[22] **Rachel Bond**, d. 1752, Boston, Suffolk Co., MA. Richard died cir 1742, Boston, Suffolk Co, MA?.[23]

Richard Shute, the second son of Richard and Elizabeth Shute, was born in Boston on 31-Aug-1666. A mariner, like his father before him, the younger Richard Shute probably went to sea at a very early age. He received his first commission as a pilot from Governor Sir Edmund Andros on 10- Apr-1688. It read: "By his Excellency. These are to Require you forthwith to Repaire on board his Majesties ffriggatt the Rose (now bound to Crouse [cruise] on ye Coast Eastward under the Command of Capt. John George & to take upon you the Charge & Duty of a

Pylott for which this Shall be your Warrant." [n.b. -- See Col. Soc. MA Publs., 1918, p. 28]

The "Rose" made several cruises to the eastward [Maine & Acadia -- now Nova Scotia] during the summer of 1688, both to inspect the colony's fortifications at Pemaquid, ME, and to serve as a deterrent to coastal pirates. Ironically, Richard Shute's orders as pilot were originally issued to a Thomas Pound, mariner, of Boston, six days earlier, who had served as pilot aboard the "Rose" in May, 1687. No explanation can be given for the last minute switch in pilots, but Pounds was later (July, 1688) made pilot of the "Rose's" consort, the sloop "Mary." Within a year, Pounds, himself, had become a pirate and attempted to take the "Mary" off Martyns Vineyard Sound on 4-Oct-1689.

Pounds failed in his attempt, however; the Boston Court of Assistants ordered on 17-Jan-1689/90 that Pounds "be carryed to the place of Execution and there be hanged by the neck untill he be dead."

Richard Shute's ties to his father's farm in Malden are not clear, but it was in Malden, one presumes, that Richard Shute met his future wife, Lydia Greenland, daughter of Deacon John and Lydia (Sprague) Greenland, prior to 1692.

The Greenland family was one of the first to settle in Malden, MA; Deacon John's father, John Greenland, a carpenter, was identified as a proprietor, with his wife, Lydia, "on the Mystic Side" as early as 1638. John Sr. was born cir 1601. No information is available on his wife, Lydia.

John Greenland, Sr. was instrumental in the settlement of lands "on the Mystic Side" which, in 1649, separated from Charlestown and became Malden, MA. The Greenlands settled on "five acres of woodland in Mystic Field #10, butting to the South upon the highway toward Capt. Robert Sedgewick's meadow; to the North upon the Mystic field; bounded on the West by the highway and upon the East by Michael Barston" -- overall 80 pole in length and 10 pole in width. They subsequently acquired the Barston lands and other lots.

John, Sr. and Lydia had John Greenland, Jr. (b. 16-Aug- 1644), Daniel (md. Elizabeth Ballantine), and Abigail (md. Abraham Ireland who later removed to Cambridge, MA). John, Sr. was active in civic affairs; was constable of Malden in 1656; and participated in the laying out of highways.

John Greenland, Sr. died in 1690/91. In his will, drawn 1-May-1685, probated 27-Mar-1691, there were bequests to his wife, Lydia, sons John and Daniel, daughter Abigail Ireland, and son Daniel's daughter, Elizabeth.

According to Corey's History of Malden, John Greenland, Jr. received his father's house and lands, as the "only surviving son," with the widow Lydia having the use of the house for the rest of her natural life. That wasn't long. The house was sold in January,1699/00, to John Ridgeway (mariner) who already occupied it.

John Greenland, Jr. probably took up residence in Malden at about the time of his marriage to Lydia Sprague (b. Sep-1653/54; dau. of John and Lydia (Goffe) Sprague), also of Malden, in 1670. He built upon a piece of land in the woodland west of the great swamp (a portion of the lot numbered 31), that his father had acquired in 1655 as part of the great allotment. There the couple had their only child, a daughter, Lydia Greenland, born 2-Feb-1672/73.

John Greenland, Jr. led a long and useful life. Malden records reflect extensive participation in town and church (he was a deacon) affairs. He saw active service in King Philip's War (1675/76) and in April, 1690/91, he was confirmed by the General Court as Ensign of the Three County Troop of Horse.

Deacon John Greenland was first elected town clerk on 6-Mar-1692/93, but refused such service after 1699. In March, 1694/95, Deacon John was listed as one of 74 proprietors who shared in land allotments in Malden.

Lydia (Sprague) Greenland died 20-Jan-1704/05, aged 51, in Malden. Deacon John Greenland died 17-Oct-1728, aged 85, also in Malden. His will, drawn in 1725, was probated 24- Jan-1728/29. The major part of his estate in Malden was left to his grandson, John Shute, the long-lived Deacon and town clerk. The estate included "one negro woman," Dinah, valued at 50 pounds, who died in Malden, 22-Jul-1768 in the service of John and Mary Shute. A salt-marsh in Charlestown was left to Deacon John Greenland's Shute grandchildren.

Richard and Lydia (Greenland) Shute had 10 children between the years of 1693 and 1718. Of the 10, seven lived to maturity. At some point, Richard and Lydia Shute removed to Boston and lived in a house given to them by Lydia's father, Deacon John Greenland, which he had purchased from William Parkman, shipwright, on 11-Jan-1699/1700. The house sat on a lot measuring 38' x 60', and was just off North Street (now Hanover) on the north side of Battery Alley, a narrow passageway, so named because it ran from North Street to the North Battery. It was later called "Shute's Lane," then "Daggett's Alley," and in 1825, "Battery Street." For many years this area of the North End of Boston was a thriving commercial center, noted for its shipbuilding, wharves, taverns, and coffee houses.

It is unclear whether Lydia returned to Malden to have each of her children (possibly because her husband was so frequently at sea), or if her children's births were simply recorded there. In all likelihood, Richard and Lydia Shute removed to Boston prior to 1702, as Lydia was "received into the Convenant" at the Second Church (Old North) of Boston on 12-Apr-1702, and many of her children were subsequently baptized there. Her husband, Richard, was "received into the Covenant and baptized" there on 24-Aug-1707, according to Second Church Records (Book 4), now held by the Massachusetts Historical Society.

Richard Shute owned land in Falmouth (now Portland) and North Yarmouth, Maine. In May, 1717, he joined with others in signing "The Memorial of the Proprietors and Settlers of the town of Falmouth in Casco Bay" delivered to Gov. Samuel Shute in Boston, petitioning that the governor grant their request for incorporation and to restore to them the "Antient Bounds" then being encroached upon by the development of North Yarmouth. He was also a petitioner for the resettlement of Falmouth in June, 1717. Shortly after 5- June-1718, Capt. Richard Shute sailed to Boston from Falmouth, to hand-deliver a letter from Samuel Moody to Paul Dudley, Attorney-General of the Province. On 28-Mar-1720, Richard Shute sold all of his Maine properties, his wife signing with him.

Lydia Greenland Shute died on 3-Oct-1721, and was buried in Copp's Hill Burial Ground in Boston, next to her sister-in-law, Mary

Rainsford Shute, the widow of Captain Michael Shute. Her stone was inscribed: "Here lyes the body of Mrs. Lydia Shute, Aged 42 years Dec'd Oct'r ye 3d 1721."

"At a Meeting of the freeholders and other Inhabitants of the Town of Boston duly Qualified being Regurly assembled in a Publick Town meeting at the Town house in Boston upon Monday the 9th day of of March 1723," Richard Shute was chosen to serve as a constable for the ensuing year, and duly sworn in [See Boston Town Records from 1700 to 1728 (1883)].

On 29-Nov-1723, Richard married Rachel (Bond) Freeman, widow of the late James Freeman, an affluent brewer of Boston, who had died in 1721. Samuel Freeman (H.C. 1725), Rachel's only child to live to maturity, died of consumption on 18-Apr-1728. At the time, he was betrothed to Abigail Boardman of Cambridge, MA, and employed as an apprentice in the Boston mercantile house of Hugh Hall, Jr., that dealt in such commodities as sugar, rum, illegal brandy and slaves.

Samuel Freeman's will, written two days before his death, stipulated that this estate, valued at 2,262 pounds, was to be equally divided between Harvard College and the Anglican Christ Church in Boston, after his mother's death. Rachel and Richard Shute, Samuel Freeman's mother and stepfather, however, had other ideas. In a scheme that landed all parties in court, Rachel and Richard Shute attempted to sell Samuel Freeman's estate ["all the real and personal estate, goods, and chattels"] to the Barbadian, Hugh Hall, Jr., who was also the executor of Samuel Freeman's estate, through a dummy buyer, Enoch Freeman. Enoch Freeman was Samuel Freeman's cousin, and Hugh Hall, Jr.'s partner in the mercantile concern in which Samuel Freeman had been apprenticed.

In Boston, on 3-Mar-1735, at a meeting of the "Select Men," Richard Shute's petition for a license "to Sell Strong Drink by Retail out of Doors in the year 1735" was approved. Richard Shute's packaged liquor shop, for lack of a better modern-day equivalent, was on Lynn St. (now Commercial St., north of Battery St.) in Boston's North End. Two years later, at a 10-Aug-1737 meeting of the Select Men, it was noted that "whereas Mr. Richard Shute was return'd as Removed in the List of Licences transmitted to the Clerk of the Peace and it happen'd thro' a Misinformation, The Town Clerk is Order'd to Certify That the Select men do approve of the Renewing his Licence as a Retailer for the year ensuing." [See the published Records of Boston Selectmen, 1716 to 1736, and the same, 1736 to 1742.]

Richard Shute made his will on 16-Apr-1736, naming as his executor, the Honorable Enoch Freeman (1706-1788) of Eastham, Boston, and later Portland, Maine. In his will, Richard indicated that sons John, Michael and Nathan, and daughter, Lydia Maxwell, were all to receive five shillings each (son John being in possession of the major part of his grandfather's [Greenland] estate, and the others already having received their portions). The remainder of his estate was to go to his daughter, Mary Shute, after debts and expenses were paid.

Richard Shute's will was presented for probate on 4-Jan- 1742, Enoch Freeman, executor. By 18-Oct-1743, Freeman, "apprehensive that the same [estate] would turn out [to be] insolvent," requested that the Court appoint a committee to assess the estate. The very next day, 19-Oct-1743, the estate was inventoried and valued (old tenor) at

9 pounds, 7 shillings, by Thomas Lee, James Cary, and Nicholas Lash. This valuation is somewhat suspect, given that Richard Shute, alone, received over 415 pounds from his stepson's estate in 1732, but as no information has been found on the final resolution of Richard Shute's estate, the subject is moot.

Rachel (Bond) Freeman Shute was not mentioned in her husband's will -- probably because she still accrued a sizeable income from her first husband's, and son's estates -- but she did, indeed, survive Capt. Richard Shute. On 6- Mar-1745, in Boston, she married Ralph Morgan, also of Boston. She died seven years later in 1752.

Capt. Richard Shute's exact date of death is unknown. It is probable, however, that he died in December, 1742, in Boston, then aged 76, as his will was first presented to the probate authorities on 4-Jan-1742/43. Noyes, Libby & Davis's Genealogical Dictionary of Maine and New Hampshire records that Richard Shute gave a deposition in January, 1737/38, then aged 72, that about 50 years before he "happened to be at Pemaquid." Enoch Freeman (executor of Richard Shute's estate) noted his business dealings with Capt. Richard Shute in his annotated almanac (now in the possession of the Portland, ME, Public Library). On 31-Aug- 1736, he made the notation that "Capt. Richard Shute this day is 70 years old." References to Capt. Shute extend at least as far as 8-Mar-1738/39, when Richard again debits his account with Freeman for cash. Other notes by Freeman show that Capt. Richard Shute debited his account to buy casks, meat and cordwood, and credited his account by selling rum, among other commodities.

Children by Lydia Greenland:

+ 18. i **John Shute** b. 26-Mar-1693.
+ 19. ii **Lydia Shute** b. 14-Jul-1696.
+ 20. iii **Elizabeth Shute** b. 20-Feb-1698/99.
  21. iv **Joanna Shute** b. 20-Feb-1698/99, Malden, MA,[24] d. 12-Sep-1700, Malden, MA.[24]
  22. v **Richard Shute** b. 23-Aug-1702, Malden, MA,[25] Baptized: 20-Jun-1703, Second Church of Boston,[26] m. 2-Jun-1725 int, in Boston, Suffolk Co., MA,[27] **Ann Adams**. Richard died cir 1725.

Richard Shute's betrothal to Ann Adams is documented in a Boston marriage intention, only. As neither Richard nor a spouse or children is mentioned in his father's will of 1736, it may be assumed that Richard died prior to 1736, and may have died shortly after his marriage intention in 1725.

Shute's finacee, Ann Adams, may very well have been the daughter of Nathaniel and Anna (Coolidge) Adams, of Charlestown, from whom Richard Shute's grandfather, Richard Shute, Sr., mortgaged a wharf and lands above, in the year 1700/01. Nathaniel Adams' daughter, Ann[a], later married Isaac Child of Waltham, MA, on 7-Dec-1727.

  23. vi **Michael Shute** b. 16-Sep-1704, Malden, MA,[28] Baptized: 17-Sep-1704, Second Church of Boston,[29] d. 10-Apr-1706, Malden, MA.[24]
+ 24. vii **Michael Shute** b. 21-Apr-1707.
  25. viii **Mary Shute** b. 18-Apr-1710, Malden, MA,[24] d. bef 24-Mar-1717.

26. ix **Nathan Shute** b. 21-Aug-1713, Malden, MA,[30] Occupation: Housewright, m. 14-Nov-1745, in Malden or Chelsea, MA,[31] **Mary Brintnall**, d. aft 1780, Woburn, MA.[32] Nathan died Jul-1778, Malden, MA.[24]

On 29-Jan-1770, the Town Clerk of Chelsea, MA, wrote to the selectmen of Boston, informing them "that one Nathan Shute, a poor Man belonging to your Town is now in Town, and in so distressed a situation, that we are obliged to supply him with some necessaries, for the amount of which we shall apply to you for a discharge." The Boston selectmen ordered the bill paid, yet it was not the last time they would have to deal with Nathan Shute. On 15-Jun-1774, the selectmen were asked to consider the "Application being made by the Friends & Relations of Nathan Shute that he may be permitted to go in the Country to the House of Ebenezer Shute [his nephew] of Malden for his better health & that they will make such addition to the Province support as may be necessary." The selectmen agreed to "permit his going out." [See the published Boston Selectmen's Minutes, 1769-1775.]

Nathan Shute was recorded as a member "in full Communion with the first Chh of Christ in Malden," in 1772. Other members included his elder brother, Deacon John Shute, and his nephews, Samuel and Amos Shute, sons of Deacon John Shute.

27. x **Mary Shute** b. 24-Mar-1717/18, Boston, Suffolk Co., MA,[8] m. 15-Mar-1738, in Boston, Suffolk Co., MA,[27] **Thomas Farmer**, b. 7-Oct-1714, Boston, Suffolk Co., MA,[8] (son of **Paul Farmer** and **Elizabeth -----**).

Third Generation

8. Elizabeth Shute b. 19-Dec-1682, Boston, Suffolk Co., MA,[33] m.
(1) 17-Jun-1701, in Boston, Suffolk Co., MA,[34] **John Blew**,
Occupation: Captain/mariner, d. cir 1709-13, m. (2) 10-Aug-1713, in
Boston, Suffolk Co., MA,[35] **Philip Viscount**, b. 1689, Occupation:
Mariner/Captain, d. 22-Sep-1751, Boston, Suffolk Co., MA,[36] Buried:
Copp's Hill Burial Ground, Boston, MA.[2] Elizabeth died bef 1715,
Charlestown, MA. John:

 The surname, Blew, is virtually non-existent in New England
records. As such, John Blew may well be the man recorded in Samuel
Sewall's diary of 12-Aug-1709: "At Council 'twas enquired whether
Blew should go to Edgartown to convoy vessels there loaden with Bread
[...] At last it was agreed, that if at the foot of the Shoals,
whether his cruise led him, he had a fair wind, he might goe. I had
urg'd teh Certainty of doing good if Blew went."

 Capt. John Blew may have been lost at sea, returning from
Bermuda. Handley Chipman (1717-1799) of Newport, RI, wrote a short
family history, circa 1790 (published in NEHGS Register, Vol. 91), in
which he remembered that, "my dear Mother took passage twice with a
Relation, or a particular acquaintance, with others, in order to See
her Relations in Bermudas, and did whether both times before Marriage
or once while a widow, I cannot tell. But the last time she went, in
her return home in Company with another Vessel, one Capt. Blue [sic],
Master, they was overtaken with a terrible storm and said Capt. Blue's
vessel foundered and sunk in their Sight, with all the Vessels crew in
her and they in the Vessel wherein my dear Mother was, could not by
any means give the other sd. Capt. Blue any releaf at all, being in
very great danger and distress themselves, which sad affair I have
hear my dear father say, my dear Mother has told him, fully determined
her never to attempt any very distant Voyage again, &c."

 Children by John Blew:
28. i **John Blew** b. 1710, Boston, Suffolk Co., MA, d. 1710,
  Boston, Suffolk Co., MA,[2] Buried: Copp's Hill Burial
  Ground, Boston, MA.

12. Joanna Shute b. cir 1694, m. 21-Apr-1715, in Boston, Suffolk
Co., MA,[37] **Joseph Langdon**, b. 22-Nov-1692, Boston, Suffolk Co.,
MA,[6] (son of **David Langdon** and **Martha -----**).
 Children:
29. i **Mary Landon** b. 24-Jan-1715/16, Boston, Suffolk Co.,
  MA.[8]

13. Elizabeth Nichols b. 14-Apr-1682, Charlestown, MA,[38] Baptized:
1687, Charlestown, MA,[17] m. 29-May-1712, in Boston, Suffolk Co.,
MA,[22] **Joshua Pickman**, b. 28-Aug-1681, Salem, MA, (son of **Benjamin
Pickman** and **Elizabeth Hardy**). Elizabeth died aft 1718.
 Children:
30. i **Joshua Pickman** b. 7-May-1713, Boston, Suffolk Co.,
  MA.[8]
31. ii **Nathaniel Pickman** b. 28-Jul-1718, Boston, Suffolk Co.,
  MA.[8]

14. **Hannah Nichols** Baptized: 1687, Charlestown, MA,[17] m.
7-Jan-1702, in Boston, Suffolk Co., MA,[13] **Jonathan Mountfort**, b.
15-Jun-1678, Boston, Suffolk Co., MA,[39] (son of **Edmund Mountfort**
and **Elizabeth Farnham**) Occupation: Physician/apothecary, d. 1724,
Boston, Suffolk Co., MA,[40] Buried: Tomb #59, Copp's Hill Burial
Ground. Hannah died aft 1726, Boston, Suffolk Co., MA. Jonathan:

Jonathan Mountfort has been described as a man of liberal
education, a physician and apothecary, who was independent in his
means and eccentric in his habits. He resided for many years at what
was called "Mountfort's Corner," on North Street at the North Square,
in Boston, on a lot that had been bought by his father, Edmund
Mountfort, in 1670/71. The elder Mountfort had fled from England in
1656 to Boston, in consequence of political offences. "Mountfort's
Corner" remained in family hands until his heirs sold it in 1797. The
lot stood directly across the triangular Square, south of the original
Second Church building, and southeast of the still extant Paul Revere
House.

In 1719, Jonathan Mountfort was one of the seceders from the New
North Church, and was a founder, and member of the building committee,
for the "New Brick" or "Weathercock" Church for whom he was treasurer.
His descendants in the male line are extinct; in the female line,
they are merged with the Greenough and Pitts families.

The Mountfort family coat of arms, displayed on Jonathan
Mountfort's tomb in Copp's Hill Burial Ground in Boston, belonged to
Hugo de Mountfort, a Norman, who, in 1066, commanded the cavalry of
William the Conqueror at the Battle of Hastings. Dugdale's "History
of Warwickshire" provides a pedigree of the Mountfort family from
Turstain de Montfort (1030), father of Hugo, above, to Simon Mountfort
(1633), Jonathan's grandfather.

Children:

32. i **Joanna Mountfort** b. 2-Jun-1704, Boston, Suffolk Co.,
MA.[8]

33. ii **Elizabeth Mountfort** b. 26-Jan-1705, Boston, Suffolk
Co., MA.[8]

34. iii **Hannah Mountfort** b. 22-Oct-1707, Boston, Suffolk Co.,
MA.[8]

35. iv **Jonathan Mountfort** b. 20-Nov-1710, Boston, Suffolk Co.,
MA.[8]

36. v **Sarah Mountfort** b. 6-Mar-1712/13, Boston, Suffolk Co.,
MA.[8]

37. vi **Jonathan Mountfort** b. 11-Jan-1714, Boston, Suffolk Co.,
MA.[8]

38. vii **Johanna Mountfort** b. 12-Aug-1717, Boston, Suffolk Co.,
MA.[8]

39. viii **Mary Mountfort** b. 2-Aug-1718, Boston, Suffolk Co.,
MA.[8]

40. ix **Abigail Mountfort** b. 24-Sep-1719, Boston, Suffolk Co.,
MA.[8]

41. x **Nathaniel Mountfort** b. 13-Nov-1722, Boston, Suffolk
Co., MA.[8]

In 1745, Nathaniel Mountfort formed a partnership
with Capt. John Gardner, another Boston merchant, to

supply the Louisbourg garrison with rum, turnips, onions and cider.
42.   xi **Hannah Mountfort** b. 5-Feb-1724, Boston, Suffolk Co., MA.[8]
43.   xii **Lydia Mountfort** b. 6-Jun-1726, Boston, Suffolk Co., MA.[8]

16. **Richard Buckley** b. 9-Oct-1695, Charlestown, MA,[41] Occupation: Mariner, m. 12-Sep-1728, in Boston, Suffolk Co., MA,[42] **Mary Noyes**. Richard died 21-May-1767,[43] Buried: Copp's Hill Burial Ground, Boston, MA.

In 1719, Richard Buckley lived in Henchman's Lane, now Henchman Street, in Boston. He was elected constable of Boston in 1726, but declined to serve and paid the fine, and served as an assessor from 1730 to 1748. Elected to the Ancient and Honorable Artillery Company in 1722, he was third sergeant of the Artillery Company in 1725, and captain in the militia. He was bondsman for Capt. Daniel Pecker, collector in the sum of 8,100 pounds in 1734, and again in 1736. By virtue of this office, he made the general walk or visitation of the town, with the justices and others, for several years.

Children:
44.   i **Mary Buckley** b. 7-Jun-1729, Boston, Suffolk Co., MA.[8]
45.   ii **Susanna Buckley** b. 5-Jun-1730, Boston, Suffolk Co., MA.[8]
46.   iii **Joseph Buckley** b. 10-Jan-1731, Boston, Suffolk Co., MA,[8] Occupation: Mariner/Captain, d. 2-Jan-1764,[44] Buried: Copp's Hill Burial Ground, Boston.
47.   iv **Richard Buckley** b. 17-Oct-1733, Boston, Suffolk Co., MA,[8] d. bef 1734, Boston, Suffolk Co., MA.
48.   v **Richard Buckley** b. 27-Jan-1734, Boston, Suffolk Co., MA.[8]
49.   vi **Joanna Buckley** b. 15-May-1737, Boston, Suffolk Co., MA,[8] d. 3-Jan-1802,[44] Buried: Copp's Hill Burial Ground, Boston, MA.

18. **John Shute** b. 26-Mar-1693, Malden, Middlesex Co., MA,[45] Baptized: 12-Apr-1702, Second Church of Boston,[26] Occupation: Farmer/Deacon/Town Clerk, m. 27-Oct-1714, in Malden, MA,[46] **Mary Waite**, b. 11-Aug-1685, (daughter of **John Waite** and **Sarah Mussey**) d. 31-Jan-1774, Malden, Middlesex Co., MA.[24] John died 20-Sep-1780, Malden, Middlesex Co., MA.[47]

Deacon John Shute occupied the post of Town Clerk of Malden (now Everett), MA, for 36 years. And although a resident of South Malden, he remained with the First Church of Christ in the North Precinct even after the division of North and South Malden. John Shute's grandfather, Deacon John Greenland, had removed to South Malden about 1670, and built upon a piece of land he had inherited from his father, also named John Greenland, who had acquired it in the Great Land Allotment of 1639. It was on this land that Deacon John Shute built his home and, which was located east of Ferry Street and ran into the present Shute Street.

A gentleman-farmer and patriot, Deacon John Shute served on the Chelsea Committee of Safety and donated money to the town of Chelsea

to pay for hiring soldiers during the Revolutionary War.
Children:
50.   i **John Greenland Shute** b. 10-Dec-1715, Malden, Middlesex Co., MA,[24] d. 4-Jun-1768, Malden, Middlesex Co., MA.[24]
+ 51.   ii **Samuel Shute** b. 27-Feb-1717/18.
52.   iii **Thomas Shute** b. 23-Apr-1720, Malden, Middlesex Co., MA,[48] m. 21-Jan-1747/48, in Malden, Middlesex Co., MA,[49] **Sarah Baldwin**, b. 10-Oct-1719, Malden, Middlesex Co., MA,[24] (daughter of **Joseph Baldwin** and **Sarah -----**) d. 6-Dec-1799, Malden, Middlesex Co., MA.[24] Thomas died 9-Jan-1770, Malden, Middlesex Co., MA.[24]
+ 53.   iv **Daniel Shute** b. 19-Jul-1722.
54.   v **Solomon Shute** b. 16-Nov-1724, Malden, Middlesex Co., MA,[50] d. Apr-1747, Malden, Middlesex Co., MA.[24]
+ 55.   vi **Mary Shute** b. 11-Mar-1727.
+ 56.   vii **Richard Shute** b. 25-Jul-1729.
+ 57.   viii **Jacob Shute** b. 28-Aug-1731.
+ 58.   ix **Benjamin Shute** b. 6-Jun-1734.
+ 59.   x **Amos Shute** b. 3-May-1737.
+ 60.   xi **Ebenezer Shute** b. 28-Sep-1740.
+ 61.   xii **Lydia Shute** b. 30-Nov-1743.

19. **Lydia Shute** b. 14-Jul-1696, Malden, Middlesex Co., MA,[24] Baptized: 12-Apr-1702, Second Church of Boston,[29] m. 23-Aug-1717, in Boston, MA,[37] **William Maxwell**. Lydia died bef 1740, Boston, Suffolk Co., MA?. William:
    In January, 1726/27, William Maxwell wrote a promissory note to his sister-in-law's husband, Samuel Watts, for the value of 30 pounds. The original note is to be found in the Massachusetts Historical Society's Chamberlain papers.
Children:
62.   i **Lydia Maxwell** b. 6-Jul-1721, Boston, Suffolk Co., MA.[8]
63.   ii **George Maxwell** b. 1-May-1725, Boston, Suffolk Co., MA.[8]
64.   iii **James Maxwell** b. 1727, Boston, Suffolk Co., MA, d. 3-Jul-1729, Boston, Suffolk Co., MA,[2] Buried: Copp's Hill Burial Ground, Boston, MA.
65.   iv **Mary Maxwell** b. 11-Mar-1728, Boston, Suffolk Co., MA,[8] m. 22-Jul-1749 int, in Boston, Suffolk Co., MA,[51] **Richard Watts**.
66.   v **Elizabeth Maxwell** b. 20-Oct-1731, Boston, Suffolk Co., MA,[8] m. 3-May-1750, in Boston, Suffolk Co., MA,[52] **Nathaniel Barber**.

20. **Elizabeth Shute** b. 20-Feb-1698/99, Malden, Middlesex Co., MA,[24] Baptized: 12-Apr-1702, Second Church of Boston,[26] m. 8-Mar-1715/16, in Boston, MA,[53] **Samuel Watts**, b. cir 1698, England, Occupation: Innkeep/Ferryman/J.P., d. 5-Mar-1770, Chelsea, Suffolk Co., MA.[31] Elizabeth died 16-Mar-1730/31, North Chelsea, Suffolk Co., MA,[54] Buried: North Chelsea, MA. Samuel:
    Samuel Watts, yeoman, was the leading inhabitant of the Rumney Marsh district of Boston, where about 1730 he built a fine home on the site of the modern Chelsea Marine Hospital, at the terminus of the

Chelsea ferry, in which he owned an interest. In 1733 he bought a town house on State Street in Boston, and the next year he was appointed a Justice of the Peace.

In 1728, Samuel Watts had petitioned the selectmen for a "Tavernars or Innholders" license at Winnisimmet, which petition was approved and the license granted. He kept the Winnisimmet Tavern for a year and a half, when on 18-Feb- 1729, he also leased the Winnisimmet Ferry for seven years. The ferry remained in Watt's care in 1741.

In 1733, Samuel Watts was elected to the Ancient and Honorable Artillery Company, was chosen moderator of Rumney Marsh (Chelsea), and chaired a committee appointed by the General Court to supervise the settlement of 1,000 French nationals from Nova Scotia in Massachusetts.

Watts was elected to the Legislature several terms, and in 1741, was elected speaker of the House of Representatives. He was elected a member of the council for 22 successive years, from 1742 to 1763. He was appointed justice of the peace on 28-Jun-1734, and justice of the inferior Court of Common Pleas on 6-Apr-1748.

The house that Samuel Watts built in 1730, passed to his son, Samuel Watts, in 1770, along with his black slaves. After the son's death in 1791, the house became the ferry hotel at Chelsea.

Children:

67.   i **Samuel Watts** b. 28-Mar-1717, Rumney Marsh, Boston, Suffolk Co., MA, m. 8-Jan-1740/41, in MA, **Hannah Rachel**, b. cir 1717, Chelsea, Suffolk Co., MA, (daughter of **John Rachel** and **Hannah** -----) d. Nov-1780, Chelsea, Suffolk Co., MA, Buried: 19-Nov-1780, Chelsea, Suffolk Co., MA.[31] Samuel died Nov-1791, Chelsea, Suffolk Co., MA, Buried: 30-Nov-1791, Chelsea, MA.[31]

Samuel Watts, son of Justice Samuel Watts, graduated from Harvard College in 1738 (A.B.). The births of his ten children by wife, Hannah Rachel, were recorded in Chelsea, MA, but Samuel lived for at least part of the time in Rhode Island from which he drove up cattle to be fattened for the Boston market on his father's farms.

After 1760, Samuel Watts became active in Chelsea affairs, being at times Selectman, Assessor, Town Clerk, and Collector of Taxes. In August, 1774, he was a member of the Committee of Correspondence for Suffolk Co. which met at Dedham. In October, Chelsea sent him to the meetings of the Provincial Congress at Salem and Concord.

In January, 1775, he was sent to the Second Provincial Congress. He was appointed a Justice of the Peace for Suffolk Co. on 24-Aug- 1775. During the siege of Boston he served on the executive committee of the town which handled such problems as the protection of cattle.

+ 68.   ii **Richard Watts** b. 23-Jan-1718/19.
+ 69.   iii **Elizabeth Watts** b. 25-Nov-1720.
  70.   iv **Edward Watts** b. 1-Aug-1724, Boston, Suffolk Co., MA.[8]
  71.   v **Ann Watts** b. 9-Mar-1726, Boston, Suffolk Co., MA.[8]

24. Michael Shute b. 21-Apr-1707, Malden, Middlesex Co., MA,[55]

Baptized: 24-Aug-1707, Second Church of Boston,[26] Occupation: Shipwright/Trader, m. (1) 8-Apr-1731, in First Church of Boston, Suffolk Co., MA,[56] **Welthen Walters**, b. cir 1708, (daughter of **William Walters** and **Loise Adams**) d. 14-Mar-1753, Newbury, MA,[57] Buried: Old Burying Ground, Newburyport, MA, m. (2) 19-Dec-1754, in Newburyport, MA,[58] **Elizabeth Boardman**, b. 7-Mar-1726, Newbury, Essex Co., MA, (daughter of **Offin Boardman** and **Sarah Woodman**) d. 1793, Exeter, Rockingham Co., NH. Michael died 23-Nov-1784, Newmarket (now Newfields), NH,[59] Buried: Hilton Burial Ground, Newfields, NH.

Michael Shute, the seventh child of Richard and Lydia (Greenland) Shute, was born in Malden, MA, on 21-Apr-1707. Unlike his father or grandfather (both mariners), Michael Shute became a shipwright, or shipbuilder, and settled first in Newbury, Essex Co., MA.

Michael Shute was married to Welthen Walters (dau. of William and Loise (Adams) Walters) by Rev. Charles Chauncy of the First Church of Boston on 8-Apr-1731.

On 9-Apr-1735, his father, Captain Richard Shute, conveyed to Michael and his brother, Nathan (a housewright), the house with land at the north end of Boston which had been given to him by his father-in-law, John Greenland. Michael and Welthen sold their half interest in the house to Ralph Cross of Newbury on 14-Feb-1745. With the proceeds they purchased three acres of land in the "great field" in Newbury from Benjamin Coker.

Michael and Welthen Shute's first two children died young; the six following survived.

Welthen (Walters) Shute died on 14-Mar-1753, and was buried in Newburyport's Old Burial Hill Cemetery. There is also a stone to her memory in the Hilton Graveyard in Newmarket (now Newfields), NH. At her death, her oldest child, Michael, Jr. was 17 years old; her youngest, Elizabeth, was only two years old.

On 19-Dec-1754, in Newbury, at the age of 47, Michael Shute married Elizabeth (Boardman) Pearson, presumably the widow of John Pearson III, and daughter of Offin and Sarah (Woodman) Boardman of Newbury.

In 1755, Michael Shute purchased land with a house in Newmarket, Rockingham Co., NH, from Richard Mattoon, carpenter. Between 1755 and 1757, Michael built a two- story, Georgian, center-chimney "Mansion House" which connected with the original one-room-with-loft Mattoon structure. The house, situated on the Squamscot River, was modified somewhat by subsequent owners, but was significantly restored by the late Margery P. Brooke in the 1970s and 1980s.

Michael and Elizabeth (Boardman) Pearson Shute moved to Newmarket, NH, when the new house was completed. Elizabeth became a member of the Stratham Church (just across the Squamscott River) in May, 1759.

Michael Shute was a major landholder in the Newmarket area, owning most of the acreage north of the River Road and east of the Exeter-Durham Road, plus acreage in Stratham. Exeter and Sanbornton, NH.

As Michael's sons reached adulthood, he helped each of them build homes of their own. Several of the sons moved on to newer settlements beyond Newmarket such as Sanbornton (Michael, Jr. and Thomas),

Londonderry (Benjamin), and Northwood (Joseph). Michael's son, John, started in the shipbuilding business, but later became an innkeeper and operated the "Shute House" on Main Street in Newmarket for several years. Sons William and Walter, however, continued in the family shipyards and, indeed, William's son, William, Jr. and grandsons, John William and Andrew Breden Shute, extended the Newmarket Shute shipbuilding trade through a fourth generation.

In civil affairs, Michael Shute petitioned for a lottery in aid of the Squamscot Bridge and its location at Newmarket (1759-60); for opening a road from the upper ferry to the main road "which is a great advantage to the north end of Newmarket" (1766); and for a bridge at Newmarket (1772).

Michael Shute was received into membership in the West Religious Society on 12-Apr-1779, and sold a pew in the Stratham meeting house on 28-Jun-1782. His wife, Elizabeth, and son, Benjamin, were baptized at Stratham on 6-May-1759; his twin daughters, Anna and Mary, were baptized there on 6- Sep-1767.

In politics, it can be assumed that the Shutes of Newmarket were conservative. When, in the Spring of 1776, the New Hampshire Committee of Safety ordered all males above 21 years of age ("Lunatics, Idiots and Negroes excepted") to sign the "Association Test," thereby signalling their willingness to "defend by Arms, the United Colonies, against the Hostile Attempts of the British Fleets and Armies" -- or have their refusal to sign reported -- the Shutes of Newmarket abstained. Indeed, Michael Shute was joined by each of his sons, then of age (William, John, and Walter), as well as his sons-in-law, Henry Wiggin and Dr. John Marsters, in refusing to sign.

Michael Shute drew up his will on 1-Sep-1778, styling himself a "Trader." He died 23-Nov-1784, in Newmarket, NH. His will was proved on 15-Dec-1784, but the disbursement of his bequests was not completed until May, 1791. Michael had a very substantial estate, and he had put in a provision in several clauses of his will, that final resolution not occur until a "term of four years from the twentieth of October next after the date, hereof," at which time all of his children would have been of age. Resolving the complicated land and house allocations, as well as the complex administrative processes extended the time considerably.

Elizabeth (Boardman) Pearson Shute survived her husband, and removed to Exeter, NH, soon after his death, to live with her daughter, Mrs. Jacob Randall. An exact date of death is not known, but Elizabeth Shute's estate was inventoried on 30-Mar-1793. Both Michael and Elizabeth Shute are buried in the Hilton Family Graveyard, Newfields (formerly Newmarket), NH. A replacement stone reads: "Here Lies / Mr. Michael Shute / Who Departed / This Life / Nov. 23 A.D. 1784 / In The 76 Year / Of His Age." The reverse of the same stone is simply inscribed: "Elizabeth / Wife Of / Michael Shute."

Children by Welthen Walters:

72.   i **Michael Shute** b. 31-May-1733, Newbury, MA,[60] d. bef Oct-1736, Newbury, MA.

73.   ii **Lydia Shute** b. 1734/35, Newbury, MA, Baptized: 02-Mar-1734/35, Third Church, Newburyport, MA,[61] d. bef Dec-1740, Newbury, MA.

```
+  74.    iii  Michael Shute b. Oct-1736.
+  75.     iv  William Shute b. 21-Sep-1738.
+  76.      v  Lydia Shute b. 2-Dec-1740.
+  77.     vi  John Shute b. 4-Jun-1744.
+  78.    vii  Walter Shute b. 15-Oct-1749.
+  79.   viii  Elizabeth Shute b. 9-Oct-1751.
               Children by Elizabeth Boardman:
+  80.     ix  Thomas Shute b. 11-Apr-1756.
+  81.      x  Joseph Shute b. 1757.
+  82.     xi  Benjamin Shute b. 16-Apr-1759.
   83.    xii  Sally Shute b. 1761, Newmarket, Rockingham Co., NH, d.
               aft Nov-1784.
+  84.   xiii  Anna Shute b. 1767.
   85.    xiv  Mary Shute b. 1767, Newmarket, Rockingham Co., NH,
               Baptized: 6-Sep-1767, Stratham, Rockingham Co., NH, d.
               aft Nov-1784.
```

Fourth Generation

51. **Samuel Shute** b. 27-Feb-1717/18, Malden, Middlesex Co., MA,[62] m. 23-May-1744, in Malden, Middlesex Co., MA,[49] **Elizabeth Pratt**, b. 25-Sep-1723, Malden, Middlesex Co., MA, (daughter of **Richard Pratt** and **Joanna Ong**) d. 1-Oct-1784, Malden, Middlesex Co., MA.[24] Samuel died 16-Apr-1786, Malden, Middlesex Co., MA.[24]

        Children:
+ 86.   i **Elizabeth Shute** b. 3-Mar-1744/45.
  87.   ii **Hannah Shute** b. 24-Oct-1752, Malden, Middlesex Co., MA,[24] d. 25-Feb-1833, Malden, Middlesex Co., MA.[24]
  88. iii **Lois Shute** b. 21-Mar-1755, Malden, Middlesex Co., MA,[24] d. 13-Feb-1834, Malden, Middlesex Co., MA.[24]
  89.   iv **Rhoda Shute** b. 26-Oct-1757, Malden, Middlesex Co., MA.[24]
  90.   v **Lydia Shute** b. 1-Aug-1760, Malden, Middlesex Co., MA,[24] d. 15-Jun-1840, Malden, Middlesex Co., MA.[24]
  91.   vi **Susanna Shute** b. 20-Feb-1765, Malden, Middlesex Co., MA,[24] d. 1-May-1766, Malden, Middlesex Co., MA.[24]

53. **Daniel Shute** b. 19-Jul-1722, Malden, Middlesex Co., MA,[63] Occupation: Congregationalist Min., m. (1) 25-Mar-1753, in Hingham, Plymouth Co., MA,[64] **Mary Cushing**, b. 28-Jan-1731/32, Hingham, Plymouth Co., MA,[65] (daughter of **Abel Cushing** and **Mary Jacob**) d. 12-Feb-1756, Hingham, MA, m. (2) 6-Jan-1763, in Pembroke, MA,[66] **Deborah Cushing**, b. 1738, Pembroke, MA, (daughter of **Elijah Cushing** and **Elizabeth Barker**) d. 26-Oct-1823, Hingham, Plymouth Co., MA.[66] Daniel died 31-Aug-1802, Hingham, Plymouth Co., MA.[67]

    Daniel Shute, the first minister of the Second Congregational Church of Hingham, MA, graduated from Harvard College in 1743 (A.B.). Following his first wife's death in 1756, Daniel Shute was appointed "Chaplain of a Regiment of Foot commanded by Colonel Joseph Williams, raised [...] for a general Invasion of Canada," on 13-Mar-1758. Daniel Shute accompanied the regiment to Albany, and was on hand for Gen. Abercrombie's attack on Ft. Ticonderoga, and the death of Lord Howe on 7-Jul-1758. Two months later, in September, 1758, Daniel Shute was exposed to smallpox, while working in the camp's hospital. He retired to Schenectady, NY, to recover and, by 20-Oct-1758, was back in Hingham, MA. [n.b. -- Rev. Daniel Shute's journal of the expedition to Canada in 1758 was published in the Essex Institute's Collections, vol. 12, pp. 132-151.]

    Stiffly opposed to the Stamp Act of 1765, Daniel Shute was described by John Adams, the future U.S. president, as "a jolly, merry droll, social Christian; he loves to laugh, tells a story with a good grace, delights in banter, but yet reasons well; is inquisitive and judicious; has an eye that plays its lightnings; sly, and waggish, and roguish; is for sinking every person who either favors the stamps or trims about them, into private station; expects a great morality among the counsellors next May."

    Daniel Shute preached before the Ancient and Honourable Artillery Company in 1767, and gave the annual Election Sermon before the legislature in 1768.

    In 1779, Hingham sent him as a delegate to the convention which

drafted the Constitution of Massachusetts; and in 1788, sent him to
the convention called to ratify the Constitution of the United States.

Daniel Shute received the D.D. from Harvard in 1790, and
relinquished public labors in March, 1799, having discharged the
duties of pastor for a period of 56 years. He resided in Hingham, MA,
on the corner of Main Street and South Pleasant Street. The lot was
purchased in 1754, and the house -- which still stands -- was built by
1762, prior to Daniel Shute's second marriage to Deborah Cushing.

                Children by Mary Cushing:

92.   i **Mary Shute** b. 8-Mar-1754, Hingham, Plymouth Co., MA,[64]
           d. 14-Aug-1825, Hingham, Plymouth Co., MA.[64]

+ 93.   ii **Daniel Shute** b. 30-Jan-1756.

55. **Mary Shute** b. 11-Mar-1727, Malden, Middlesex Co., MA,[24] m.
26-Apr-1750, in Malden, Middlesex Co., MA,[49] **Thomas Hills**, b.
25-Apr-1719, Malden, Middlesex Co., MA,[24] (son of **Benjamin Hills**
and **Mary** -----) Occupation: Shipwright/Constable, d. 6-Oct-1804,
Malden, Middlesex Co., MA.[24] Mary died 31-Mar-1810, Malden,
Middlesex Co., MA.[24]

                Children:

94.   i **Benjamin Hills** b. 10-Feb-1750/51, Malden, Middlesex
           Co., MA.[24]

95.   ii **John Hills** b. 28-Dec-1752, Malden, Middlesex Co.,
           MA.[24]

96. iii **Mary Hills** b. 3-Dec-1754, Malden, Middlesex Co., MA.[24]

97.   iv **Sarah Hills** b. 26-Jan-1757, Malden, Middlesex Co.,
           MA.[24]

98.   v **Nathan Hills** b. 18-Apr-1759, Malden, Middlesex Co.,
           MA.[24]

99.   vi **Nathan Hills** b. 27-Jun-1761, Malden, Middlesex Co.,
           MA.[24]

100. vii **Martha Hills** b. 12-May-1763, Malden, Middlesex Co.,
           MA.[24]

101. viii **Elizabeth Hills** b. 5-Nov-1771, Malden, Middlesex Co.,
           MA.[24]

56. **Richard Shute** b. 25-Jul-1729, Malden, Middlesex Co., MA,[68] m.
(1) 4-Jan-1750/51, in Malden, Middlesex Co., MA,[49] **Mary Green**, b.
cir 1730, Malden, Middlesex Co., MA, d. 21-Oct-1787, Malden, Middlesex
Co., MA,[24] m. (2) 11-Nov-1788, in Malden, Middlesex Co., MA,[24]
Lydia Porter, b. Malden, Middlesex Co., MA, d. 11-Oct-1825, Malden,
Middlesex Co., MA.[69] Richard died 27-Jan-1818, Malden, Middlesex
Co., MA.[24]

    Pvt. Richard Shute served in Capt. Samuel Sprague's (Chelsea)
company, MA militia, and was on the Lexington Alarm list of 1775. By
15-Jul-1780, however, Richard Shute of Chelsea was willing to pay a
150 pound fine, rather than be drafted as one of "The Six Months Men."
The original receipt is in the Massachusetts Historical Society's
Chamberlain papers. It is not clear, however, whether the fine was
paid by the elder Richard Shute for himself, or possibly for his son,
Richard Shute, later of Lynn, MA.

                Children by Mary Green:

102. i **Mary ("Polly") Shute** b. 19-Jul-1751, Malden, Middlesex Co., MA,[24] m. 5-May-1782, in Boston, Suffolk Co., MA,[70] **William Smith**.

+ 103. ii **Solomon Shute** b. 1-Oct-1752.

104. iii **John Shute** b. 8-Sep-1754, Malden, Middlesex Co., MA,[71] d. aft 1820, Malden, Middlesex Co., MA.[72]

Pvt. John Shute of Chelsea, MA, served under Capt. Isaac Hall of Col. Gardner's Massachusetts troops for eight months, and in January, 1778, served as a Marine aboard the U.S. Brig "General Gates," commanded by Capt. John Skinner. Like his brother, Pvt. Solomon Shute (on board the same ship), John qualified for 1 share of prize shares. The two brothers are included in a list of Chelsea men, compiled by the Chelsea Committee of Correspondence, who had enlisted into the Continental Army in or about February, 1777, certifying that they had enlisted on board Continental and State vessels.

In making his application for a Revolutionary service pension on 11-Apr-1818, John Shute of Malden, MA, then aged 62, stated he had "never had either wife or child."

+ 105. iv **Rachel Shute** b. 16-Oct-1756.

106. v **Huldah Shute** b. 28-Feb-1758, Malden, Middlesex Co., MA,[24] d. 20-Sep-1822, Chelsea, MA.[31]

107. vi **Eunice Shute** b. 15-Jan-1760, Malden, MA,[24] d. Oct-1813.

+ 108. vii **Richard Shute** b. 2-Oct-1761.

109. viii **Eleanor Shute** b. 15-May-1763, Malden, Middlesex Co., MA.[24]

110. ix **Bathsheba Shute** b. 16-Jun-1765, Malden, Middlesex Co., MA,[24] d. 25-Jan-1770, Chelsea, MA.[31]

111. x **David Shute** b. 15-Jan-1767, Malden, Middlesex Co., MA,[73] d. 25-Sep-1767, Malden, Middlesex Co., MA.[24]

112. xi **Sarah Shute** b. 26-Apr-1769, Malden, Middlesex Co., MA.[31]

+ 113. xii **David Shute** b. 25-Jan-1771.

57. Jacob Shute b. 28-Aug-1731, Malden, Middlesex Co., MA,[74] m. 28-Dec-1750, in Malden, Middlesex Co., MA,[49] **Mary Pratt**, b. 3-Apr-1730, Malden, Middlesex Co., MA,[24] (daughter of **William Pratt** and **Ruth -----**). Jacob died 28-Nov-1783, Malden, Middlesex Co., MA.[24]

Pvt. Jacob Shute served in Capt. Benjamin Blaney's company, Col. Brooks' regiment of guards, from 2-Feb-1778 to 3-Apr-1778; 60 days service at Cambridge.

Children:

114. i **Mary Shute** b. 8-May-1751, Malden, Middlesex Co., MA,[24] m. 2-Apr-1775, in Malden, Middlesex Co., MA,[75] **Benjamin Waite Jr.**, b. 4-May-1752, Malden, Middlesex Co., MA,[24] (son of **Isaac Waite** and **Deborah Wayte**).

115. ii **William Shute** b. 20-Mar-1753, Malden, Middlesex Co., MA.[76]

+ 116. iii **Jacob Shute Jr.** b. 6-Dec-1755.

+ 117.   iv **Sarah Shute** b. 22-Sep-1759.
  118.   v **Phebe Shute** b. 5-Dec-1763, Malden, Middlesex Co.,
           MA,[24] m. **Ebenezer Sargent**.
  119.   vi **Susanna Shute** b. 31-Mar-1766, Malden, Middlesex Co.,
           MA.[24]

58. **Benjamin Shute** b. 6-Jun-1734, Malden, Middlesex Co., MA,[77]
Occupation: Militia/Innkeeper, m. 29-Mar-1759, in Chelsea, MA,[78]
Elizabeth Stowers, b. 17-Nov-1739, Chelsea, Suffolk Co., MA,[31]
(daughter of **James Stowers** and **Elizabeth -----**) d. 17-Jul-1806,
Prospect, Waldo Co., ME.[79] Benjamin died 22-Jan-1807, Prospect (now
Stockton Springs), ME.[80]

Corporal Benjamin Shute of Malden, and later, Marblehead, MA,
served in a company under Captain Benjamin Johnson of Woburn in the
Crown Point expedition of 1755. At the time, he was 21 years old. On
28-Feb-1756, he petitioned the General Court for expenses incurred
while in service:

"That whereas in September last I voluntarily inlisted [sic] in
his Majesty's Service in an expedition against Crown Point in A
Rigament under the command of Collonel Plaisted and Captain Jonson
while at Fort Edward was seized with a violent fever and when the
forces were dismised [sic] was unable to come with them and lay
confined to my bed for many days after. And whereas after the fever
had left me I was a great expenc [sic] to get back to my native place
(viz) ten dollars for a man to assist me, two pound is charged for a
horse and two pounds eighteen and ten pence for the mans and my
maintainnnance [sic]. Besides A Considerable of provision sent by the
man for himself and to me, by my friends, I am yet remaining under
such great indisposition of body as to unable me to do anything for my
present support. wherefor your petitioner humbly prayeth that your
excellency and honours would take these things under your wise
consideration And I humbly trust you will make me a consideration for
the money that I have necessarily been out for my return home, the
whole is L7-18- 10." Benjamin Shute's request was allowed and ordered
paid.

The same Benjamin Shute signed a petition at Kennebeck, ME, on
20-May-1762, addressed to Francis Bernard, Esq., Capt. Gen. Governor
of Massachusetts, asking that the inhabitants be incorporated into a
town so as to enable them to provide a school and a church for their
children. On 7- Jun-1775, patriot Benjamin Shute joined with other
"inhabitants of the Penobscot River" in signing a letter to the
Provincial Congress, alerting them to the scarcity of corn and
ammunition in their area.

Captain Benjamin Shute, aged 42, was commissioned in Col. Josiah
Brewer's (Penobscot) regiment on 20-Jul-1776. Within a year, on
26-July-1777, Benjamin Shute of Frankfort, ME, was named to represent
the town on The Committee of Safety. On 5-Nov-1777, Capt. Benjamin
Shute joined in yet another petition directed toward the Council and
House of Representatives at Boston, for the return of Col. Jonathan
Buck's regiment to their own. Lt. Colonel Benjamin Shute was later of
the 1st Reg't of the 2nd Brigade of the 8th Division of the
Massachusetts Militia. On 8-Oct-1977, the Penobscot Expedition
Chapter of the DAR dedicated a bronze plaque at Hersey Retreat on

French's Point to Col. Shute. The marker details the life of Col. Shute (1734-1807), who was the first colonial settler on the point.

In 1789, Benjamin Shute, along with his son, Benjamin Shute, Jr., signed a petition of Frankfort, ME, residents to the Massachusetts General Court, asking that the town be incorporated.

By 1793, Col. Shute and his wife operated a tavern at Sandy Point, near Prospect, ME. One reviewer, Thomas Cobb, who spent the winter of 1794/95 in Maine, had a poor opinion of the establishment. In a letter to his father, dated 26- Nov-1794, Cobbs complained of the scarcity of lodgings in Prospect, noting that he knew "of none but Colonel Shute's, which beside its being a tavern is by no means a reputable house; for it often happens that the Colonel and his wife are noding over the fire by the power of 'New England' [i.e. rum], while the girls are in bead [sic] with there sweethearts." [see Col. Soc. of MA Publs., vol. 36, p. 211]

Children:

120.	i	**Elizabeth Shute** b. 25-Sep-1759, Malden, Middlesex Co., ME,[81] Baptized: 20-Apr-1760, Chelsea, MA.[31]
+ 121.	ii	**Benjamin Shute Jr.** b. 10-Oct-1761.
122.	iii	**Dorothy ("Dolly") Shute** b. 11-Jan-1764, Chelsea, MA,[82] m. **Jonathan Haskell**, b. 19-Dec-1755, Gloucester, MA,[83] (son of **Francis Haskell** and **Elizabeth Wheeler**) d. 24-Dec-1830, Deer Isle, ME.[84] Dorothy died 23-Dec-1849.[85]
+ 123.	iv	**Sarah ("Sally") Shute** b. 16-Nov-1765.
124.	v	**Thomas Shute** b. 1-Oct-1769, Chelsea, MA,[86] Baptized: 8-Jul-1770, 1st Unitarian Soc., Revere, MA,[31] Occupation: Mariner, d. 18-Jul-1800, Prospect, Waldo Co., ME.[79]
125.	vi	**Mary ("Polly") Shute** b. 18-Nov-1771, Prospect, Waldo Co., MA,[81] m. **James Blanchard Jr.**, b. 4-Nov-1769, Woolwich, ME,[84] (son of **James Blanchard** and **Susannah Thomas**) d. 5-Jan-1855, Prospect, Waldo Co., ME.[87] Mary died 1854, Prospect, Waldo Co., MA.[84]
+ 126.	vii	**Samuel Shute** b. 3-Dec-1773.
+ 127.	viii	**Catherine Shute** b. 12-Mar-1776.
128.	ix	**Lydia Shute** b. 22-Jan-1779, Prospect, ME,[81] d. bef 1781.
+ 129.	x	**Lydia Shute** b. 12-May-1781.
130.	xi	**John Shute** b. 9-Apr-1783, Prospect, ME,[88] m. ----- **Lancaster**.

59. **Amos Shute** b. 3-May-1737, Malden, Middlesex Co., MA,[89] m. 7-Feb-1760, in Malden, Middlesex Co., MA,[49] **Phebe Sprague**, b. Malden, MA, (daughter of **Stowers Sprague** and **Phoebe Brintnall**). Amos died 19-Feb-1784, Malden, Middlesex Co., MA.[24]

Pvt. Amos Shute marched in the Fort William Henry Alarm of August, 1757, under Capt. Michael Brigden. He later served in a company under Capt. Ebenezer Marrow in the campaign of 1758, and was in service until 9-Oct-1758, then aged 21, when "my health being impaired, having liberty to repair homeward I had help by the teams in my way to Albany. And then not able to travel, one of my fellow Soldiers procuered me a horse such a one as he was able to purchase and at the owners price. ... When I came home I was very Sick and under the Docters hands." [n.b. -- See Corey's History of Malden, page 713, for the full transcript of Pvt. Shute's petition.]

Seventeen years later, Sgt. Amos Shute, of Capt. Benjamin Blaney's company of MA militia, marched on the alarm of 19-Apr-1775 to Watertown, by order of Col. Gardner; service, one day. He is also recorded on the payroll of the same company for service of three days, in the march to Point Shirley, 13-Jun-1776.

Amos Shute's wife, Phebe (Sprague) Knower, was the widow of John Knower, also of Malden. She brought to their marriage John Knower's home, which originally was built for James Hovey, a Malden weaver, circa 1695. The "Shute House," as it was later called, stood until 1927, at 250 Shute Street, Everett, MA. It is now owned by the Smithsonian Institution in Washington, DC. Now in storage, the "Shute House" was last exhibited in 1976 for the Bicentennial.

The administration of Amos Shute's estate was granted to his only surviving son, George, on 3-Nov-1784 (Middlesex Co. Probate Rec. #20370).

Children:
131. i **Amos Shute** b. 10-Nov-1760, Malden, Middlesex Co., MA,[24] d. 29-Feb-1764, Malden, Middlesex Co., MA.[24]
+ 132. ii **George Shute** b. 29-May-1763.
133. iii **Phebe Shute** b. 26-Jun-1765, Malden, Middlesex Co., MA,[24] m. 1-Jul-1792, in Malden, Middlesex Co., MA,[90] **Abraham French**.
+ 134. iv **Nancy Shute** b. 6-Oct-1767.
135. v **Mary Shute** b. 5-Nov-1769, Malden, Middlesex Co., MA,[24] m. 14-Apr-1793, in Malden, Middlesex Co., MA,[91] **John Trevalley**, b. Roxbury, MA.
136. vi **Amos Shute** b. 21-Oct-1771, Malden, MA.[24]

60. **Ebenezer Shute** b. 28-Sep-1740, Malden, Middlesex Co., MA,[92] m. 16-Nov-1769, in Malden, Middlesex Co., MA,[93] **Phebe Hitchings**, b. cir 1731, (daughter of **Elkanah Hitchings** and **Phebe Baldwin**) d. 23-Jun-1817, Malden, MA. Ebenezer died 31-Aug-1801, Malden, Middlesex Co., MA.[24]

Pvt. Ebenezer Shute served for three days in the company commanded by Capt. Benjamin Blaney of Malden, MA, and ordered to Point Shirley 13-Jun-1776 by order of Gen. Lincoln.

Children:
137. i **Phebe Shute** b. 25-Jun-1771, Malden, Middlesex Co., MA,[24] d. 1-Mar-1782, Malden, Middlesex Co., MA.[24]
+ 138. ii **Samuel Shute** b. 4-Mar-1773.
+ 139. iii **Ebenezer Shute** b. 5-Jan-1775.
140. iv **Thomas Shute** b. 22-Oct-1776, Malden, Middlesex Co., MA,[94] d. 25-Nov-1777, Malden, Middlesex Co., MA.[24]
141. v **Susanna Shute** b. 22-Dec-1778, Malden, Middlesex Co., MA.[24]
142. vi **Thomas Shute** b. 17-Jan-1781, Malden, Middlesex Co., MA,[95] d. 19-Sep-1803, Malden, Middlesex Co., MA.[24]
+ 143. vii **Isaac Shute** b. 8-Oct-1782.
144. viii **Joseph Hitchings Shute** b. 21-May-1785, Malden, Middlesex Co., MA.[96]

61. Lydia Shute b. 30-Nov-1743, Malden, Middlesex Co., MA,[24] m. 6-Jun-1765, in Malden, Middlesex Co., MA,[93] **William Watts**. Lydia died 11-Oct-1825, Malden, Middlesex Co., MA.[24]

        Children:
145.   i **William Watts** b. 7-Aug-1766, Malden, Middlesex Co., MA.[24]

68. Richard Watts b. 23-Jan-1718/19, Rumney Marsh, Boston, Suffolk Co., MA,[97] m. 11-Jun-1740, in Hampton Falls?, NH,[97] **Sarah Rachel**, b. cir 1722, Chelsea, Suffolk Co., MA, (daughter of **John Rachel** and **Hannah -----**) d. 20-Feb-1758, Chelsea, Suffolk Co., MA.[31] Richard died Jul-1771, Chelsea, Suffolk Co., MA, Buried: 10-Jul-1771, Chelsea, Suffolk Co., MA.[31]

    Richard Watts graduated from Harvard College in 1739 (A.B.). Shortly thereafter he went on a voyage to Newfoundland. Back in Chelsea before winter, he courted Sarah Rachel, sister-in-law of his brother, Samuel Watts. They ran off to New Hampshire together where, on 11-Jun- 1740, they were married by Joseph Whipple of Hampton Falls. Their child, Richard, was baptized 14-Sep-1740, in Christ Church, Boston, probably as Sibley's Harvard Graduates notes, "because the Episcopalians asked fewer questions."

    In 1756, Richard Watts became insolvent. For the rest of his life he was described as sick and near poverty. Upon his death in 1771, his first cousin, Jacob Shute, still billed the estate for 17 days' labor commissioned between December, 1757 and January, 1758, as well as "2 bushels of pertatoes" and "one quarter of veal." Other creditors, such as Nathan Cheever, also of Chelsea, were still billing for debts acrued as far back as 1744. Another cousin, John Shute, billed for the May, 1754, purchase of "2 new shooes."

    Capt. Richard Watts and his wife had six children.

        Children:
146.   i **Richard Watts** b. 2-Sep-1740, Chelsea, Suffolk Co., MA,[31] Baptized: 14-Sep-1740, Christ Ch., Boston, Suffolk Co., MA, d. Sep-1747, Buried: 19-Sep-1747.
147.   ii **Elizabeth Watts** b. 9-Mar-1742, Chelsea, Suffolk Co., MA,[31] Baptized: 28-Mar-1742, Christ Ch., Boston, Suffolk Co., MA.
148.   iii **Sarah Watts** b. 2-Oct-1744, Chelsea, Suffolk Co., MA,[31] Baptized: 7-Oct-1744, Christ Ch., Boston, Suffolk Co., MA.
149.   iv **Richard Watts** b. 16-Dec-1746, Chelsea, Suffolk Co., MA.[31]
150.   v **Anna Watts** b. 1-Jan-1748, Chelsea, Suffolk Co., MA.[31]
151.   vi **Mary Watts** b. 18-Mar-1749, Chelsea, Suffolk Co., MA,[31] Baptized: 15-Apr-1750, Christ Ch., Boston, Suffolk Co., MA, d. 7-May-1750, Chelsea, Suffolk Co., MA,[31] Buried: 28-May-1750.
152.   vii **Richard Watts** b. 7-Mar-1754, Chelsea, Suffolk Co., MA,[31] Baptized: 14-May-1754, Christ Ch., Boston, Suffolk Co., MA, d. Nov-1793, Buried: 29-Nov-1793, Chelsea, Suffolk Co., MA.[31]
153.   viii **Ebenezer Watts** b. 9-Apr-1756, Chelsea, Suffolk Co.,

MA,[31] Baptized: 11-Apr-1756, Christ Ch., Boston, Suffolk
Co., MA.

69. Elizabeth Watts b. 25-Nov-1720, Boston, Suffolk Co., MA,[8]
Baptized: 16-Sep-1722, Chelsea, MA, m. 6-Nov-1740, in Chelsea, MA,[98]
Benjamin Kent, b. 1708, Charlestown, Suffolk Co., MA, Baptized:
13-Jun-1708, First Church of Cambridge, MA, (son of **Joseph Kent** and
Rebecca Chittenden) Occupation: Barrister, d. 22-Oct-1788, Halifax,
NS,[99] Buried: St. Paul's Cem., Halifax, NS. Elizabeth died
2-Aug-1802, Halifax, NS,[100] Buried: St. Paul's Cem., Halifax, NS.
Benjamin:
   Benjamin Kent graduated from Harvard College in 1727, and was
ordained a minister at Malborough in 1733. Found "unsound in the
faith" in 1735, he removed to Boston, studied law and became a
barrister. John Adams said of him, "Kent is for fun, drollery, humor,
flouts, jeers, contempt. He has an irregular, immethodical head, but
his thoughts are often good, and his expressions happy."
   Labeled a Loyalist Tory for leaving Boston for Halifax in 1784,
Kent actually served throughout the revolution on various important
Boston committees and, in 1785, at the request of Gov. Hancock, was
intrumental in negotiating the return of Suffolk Co. Probate records
which had been evacuated to Halifax by the British fleet in 1776. On
24- Apr-1776, Kent wrote to John Adams in Philadelphia, "What in the
name of Common Sense are you Gentlemen of the Continental Congress
about? [...] the present time to make a final Declaration of
Independence is the best." Adams' response included the rejoinder:
"You cannot make thirteen clocks strike precisely alike at the same
second."
   Of Kent's removal to Halifax, it is far more likely that he bowed
to familial pressure from his wife to rejoin their daughter, Sarah,
and son-in-law, Sampson Salter Blowers who, as Boston Loyalist
refugees, had sailed with the British fleet from Boston years earlier.
         Children:
   154.   i **Elizabeth Kent**.
   155.   ii **Benjamin Kent**.
   156.   iii **Ann Kent**.
   157.   iv **Sarah ("Sally") Kent** m. 5-Apr-1774,[101] **Sampson Salter
             Blowers**, b. 10-Mar-1741, Boston, Suffolk Co., MA,[102]
             Occupation: Chief Justice, d. 25-Oct-1842.[102] Sarah
             died 1845.[103] Sampson:
                Sampson Salter Blowers, a Boston Loyalist refugee,
             later became Chief Justice of the Supreme Court of Nova
             Scotia, Canada.

74. Michael Shute b. Oct-1736, Newbury, MA,[104] Baptized:
17-Oct-1736, Third Church, Newburyport, MA,[61] Occupation:
Boatbuilder, m. cir 1777, ----- -----. Michael died 1791,
Newmarket, Rockingham Co., NH.[105]
   Mical [sic] Shute served in the French and Indian War under Capt.
Gerrish with other men from Newburyport and Ipswich. Their unit was
in the attack against Ft. Ticonderoga in 1758. Benjamin Glasier, an
Ipswich native, kept a daily journal of his serice under Capt. Gerrish
from 28-Feb-1758 to 20-Nov-1758. On 8-Apr-1758 he wrote: "Day fair

weather and mical Shute is very Bad." At the time, smallpox was rampant.

Children:
- 158. i **Michael Shute** b. cir 1777-1781,[106] d. aft 1802.
- 159. ii **Hiram Shute** b. cir 1777-1791.
- 160. iii **William Shute** b. cir 1777-1783, d. aft 1802.
    This may be the William Shute, shipbuilder, credited with the 1822 construction of the "Izette" at Newmarket, NH, by the firm of Shute & Tarlton for Abraham Shaw [see Ray Brighton's "Port of Portsmouth Ships and the Cotton Trade 1783-1829" (1986)].
- 161. iv **Lydia Shute** b. cir 1782-1791, d. aft 1802.

75. William Shute b. 21-Sep-1738, Newbury, Essex Co., MA,[107] Occupation: Shipbuilder, m. (1) **Phebe Jewett**, b. 18-Oct-1741, (daughter of **Joseph Jewett** and ----- -----) d. 13-Jun-1818, m. (2) **Margery** -----. William died 11-Jun-1791.

William Shute was a shipbuilder of Newmarket and Stratham, NH. He petitioned for a lottery in aid of a Squamscot Bridge and its location in Newmarket on 20-Jan- 1760; for a bridge at Newfields, 1766; and at Newmarket in 1769. He refused to sign the Association Test posted at Newmarket in 1776, and was admitted to the West Religious Society in Stratham, NH, on 12-Apr-1779.

Children by Phebe Jewett:
- 162. i **Anna Shute** b. 5-Dec-1762, Newmarket, Rockingham Co., NH.
- + 163. ii **William Shute Jr.** b. 22-Jun-1766.
- 164. iii **Nancy Shute** b. cir 1769, Newmarket, Rockingham Co., NH.
- 165. iv **James Shute** b. cir 1770, Newmarket, Rockingham Co., NH.

76. Lydia Shute b. 2-Dec-1740, Newburyport, Essex Co., MA,[108] m. 31-Mar-1765, in Newmarket, Rockingham Co., NH,[109] **Henry Wiggin**, b. 8-May-1740, Stratham, NH,[109] (son of **Simon Wiggin** and **Susanna** -----). Lydia died 22-Jul-1784, Newmarket, Rockingham Co., NH.[109] Henry:

Henry Wiggin was descendant from English Royalty, courtesy of his great-great-great-grandmother, Dorothy Yorke, first wife of Governor Thomas Dudley (1576-1653) of Rowley, MA. She descended from King Henry II (1154-1189) by his liaison with an unnamed, or now forgotten, mistress.

To trace that connection, follow Henry Wiggin, son of Simon and Susanna Wiggin; to Simon Wiggin son of Jonathan Wiggin and Mary Emery; to Jonathan Wiggin son of Andrew Wiggin and Hannah Bradstreet. Hannah Bradstreet was the daughter of Simon Bradstreet and Anne Dudley, the Governor's daughter and, incidentally, the first published New England poetess. Anne Dudley's mother was Dorothy Yorke.

As Governor Dudley's second wife, Katherine Deighton, was also of Royal descent, all descendants of Governor Dudley, by either of his two wives, are of similar ancestry.

Children:
- 166. i **Michael Wiggin** b. 12-Dec-1765, Newmarket, Rockingham Co., NH.[109]
- 167. ii **Henry Wiggin** b. 5-Jan-1767, Newmarket, Rockingham Co.,

NH,[109] m. 11-Dec-1794, in Newmarket, Rockingham Co., NH,[109] **Hannah Hill**, b. 27-Mar-1775, Newmarket, Rockingham Co., NH,[109] (daughter of **James Hill** and **Sarah Burleigh**).

168.   iii **Lydia Wiggin** b. 15-Sep-1768, Newmarket, Rockingham Co., NH,[109] d. 25-Mar-1776, Newmarket, Rockingham Co., NH.[109]

169.   iv **Welthen Wiggin** b. 14-May-1771, Newmarket, Rockingham Co., NH.[109]

170.   v **Susanna Wiggin** b. 5-Jan-1774, Newmarket, Rockingham Co., NH,[109] d. 14-Dec-1793, Newmarket, Rockingham Co., NH.[109]

171.   vi **Elizabeth Wiggin** b. 21-Sep-1775, Newmarket, Rockingham Co., NH.[109]

172.   vii **Lydia Wiggin** b. 17-Dec-1778, Newmarket, Rockingham Co., NH.[109]

77. **John Shute** b. 4-Jun-1744, Newbury, MA,[110] Occupation: Shipbuilder/Innkeeper, m. (1) 24-Jan-1771, in Kittery, ME,[111] **Mary Hill**, b. 22-Jul-1733, (daughter of **Benjamin Hill** and **Mary Neal**) d. 9-Mar-1800, Newmarket (Newfields), Rockingham, NH, Buried: Junction Cem. nr. Newmarket, NH, m. (2) 1801, in Newmarket, Rockingham Co., NH,[112] **Fanny Noble**, b. cir 1754, Swan-Island, Kennebeck River, ME, (daughter of **Lazarus Noble** and ----- **Whidden**) d. Sep-1819, Newfields, Rockingham Co., NH. John died 26-Sep-1819, Newmarket (Newfields), Rockingham, NH, Buried: Junction Cem. nr. Newmarket, NH.

    John Shute trained as a shipbuilder, but is perhaps best remembered as the innkeeper of the "Shute House" in Newmarket, NH. [n.b. -- The inn was known as the "Shute House" from 1785 to 1884; it thereafter was called "Newfields House.] Newmarket licensed John Shute, "Taverner," in 1806, 1809-10, 1812, and 1814-17.

    Though he refused to sign the Association Test of 1776, John Shute did enlist at Portsmouth, NH, on 29-Mar-1777; deserted on 1-May-1779; and returned 1-May-1780 to rejoin Col. Henry Dearborn's regiment. Portsmouth furnished supplies for his family from 30-Mar-1780 to 1-Jun-1781.

    Active in parish affairs, John Shute served as executor for the wills of his father, mother and other family members.

    John's first wife, Mary, was the sister of Gen. James Hill, with whom John Shute, briefly, was in the shipbuilding business in Newmarket.

    John's second wife, Fanny Noble Tilton, was the widow of Johnathan Tilton of Kensington. She had been captured by the Indians when only 13 months old, on 5-Sep-1743; was sold into Canada; and educated at a French-Canadian convent. She was noted for her "excellent qualities," and was "very much esteemed by all who knew her." [n.b. -- See "Narrative of Mrs. Shute's Captivity," in Farmer's Collections (1822), vol. 1, p. 116]

          Children by Mary Hill:

173.   i **Betsey Shute** b. 1772, d. 21-Feb-1844.

+ 174.   ii **John Shute Jr.** b. 1773.

175.   iii **Robert Shute** b. 1775/76.[113]

78. **Walter Shute** b. 15-Oct-1749, Newbury, MA,[114] Baptized:
22-Oct-1749, Old South Church, Newburyport, MA,[61] Occupation:
Shipbuilder, m. 13-Sep-1778, in Newmarket, Rockingham Co., NH,[109]
Elizabeth Furber, b. 15-Aug-1759, Newmarket, Rockingham Co., NH.[109]
Walter died aft 1799.

       Walter Shute refused to sign the Association Test of 1776, posted
at Newmarket, NH.

       Children:

176.	i	**Sarah Shute** b. 6-Jun-1779, Newmarket, Rockingham Co., NH,[109] d. 9-Jun-1779, Newmarket, Rockingham Co., NH.[109]
+ 177.	ii	**Nathaniel Shute** b. 13-May-1781.
178.	iii	**Sarah Shute** b. 26-Aug-1784, Newmarket, Rockingham Co., NH,[109] m. 29-Aug-1806, **Edward Ordway**. Sarah died 12-Jun-1865.
179.	iv	**Robert Shute** b. 26-Jul-1788, Newmarket, Rockingham Co., NH,[115] m. 5-Oct-1817, in Exeter, NH,[116] **Emma Smith**.
180.	v	**Walter Shute** b. 23-Aug-1791, Newmarket, Rockingham Co., NH,[115] d. 12-Sep-1798, Newmarket, Rockingham Co., NH.[109]
+ 181.	vi	**Henry Shute** b. 18-Apr-1794.
182.	vii	**Nancy Shute** b. 2-Apr-1799, Newmarket, Rockingham Co., NH.[109]

79. **Elizabeth Shute** b. 9-Oct-1751, Newbury, MA,[61] m. **John
Marsters**, b. Exeter, NH?, Occupation: Physician. Elizabeth died aft
Nov-1784.

       Children:

+ 183.	i	**Rebecca Marsters**.

80. **Thomas Shute** b. 11-Apr-1756, Newburyport, MA,[117] Baptized:
25-Apr-1756, Old South Church, Newburyport, MA,[61] Occupation:
Shipbuilder/Farmer, m. 3-Feb-1783, in Stratham, NH,[118] **Elizabeth
Barker**, b. 25-Aug-1760, Stratham, NH,[119] (daughter of **David Barker**
and **Mary -----**) d. 29-Dec-1837, Sanbornton, NH.[120] Thomas died
24-May-1837, Sanbornton, NH,[120] Buried: Sanbornton, NH.

       Thomas Shute worked as a shipbuilder in Stratham, NH, then
purchased a farm in Sanbornton, NH, north of Franklin, and just west
of Lake Winnepesaukee.

       Children:

+ 184.	i	**Betsey (Betty) Shute** b. 13-Dec-1783.
185.	ii	**Michael Shute** b. 6-Apr-1785, Sanbornton, NH,[120] d. 22-Feb-1795, Sanbornton, NH.[120]
+ 186.	iii	**Ebenezer Shute** b. 13-Feb-1787.
187.	iv	**Thomas Shute Jr.** b. 4-Oct-1789, Sanbornton, NH,[120] m. 24-Feb-1844,[120] **Sally Gilman Dudley**, b. 1-Apr-1795, Sanbornton, NH,[120] (daughter of **Samuel Conner Dudley** and **Mercy Thorn**) d. 3-Feb-1872, N. Sanbornton, NH.[120] Thomas died 17-Oct-1851, Sanbornton, NH.[120]
188.	v	**Sally Shute** b. 4-Dec-1791, Sanbornton, NH,[120] d. 3-Mar-1815, Sanbornton, NH.[120]
189.	vi	**John Shute** b. 4-Dec-1791, Sanbornton, NH,[120] d. Canada.[120]

+ 190.   vii **Joseph Shute** b. 4-Nov-1793.
+ 191.   viii **Benjamin Shute** b. 23-Jan-1797.
  192.   ix **Michael Mitchell Shute** b. 26-Sep-1799, Sanbornton,
            NH,[121] Occupation: Farmer, m. 3-Apr-1829, in Littleton,
            NH,[120] **Lydia Carter**, b. 1803, Littleton, NH, d.
            17-Mar-1872, Littleton, NH.[120] Michael died 3-May-1885,
            Littleton, NH.
+ 193.   x **Nathaniel Shute** b. 20-Aug-1801.
+ 194.   xi **Nancy Shute** b. 30-Aug-1803.
+ 195.   xii **Noah Shute** b. 25-Aug-1806.

81. **Joseph Shute** b. 1757, Newmarket, NH,[122] Baptized: 25-Sep-1757,
Newbury, MA,[123] Occupation: Master Shipbuilder, m. 18-Oct-1778, in
Newmarket, Rockingham Co., NH,[109] **Sarah Mead**, b. 1760, Portsmouth,
NH, Baptized: 5-Oct-1760, North Church, Portsmouth, NH,[124] (daughter
of **Joseph Mead** and **Lettice -----**). Joseph died aft Nov-1784.
        Children:
+ 196.   i **John M. Shute** b. cir 1790.

82. **Benjamin Shute** b. 16-Apr-1759, Newmarket (now Newfields),
NH,[125] Baptized: 6-May-1759, Stratham, Rockingham Co., NH,
Occupation: Husbandman/Farmer, m. (1) 21-May-1785, in Newburyport, MA,
Rebeckah Boardman, b. 29-Sep-1764, Newburyport, Essex Co., MA,
(daughter of **Jonathan Boardman** and **Rebecca Moody**) d. 5-Sep-1802,
Londonderry, Rockingham Co., NH,[126] Buried: Forest Hill Cem., East
Derry, NH, m. (2) 10-Feb-1803, in Londonderry, NH,[127] **Lucy Cross**,
b. 7-Sep-1763, (daughter of **John Cross** and **Elizabeth Warner**) d.
16-Feb-1842, Londonderry, NH,[126] Buried: Forest Hill Cem., East
Derry, NH. Benjamin died 25-Dec-1847, Derry, Rockingham Co., NH,[126]
Buried: Forest Hill Cem., East Derry, NH.
    Benjamin Shute enlisted 28-Sep-1779 at Portsmouth, NH, as
corporal of the marines on board the U.S. Sloop of War "Ranger," which
was commanded by Capt. Thomas Simpson. The "Ranger" went to Boston,
where she joined the frigates "Providence" and "Boston," as well as
the sloop of War "Queen of France," and sailed to Charleston, SC.
There she was blockaded and captured by the British in May, 1780.
Benjamin Shute was taken prisoner. He was sent to Philadelphia, PA,
arriving there in June, 1780. He was issued a passport on 30-Jun-1780,
and was soon released. He reached his home in New Hampshire on
17-Jul-1780.
    He was allowed pension on his application executed 7-Apr- 1818,
at which time he was living in Londonderry, Rockingham Co., NH. In
1832, he was living in Derry, Rockingham Co., NH, with his second
wife, Lucy (Cross) Orr, the widow of James Orr.
        Children by Rebeckah Boardman:
+ 197.   i **Jonathan Shute** b. 15-Nov-1786.
  198.   ii **Rebecca Shute** b. 12-Feb-1788, Londonderry, NH,[127] m.
            1821-22 int., in Londonderry, NH,[127] **David Sargent**.
            Rebecca died aft 1849.
  199.   iii **Mary Shute** b. 11-Aug-1789, Londonderry, NH,[127] d.
            17-Apr-1815.
  200.   iv **James Shute** b. 14-Mar-1791, Londonderry, NH, d.
            23-Sep-1813.

201.   v **Samuel Shute** b. 17-May-1793, Londonderry, NH,[128] m.
         (1) 1821-22 int., in Londonderry, NH,[127] **Rhoda
         Ingerson**, m. (2) 1824/25 int., in Londonderry, NH,[127]
         Lovey Gaut. Samuel died 11-Jan-1836.
+ 202.   vi **Michael Shute** b. 20-Jan-1795.
+ 203.   vii **William B. Shute** b. 9-Sep-1796.
204.   viii **Daniel Shute** b. 17-Jul-1798, Londonderry, NH.[128]
205.   ix **Lydia Shute** b. 6-Aug-1800, Londonderry, NH, d.
         8-Sep-1813.
206.   x **John Shute** b. 17-Aug-1801, Londonderry, NH, d.
         6-Sep-1802, Londonderry, NH.
         Children by Lucy Cross:
207.   xi **Sarah Shute** b. 8-Nov-1803, Londonderry, NH,[127] d.
         25-Jan-1839.
208.   xii **John Orr Shute** b. 21-Jun-1805, Londonderry, NH, d.
         7-Nov-1810.
+ 209. xiii **George Shute** b. 19-Aug-1807.
210.   xiv **Julia Ann Shute** b. 26-Sep-1809, Londonderry, NH,[127] m.
         12-Feb-1839, in Londonderry, NH,[129] **Daniel Goodwin**, b.
         25-Jan-1809, (son of **Joshua Goodwin** and **Elizabeth
         Jones**) Occupation: Rev., d. 30-Dec-1893. Julia died
         10-Sep-1845, Londonderry, NH.[126] Daniel:
              Rev. Daniel Goodwin prepared for college at
         Pinkerton Academy, was graduated from Dartmouth in 1835,
         and from Andover Theological Seminary in 1838, and was
         ordained to the ministry 27-Feb-1839, at Brookline.
         There he remained for 16 years. After serving for short
         periods of time the churches of Hillsborough Bridge,
         Londonderry, and Derry, he served as pastor at Mason, NH,
         from 1857 to 1878, and resided there until his death.
211.   xv **Almira Shute** b. 12-Mar-1812, Londonderry, NH,[127] d.
         9-Jun-1842, Londonderry, NH,[130] Buried: 11-Jun-1842,
         Forest Hill Cem., East Derry, NH.

84. **Anna Shute** b. 1767, Newmarket, Rockingham Co., NH, Baptized:
6-Sep-1767, Stratham, Rockingham Co., NH, m. 5-Jun-1787, in Newmarket,
Rockingham Co., NH,[131] **Jacob Randall**, b. Portsmouth, NH, (son of
Jacob Randall and ----- -----) Occupation: Barber. Anna died
28-Mar-1792, Exeter, Rockingham Co., NH.[132]
              Children:
+ 212.   i **Jacob Randall Jr.** b. 25-Dec-1788.
213.   ii **Sarah Randall** b. 6-Oct-1790, Exeter, Rockingham Co.,
         NH.[132]

Fifth Generation

86. Elizabeth Shute b. 3-Mar-1744/45, Malden, Middlesex Co., MA,[24] m. (1) 25-Jan-1770, in Malden, Middlesex Co., MA,[93] **John Grover**, b. Malden, Middlesex Co., MA, d. cir 1800, Malden, Middlesex Co., MA, m. (2) 13-Oct-1806, in Malden, Middlesex Co., MA,[24] **Nathan Burditt**, b. 26-Nov-1745, Malden, Middlesex Co., MA,[24] (son of **Joseph Burditt** and **Tabitha -----**). Elizabeth died aft 1806.

Children by John Grover:

214.	i	**James Grover** b. 27-Jan-1771, Malden, Middlesex Co., MA.[24]
215.	ii	**John Grover** b. 1-Jul-1772, Malden, Middlesex Co., MA.[24]
216.	iii	**Asa Grover** b. 1-Mar-1774, Malden, Middlesex Co., MA.[24]
217.	iv	**Peter Grover** b. 12-Oct-1776, Malden, Middlesex Co., MA.[24]
218.	v	**Stephen Grover** b. 28-Apr-1780, Malden, Middlesex Co., MA.[24]
219.	vi	**Lois Grover** b. 9-Aug-1782, Malden, Middlesex Co., MA.[24]
220.	vii	**Lydia Grover** b. 27-Mar-1786, Malden, Middlesex Co., MA.[24]
221.	viii	**Betsey Grover** b. May-1789, Malden, Middlesex Co., MA.[24]

93. Daniel Shute b. 30-Jan-1756, Hingham, Plymouth Co., MA,[133] Baptized: 30-Jan-1756, Hingham, Plymouth Co., MA, Occupation: Physician, m. 31-Dec-1789, in Hingham, Plymouth Co., MA,[64] **Betsey Cushing**, b. 5-Apr-1768, Hingham, Plymouth Co., MA,[64] (daughter of **Isaiah Cushing** and **Betsey Cushing**) d. 4-Oct-1818, Hingham, Plymouth Co., MA.[64] Daniel died 19-Jan-1829, Hingham, Plymouth Co., MA.[64]

Daniel Shute graduated from Harvard College in 1775 (A.B.). He commanded a company during the siege of Boston and, soon after, was made a Surgeon's Mate in the Hospital Dept. In 1777-78, he was Aide-de-Camp to Gen. Benjamin Lincoln, and was Surgeon, 4th MA militia, from Apr-1778 to Jun-1783. Daniel Shute was a member of the original Society of the Cincinnati.

As a physician in Hingham, MA, Daniel Shute resided in the paternal homestead on Main Street, at the corner of South Pleasant Street.

Children:

222.	i	**Elizabeth Shute** b. 9-Oct-1791, Hingham, Plymouth Co., MA,[134] m. (1) 25-May-1815, in Salem, MA,[135] **Isaac Cushing**, b. Salem, MA, m. (2) 6-May-1840,[64] **Ezekiel Webster**, b. Northfield, MA.
+ 223.	ii	**Daniel Shute Jr.** b. 23-Jul-1793.
224.	iii	**John Shute** b. 18-Jan-1796, Hingham, Plymouth Co., MA,[136] d. 9-Jul-1876.[64]
+ 225.	iv	**Charles Shute** b. 20-Apr-1799.
226.	v	**William Shute** b. 4-Jan-1802, Hingham, Plymouth Co., MA,[136] d. 2-Mar-1884.[64]
227.	vi	**Mary Cushing Shute** b. 9-Mar-1804, Hingham, Plymouth

Co., MA,[64] d. 22-Sep-1887.[64]

   228.   vii **Deborah Barstow Shute** b. 16-Feb-1806, Hingham, Plymouth Co., MA,[64] d. 1-Jan-1888.[64]

103. Solomon Shute b. 1-Oct-1752, Malden, Middlesex Co., MA,[94] Occupation: Farmer, m. 26-Jan-1795, in Malden, Middlesex Co., MA,[93] **Elizabeth Lynde**, b. 22-Dec-1757, Malden, Middlesex Co., MA,[24] (daughter of **Jabez Lynde** and **Rachel Parker**) d. 21-Mar-1848, Malden, Middlesex Co., MA.[24] Solomon died 6-Feb-1834, Malden, Middlesex Co., MA.[24]

     Pvt. Solomon Shute marched on the Alarm of 19-Apr-1775 with his father, Richard Shute, in Capt. Sprague's company of MA militia. He also served (1777) with his brother, John Shute, as a Marine aboard the U.S. Brig "General Gates," commanded by Capt. John Skimmer.

          Children:
   229.   i ----- **Shute** b. 1798/99, Malden, Middlesex Co., MA, d. 19-Jan-1799, Malden, Middlesex Co., MA.[24]
+ 230.   ii **Solomon Shute** b. 6-Sep-1801.

105. Rachel Shute b. 16-Oct-1756, Malden, Middlesex Co., MA,[24] m. 18-Dec-1781, in Chelsea, Suffolk Co., MA,[31] **Joseph Belcher**, b. 10-May-1751, Chelsea, Suffolk Co., MA,[31] (son of **Jonathan Belcher** and **Elizabeth Tuttle**). Rachel died 7-Oct-1827, Chesea, Suffolk Co., MA.[31]

          Children:
+ 231.   i **Joseph Belcher** b. 20-Feb-1782.
   232.   ii **Rachel Belcher** b. 19-Mar-1785, Chelsea, Suffolk Co., MA.[31]
   233.   iii **Samuel Belcher** b. 24-Sep-1791, Chelsea, Suffolk Co., MA.[31]
   234.   iv **Mary Belcher** b. 28-Dec-1795, Chelsea, Suffolk Co., MA.
   235.   v **John Belcher** b. 26-Apr-1800, Chelsea, Suffolk Co., MA.[31]

108. Richard Shute b. 2-Oct-1761, Malden, Middlesex Co., MA,[137] m. (1) 18-Sep-1787, in Malden, Middlesex Co., MA,[138] **Sarah Hawks**, b. Malden, MA, d. 18-Jun-1792, Lynn, Essex Co., MA,[139] m. (2) 30-Oct-1792, in Lynn, Essex Co., MA,[139] **Elizabeth Rhoades**. Richard died aft 1792.

          Children by Sarah Hawks:
   236.   i **Sarah ("Sally") Shute** b. 3-Apr-1788, Lynn, Essex Co., MA,[139] m. 29-Nov-1810, in Lynn, Essex Co., MA,[139] **David Taggert**.
   237.   ii **Thomas Hawks Shute** b. 12-Mar-1790, Lynn, Essex Co., MA,[140] d. 18-Aug-1791, Lynn, Essex Co., MA.[139]
   238.   iii **Polly Shute** b. 15-Jun-1792, Lynn, Essex Co., MA,[139] d. 15-Aug-1792, Lynn, Essex Co., MA.[139]

113. David Shute b. 25-Jan-1771, Malden, MA,[141] m. (1) 14-Jun-1796, in Boston, Suffolk Co., MA,[142] **Hannah Christie**, d. bef 1804, m. (2) 29-Jul-1804, in Trinity Church, Boston, MA,[143] **Rebecca Woods**. David died 15-Aug-1855, E. Boston, MA,[144] Buried: 17-Aug-1855, Woodlawn Cem., Everett, MA.[144]

Children by Hannah Christie:
239.   i **Richard Shute** b. 1802, d. 26-Jan-1880, Worcester, MA,[144] Buried: 29-Jan-1880, Woodlawn Cem., Everett, MA.[144]

Children by Rebecca Woods:
240.   ii **John Shute** b. 29-Mar-1810, Malden or Chelsea, MA,[31] d. 27-Apr-1889, E. Boston, MA,[144] Buried: 29-Apr-1889, Woodlawn Cem., Everett, MA.[144]

+ 241.   iii **Mary Green Shute** b. 3-Jul-1804.

116. **Jacob Shute Jr.** b. 6-Dec-1755, Malden, Middlesex Co., MA,[145] m. (1) 22-Sep-1776, in Malden, Middlesex Co., MA,[93] **Elizabeth Hitchings**, b. cir 1750, d. 14-Dec-1816, Malden, Middlesex Co., MA, m. (2) 25-Sep-1817, in Malden, Middlesex Co., MA,[146] **Nancy Knower**, b. cir 1768, d. 1-Dec-1846, Malden, Middlesex Co., MA.[24] Jacob died 1820-1821, Malden, Middlesex Co., MA.

Children by Elizabeth Hitchings:
242.   i **Aaron Shute** d. 22-Feb-1780, Malden, Middlesex Co., MA.[147]

+ 243.   ii **William Shute** b. 30-Jan-1781.
244.   iii **Jacob Shute** b. Malden, Middlesex Co., MA.[148]
+ 245.   iv **Benjamin Sargent Shute**.
+ 246.   v **Sarah Shute**.
247.   vi **Elizabeth Shute** m. 23-Dec-1804 int, in Malden, Middlesex Co., MA,[149] **Enoch Hurlbert**, b. Thompson, CT. Elizabeth died bef Jun-1820.

117. **Sarah Shute** b. 22-Sep-1759, Malden, Middlesex Co., MA,[24] m. 25-Sep-1794, in Malden, Middlesex Co., MA,[150] **Enos Blake**, b. Charlestown, MA.

Children:
248.   i **Sarah Blake** b. 26-Jul-1795, Charlestown, MA.[151]
249.   ii **Mary Blake** b. 8-Jan-1807, Charlestown, MA.[32]

121. **Benjamin Shute Jr.** b. 10-Oct-1761, Malden, Middlesex Co., MA,[152] Baptized: 18-Oct-1761, Chelsea, MA,[31] m. (1) 10-Oct-1786, in Chelsea, Suffolk Co., MA,[31] **Mary (Polly) Tewksbury**, b. 27-Jan-1764, Chelsea, Suffolk Co., MA,[31] (daughter of **John Tewksbury** and **Anna Bill**) m. (2) **Catherine -----**, m. (3) **Sally York**. Benjamin died 1848, Prospect, ME.

Children by Mary (Polly) Tewksbury:
250.   i **Benjamin Shute** b. 31-Aug-1787, Prospect, ME.[88]
251.   ii **Thomas Shute** b. 2-Mar-1789, Prospect, ME,[88] d. bef Nov-1794.
252.   iii **Mary (Polly) Shute** b. 8-Jan-1791, Prospect, ME,[81] Baptized: 2-Oct-1791, Chelsea, MA.[31]
253.   iv **Betsy Stowers Shute** b. 28-Dec-1793, Prospect, ME.[81]
254.   v **Thomas Shute** b. 17-Nov-1794, Prospect, ME.[88]
255.   vi **John Shute** b. 26-Dec-1797, Prospect, ME.[88]
256.   vii **Nancy Shute** b. 6-Oct-1798, Prospect, ME.[81]
+ 257. viii **William Shute** b. 5-Jan-1800.
258.   ix **Henry Shute** b. 25-Aug-1802, Prospect, ME.[88]
           Children by Catherine -----:

259.   x **Charlota Shute** b. 6-Sep-1803, Prospect, ME.
             Children by Sally York:
+ 260.   xi **Alfred Shute** b. 18-Dec-1806.
  261.   xii **Robert Shute** b. 30-Aug-1808, Prospect, ME.

123. **Sarah ("Sally") Shute** b. 16-Nov-1765, Chelsea, MA,[81] Baptized:
17-Nov-1765, Chelsea, MA,[31] m. **David Partridge**. Sarah died 1855.
             Children:
  262.   i **Benjamin Partridge**.

126. **Samuel Shute** b. 3-Dec-1773, Prospect, Waldo Co., ME,[88] m.
28-Nov-1797 int, **Mary ("Polly") French**, d. 23-Mar-1860, Prospect,
Waldo Co., ME.[81] Samuel died aft 1860, Stockton, Waldo Co., ME.[153]
             Children:
+ 263.   i **Samuel Shute Jr.**.
+ 264.   ii **Zetham French Shute** b. 11-Jun-1806.

127. **Catherine Shute** b. 12-Mar-1776, Prospect, ME,[81] m. **James
Sawyer**. Catherine died Deer Island, ME.
             Children:
  265.   i **Eliza Jane Sawyer** b. Nov-1809, Prospect, Waldo Co.,
             ME.[81]

129. **Lydia Shute** b. 12-May-1781, Prospect, ME,[81] m. 16-Feb-1800
int, in Prospect, Waldo Co., ME,[84] **Thomas Shute Blanchard**, b.
31-Oct-1776, Woolwich, ME,[87] (son of **James Blanchard** and **Susannah
Thomas**) d. 11-Jan-1861, Stockton Springs, Waldo Co., ME.[87] Lydia
died 1867, Stockton Springs, Waldo Co., ME.[87]
             Children:
  266.   i **Lydia Blanchard** b. 8-Jul-1810, Prospect, Waldo Co.,
             ME,[84] m. 20-Jan-1831, in Prospect, Waldo Co., ME,[154]
             James Lunt Griffin, b. 16-Nov-1807, Stockton, Waldo
             Co., ME,[154] (son of **Nathan Griffin** and **Elizabeth
             Treat**) d. 31-Jul-1884, Stockton, Waldo Co., ME.[154]

132. **George Shute** b. 29-May-1763, Malden, Middlesex Co., MA,[155] m.
(1) 2-Jun-1785, in Malden, Middlesex Co., MA,[93] **Peternell Knower**,
b. 31-Aug-1761, Malden, Middlesex Co., MA,[24] (daughter of **Daniel
Knower** and **Abigail -----**) d. Sep-1816, Malden, Middlesex Co.,
MA,[24] m. (2) 10-Jun-1817, in Malden, Middlesex Co., MA,[156] **Sarah
Grover**, b. cir 1770, d. 25-Nov-1842, Malden, Middlesex Co., MA.[157]
George died 2-Dec-1831, Malden, Middlesex Co., MA.[24]
    George Shute served with the MA Line during the Revolutionary
War. He made his will on 4-Oct-1825, which was proved on 29-Dec-1831.
In it, he mentions his second wife, Sarah, and his nephew, Samuel
Knower, of Roxbury, to whom he leaves his estate and his pew in the
Baptist Meeting House. Witnesses to the will included: William
Shute, Jacob Shute, and Benjamin S. Shute (Middlesex Co. Probate Rec.
#20372).
    George and Sarah Shute lived at 250 Shute Street in Everett, MA,
in the circa 1695 "Hovey House," which he inherited from his father,
Amos Shute. The house stood at that location until 1927; it is now in
the possession of the Smithsonian Institution in Washington, DC.

Children by Peternell Knower:
267.   i **Charles Shute** d. 1-Jul-1818, Malden, MA.[158]

134. **Nancy Shute** b. 6-Oct-1767, Malden, Middlesex Co., MA,[24] m. 26-Jul-1787, in Malden, Middlesex Co., MA,[24] **George Knower**, b. Malden, Middlesex Co., MA.
        Children:
268.   i **Phebe Knower** b. 13-Nov-1787, Malden, Middlesex Co., MA.[24]
269.   ii **Nancy Knower** b. 17-Sep-1789, Malden, Middlesex Co., MA.[24]
270.   iii **George Shute Knower** b. 2-Apr-1792, Malden, Middlesex Co., MA.[24]
271.   iv **Peternell Knower** b. 1-Feb-1794, Malden, Middlesex Co., MA.[24]
272.   v **Abigail Knower** b. 29-Sep-1796, Malden, Middlesex Co., MA.[24]
273.   vi **Samuel Knower** b. 18-Jun-1799, Malden, Middlesex Co., MA.[24]

138. **Samuel Shute** b. 4-Mar-1773, Malden, Middlesex Co., MA,[159] m. (1) 30-Nov-1797, in Malden, Middlesex Co., MA,[156] **Lydia Waite**, b. 16-Oct-1778, Malden, Middlesex Co., MA, (daughter of **Thomas Waite** and **Lydia Hitchings**) d. 5-Sep-1801, Malden, Middlesex Co., MA,[24] m. (2) 15-Mar-1803, in Malden, MA, **Lucy Cheever**, b. 30-Nov-1784, Chelsea, MA, (daughter of **Joseph Cheever** and **Sarah ----**) d. 24-Sep-1872.
        Children by Lydia Waite:
274.   i **Lydia Shute** b. 12-Nov-1798, Malden, Middlesex Co., MA.[24]
        Children by Lucy Cheever:
275.   ii **Lucy Shute** b. 18-Jul-1804, Malden, Middlesex Co., MA,[24] d. bef 1805, Malden, Middlesex Co., MA.
276.   iii **Lucy Shute** b. 18-Jun-1805, Malden, Middlesex Co., MA,[24] m. 14-Apr-1827 int, in Malden, Middlesex Co., MA,[24] **Ezra Holden Jr.**.
277.   iv **Samuel Shute** b. 5-Nov-1806, Malden, Middlesex Co., MA,[94] d. 24-Aug-1807, Malden, Middlesex Co., MA.[24]
278.   v **Harriet C. Shute** b. 30-Sep-1808, Malden, Middlesex Co., MA,[24] m. 10-Jul-1833, in Malden, Middlesex Co., MA,[160] **Otis Chandler Wood**.
279.   vi **Phebe Shute** b. 20-Apr-1810, Malden, Middlesex Co., MA,[24] m. 29-Apr-1832, in Malden, Middlesex Co., MA,[161] **Eli Holden**.
+ 280.   vii **Samuel Shute** b. 15-Aug-1813.
281.   viii **Susan Shute** b. 20-Aug-1815, Malden, Middlesex Co., MA,[24] m. 13-Apr-1834, in Malden, Middlesex Co., MA,[160] **Robert Oliver Jr.**.   Susan died 14-Jan-1846.
282.   ix **Mary C. Shute** b. 26-Jul-1817, Malden, Middlesex Co., MA,[24] d. 8-Jun-1833, Malden, Middlesex Co., MA.[162]
283.   x **Elizabeth Shute** b. 19-Nov-1818, Malden, Middlesex Co., MA,[24] m. 7-Oct-1838, **Charles A. Boyd**.
284.   xi **Pamela Shute** b. 29-Jul-1820, Malden, Middlesex Co.,

MA.[24]

139. Ebenezer Shute b. 5-Jan-1775, Malden, MA,[163] m. 5-Oct-1800, in Boston, Suffolk Co., MA,[142] **Susanna Beals**, b. 22-Nov-1773, Hingham, Plymouth Co., MA,[2] d. 1-Feb-1847, Boston, Suffolk Co., MA,[2] Buried: Copp's Hill Burial Ground, Boston, MA. Ebenezer died 23-May-1850, Boston, Suffolk Co., MA,[2] Buried: Copp's Hill Burial Ground, Boston, MA.

Children:
+ 285.   i **Ebenezer Shute Jr.** b. cir 1804.
+ 286.   ii **Caleb B. Shute** b. 7-Jul-1806.
  287. iii **Joseph B. Shute** b. 28-Apr-1808, Boston, Suffolk Co., MA,[164] d. 15-Jun-1840,[2] Buried: Copp's Hill Burial Ground, Boston, MA.
+ 288.   iv **James M. Shute** b. cir 1813.
  289.   v **Susan G. Shute** b. 9-Jun-1815, Boston, Suffolk Co., MA,[2] m. Feb-1836, **Joshua Stetson**. Susan died 9-Aug-1844,[2] Buried: Copp's Hill Burial Ground, Boston, MA.

143. Isaac Shute b. 8-Oct-1782, Malden, Middlesex Co., MA,[94] m. (1) 19-Sep-1804, in Malden, Middlesex Co., MA,[156] **Hannah Tufts**, b. 2-May-1781, (daughter of **Stephen Tufts** and **Hannah Farmington**) d. 6-Jan-1842, Malden, Middlesex Co., MA,[24] m. (2) aft 1842, **Lydia -----**, b. cir 1788, d. 20-Jun-1849, Malden, MA.

Children by Hannah Tufts:
  290.   i **Thomas Shute** b. 20-Jun-1805, Malden, Middlesex Co., MA.[94]
  291.   ii **Peter Tufts Shute** b. 1-Jan-1807, Malden, Middlesex Co., MA.[94]
  292. iii **Isaac Shute** b. 9-Sep-1809, Malden, Middlesex Co., MA.[94]
  293.   iv **Elbridge Gerry Shute** b. 6-Sep-1811, Malden, Middlesex Co., MA.[94]
  294.   v **Mary Ann Shute** b. 15-Mar-1814, Malden, Middlesex Co., MA.[24]
  295.   vi **Hannah B. Shute** b. 9-May-1815, Malden, Middlesex Co., MA,[24] m. 26-Apr-1835, in Malden, Middlesex Co., MA,[160] **Peter Augustus Waitt**.
+ 296. vii **Stephen Tufts Shute** b. 11-Aug-1818.

163. William Shute Jr. b. 22-Jun-1766, Newmarket, Rockingham Co., NH,[165] Occupation: Shipbuilder, m. bef 1792, in Newmarket, Rockingham Co., NH, **Nancy Foss**, b. cir 1770, d. 14-Jun-1818, Newmarket, Rockingham Co., NH. William died 14-Feb-1820.

William Shute, Jr. was probably the shipbuilder credited with the construction of the "James Cook" at Newmarket, NH, in 1804 for William Charles Neil. Named in honor of the great English explorer of the South Pacific, the "James Cook" was captured by a privateer in 1810 [see Ray Brighton's "Port of Portsmouth Ships and the Cotton Trade 1783-1829" (1986)].

Children:
+ 297.   i **John William Shute** b. 21-Mar-1792.

+ 298.   ii **Andrew Breden Shute** b. 21-Mar-1794.

174. **John Shute Jr.** b. 1773,[166] m. cir 1800, **Mary Ann Rogers**, b.
27-Aug-1775, (daughter of **Nathaniel Rogers** and **Elizabeth
Carpenter**) d. 14-Mar-1823. John died 8-Jul-1818,[167] Buried:
Junction Cem., nr. Newfields, NH.
    John Shute, Jr. was active in Newmarket, NH, town affairs, and
served as Selectman (1806-08) and Assessor (1809). He and his wife,
Mary, lived in the Brodhead House.
    It was most probably this John Shute, shipbuilder (or his
father), who was credited for the Newmarket construction of the
"Patriot" in 1801, the "Manning" in 1805, and the "Eliza Sproat" in
1807 [see Ray Brighton's Port of Portsmouth Ships and the Cotton Trade
1783-1829" (1986)].
        Children:
    299.   i **Elizabeth Shute** b. cir 1800.

177. **Nathaniel Shute** b. 13-May-1781, Newmarket, Rockingham Co.,
NH,[168] Occupation: Saddler, m. 14-May-1806,[79] **Elizabeth Smith**, b.
1784, Exeter, d. 7-Sep-1816.[79] Nathaniel died 9-Aug-1821, Kennebunk,
ME.
    Nathaniel Shute removed to Kennebunk, ME in 1805, and purchased
(1809) a commercial building on Main Street from Capt. George Perkins,
from which he ran a saddlemaking business. The building was sold
circa 1842.
        Children:
+ 300.   i **Nathaniel Shute** b. 1807.

181. **Henry Shute** b. 18-Apr-1794, Newmarket, Rockingham Co., NH,[169]
m. 27-Feb-1820, in Exeter, Rockingham Co., MA,[132] **Elizabeth Rowe
Smith**, b. 7-Feb-1800, Exeter, Rockingham Co., MA.[132] Henry died
Dec-1858.
        Children:
    301.   i **Henry Augustus Shute** b. 18-Jun-1821, Exeter Twp.,
            Rockingham Co., NH,[170] d. 18-Dec-1841, Exeter Twp.,
            Rockingham Co., NH.[132]
    302.   ii **Ann Elizabeth Shute** b. 15-Nov-1824, Exeter Twp.,
            Rockingham Co., NH,[132] d. 25-May-1858, Exeter Twp.,
            Rockingham Co., NH.[132]
+ 303.   iii **George Smith Shute** b. 2-Mar-1827.
    304.   iv **Sarah Frances Shute** b. 26-May-1831, Exeter Twp.,
            Rockingham Co., NH.[132]

183. **Rebecca Marsters** b. Newmarket, Rockingham Co., NH, m.
7-Feb-1793, in Exeter, Rockingham Co., NH,[132] **Jacob Randall Jr.**, b.
25-Dec-1788, Exeter, Rockingham Co., NH,[132] (son of **Jacob Randall**
and **Anna Shute**).
        Children:
    305.   i **Anna Randall** b. 26-May-1794, Exeter, Rockingham Co.,
            NH.[132]

184. **Betsey (Betty) Shute** b. 13-Dec-1783, Sanbornton, NH,[120] m.
6-May-1804, **Richard Brown**, b. 20-Dec-1779, Sanbornton, NH,[120] (son

of **Samuel Brown** and **Sally Paine**) d. 8-Mar-1858, Sanbornton, NH.[120] Betsey died 8-Oct-1859, Sanbornton, NH.[120]

Children:
- 306.   i   **Sally Brown** b. 22-Aug-1805, Sanbornton, NH.[120]
- 307.   ii   **Noah Barker Brown** b. 5-Dec-1807, Sanbornton, NH.[120]
- 308.   iii   **Eliza Brown** b. 18-Aug-1814, Sanbornton, NH,[120] d. 25-Jul-1848, Sanbornton, NH.[120]
- 309.   iv   **Mary Ann Brown** b. 5-Mar-1821, Sanbornton, NH.[120]

186. Ebenezer Shute b. 13-Feb-1787, Sanbornton, NH,[171] Occupation: Farmer/militia captain, m. bef 1811, **Rachel Short Johnson**, b. 1-Aug-1792, Sanbornton, NH,[120] (daughter of **John Johnson** and **Mary (Molly) Smith**) d. 3-Apr-1869, Sanbornton, NH.[120] Ebenezer died 23-Nov-1853, Sanbornton, NH.[120]

Capt. Ebenezer Shute served in the NH militia.

Children:
- + 310.   i   **Elizabeth Barker Shute** b. 31-Mar-1811.
- 311.   ii   **Mary Smith Shute** b. 31-Dec-1812, Bridgewater, Grafton Co., NH,[120] d. 11-Feb-1842, Sanbornton, NH.[120]
- 312.   iii   **John Shute** b. 10-Oct-1815, Bridgewater, Grafton Co., NH,[120] d. 12-Oct-1840, Sanbornton, NH.[120]
- + 313.   iv   **Thomas Shute** b. 9-Jan-1819.
- + 314.   v   **Noah Johnson Shute** b. 30-Nov-1821.
- + 315.   vi   **Ebenezer Shute** b. 19-Jun-1824.
- 316.   vii   **Harriet Rollins Shute** b. 17-May-1827, Bridgewater, Grafton Co., NH,[120] d. 14-Mar-1845, Sanbornton, NH.[120]
- 317.   viii   **Rachel Augusta Shute** b. 13-Jun-1835, Sanbornton, NH,[120] d. 12-Feb-1839, Sanbornton, NH.[120]

190. Joseph Shute b. 4-Nov-1793, Sanbornton, NH,[121] Occupation: Farmer, m. (1) 23-Feb-1820, in Sanbornton, NH,[120] **Mary Carter**, b. 16-May-1798, New Hampton, NH, d. 1-Jan-1840, Littleton, NH,[120] m. (2) 6-Dec-1841,[120] **Phebe C. Church**, b. 6-Dec-1798, Waterford, VT, (daughter of **Perley Church** and **Jerviah Jacobs**) d. 24-Sep-1873, Littleton, NH.[120] Joseph died 18-Sep-1873, Littleton, NH.[120]

Children by Mary Carter:
- + 318.   i   **Joseph B. Shute** b. 1-Dec-1820.
- 319.   ii   **Sally Shute** b. 26-Jan-1824, Littleton, NH.[120]
- + 320.   iii   **Horace Shute** b. 17-Dec-1829.
- + 321.   iv   **Sewell Shute** b. 20-May-1833.
- 322.   v   **Harriet Shute** b. 14-Apr-1835, Littleton, NH,[120] d. 1835, Littleton, NH.[120]
- 323.   vi   **Alden Shute** b. 20-Oct-1837, Littleton, NH,[121] d. 1837, Littleton, NH.[120]

191. Benjamin Shute b. 23-Jan-1797, Sanbornton, NH,[120] m. 2-Nov-1830,[120] **Mary Dudley**, b. 4-Aug-1797, (daughter of **Samuel Conner Dudley** and **Mercy Thorn**) d. 10-Nov-1879, Thornton, NH.[120] Benjamin died 17-Mar-1884, Thornton, NH.

Children:
- 324.   i   **Charles Shute** b. 2-Aug-1833, Sanbornton, NH,[120] m. 2-Mar-1865,[120] ----- -----. Charles died Thornton, NH?.

325.   ii **Mary Elizabeth Shute** b. 19-Sep-1835, Sanbornton, NH,[120] m. 10-May-1859, in Thornton, NH,[120] **H. P. Emerson**, d. bef 1881.[120] Mary died 1-Mar-1917, Ottumwa, IA.

193. **Nathaniel Shute** b. 20-Aug-1801, Sanbornton, NH,[121] Occupation: Farmer, m. 13-Feb-1827, **Marie Dudley Bagley Smith**, b. 1802, Sanbornton, NH, (daughter of **Reuben Smith** and **Mary Dudley**) d. 1880, Littleton, NH. Nathaniel died 7-Feb-1885, Littleton, NH.
      Children:
326.   i **Charles Smith Shute** b. 14-Nov-1830, Littleton, NH,[121] d. 27-Feb-1844, Littleton, NH.[120]
+ 327.   ii **Gilman Dudley Shute** b. 18-Jun-1831.
328.   iii **Charles N. Shute** b. 14-Oct-1847, Littleton, NH,[121] d. 14-Nov-1847, Littleton, NH.[120]

194. **Nancy Shute** b. 30-Aug-1803, Sanbornton, NH,[120] m. 13-Apr-1831,[120] **Gilman Clark**, b. 20-May-1802, Candia, NH,[120] (son of **Henry Clark** and **Hannah Dudley**). Nancy died bef 1844, Sanbornton, NH.
      Children:
329.   i **Sarah E. Clark** b. 9-Jan-1834, Candia, NH.
330.   ii **Henry Gilman Clark** b. 6-Jun-1836, Candia, NH,[120] d. aft 1880, Manchester, NH.

195. **Noah Shute** b. 25-Aug-1806, Sanbornton, Belknap Co., NH,[120] Occupation: Farmer, m. 8-Oct-1825, in Sanbornton, Belknap Co., NH,[120] **Mary (Molly) Smith**, b. 11-Jun-1806, Sanbornton, Belknap Co., NH,[120] (daughter of **Shadrach C. Smith** and **Anna (Nancy) Taylor**) d. 16-Sep-1870, Sanbornton, Belknap Co., NH.[120] Noah died 21-Sep-1867, Sanbornton, Belknap Co., NH.[120]
    Noah Shute died of typhoid fever.
      Children:
+ 331.   i **Sally Shute** b. 7-Feb-1827.
332.   ii **Nancy Clark Shute** b. 29-Mar-1831, Sanbornton, NH,[120] m. 18-Jan-1859, in Sanbornton, NH,[120] **Alonzo Wadleigh**, b. 14-Jan-1833, New Hampton, NH,[120] (son of **Chase Weeks Wadleigh** and **Marcia M. Whitcher**) Occupation: Farmer/sawyer, d. aft 1880.
+ 333.   iii **Noah Brackett Shute** b. 10-Mar-1834.
334.   iv **John Barker Shute** b. 9-Feb-1837, Sanbornton, NH,[120] d. 13-Feb-1863, LA,[120] Buried: Sanbornton, NH.
      John Barker Shute served with the 15th NH Reg't. during the Civil War, under Capt. Jacob Sanborn, and died of typhoid fever at a military hospital in Louisiana, 13-Feb- 1863. His remains were sent home to Sanbornton, NH, the following April.
335.   v **Clarinda Taylor Shute** b. 28-Jul-1842, Sanbornton, NH,[120] d. 3-Jul-1850, Sanbornton, NH.[120]
336.   vi **Harriet Augusta Shute** b. 7-Dec-1845, Sanbornton, NH,[120] d. 14-Oct-1867, Sanbornton, NH.[120]

196. **John M. Shute** b. cir 1790,[172] m. bef 1813, **Nancy Small**, d.

Northwood, NH. John died Northwood, NH.
Children:
337.   i **Eliza R. Shute** b. 13-Aug-1813, Newburyport, Essex Co., MA.[173]
338.   ii **Jeremiah Shute** b. 8-Mar-1815, Newburyport, Essex Co., MA.[172]
339.   iii **John B. Shute** b. 22-Nov-1824, Newburyport, Essex Co., MA.[172]
340.   iv **Nancy Shute** b. 26-Sep-1826, Newburyport, Essex Co., MA.[173]
+ 341.   v **Charles Shute** b. 4-Nov-1829.

197. **Jonathan Shute** b. 15-Nov-1786, Newmarket, Rockingham Co., NH,[174] m. Jun-1806, in Londonderry, Rockingham Co., NH,[127] **Elizabeth (Betsey) Plumer**, b. 10-Aug-1785, Derry, Rockingham Co., NH,[175] (daughter of **Nathan Plumer** and **Mary Palmer**) d. 2-Nov-1864, Newburyport, Essex Co., MA.[176] Jonathan died 11-Aug-1824, Londonderry, Rockingham Co., NH.
Children:
342.   i **Mary Shute** b. cir 1807, Londonderry, NH, m. ----- Page.
+ 343.   ii **Rebecca Boardman Shute** b. cir 1809.
+ 344.   iii **Benjamin Shute** b. Mar-1811.
+ 345.   iv **Eliza Shute** b. 2-Mar-1813.
+ 346.   v **James Shute** b. 17-May-1815.
347.   vi **Sarah Shute** b. cir 1817, Derry, NH, m. 28-Nov-1840 int, in Newbury, MA,[61] **Jonathan Bartlett**.
+ 348.   vii **Jonathan Boardman Shute** b. cir 1819.
349.   viii **Harriet Shute** b. cir 1821, Derry, NH, m. cir 1846-50, ----- **Fethers**. Harriet died aft 1850, Charlestown, MA?.

202. **Michael Shute** b. 20-Jan-1795, Londonderry, NH,[177] m. 24-Nov-1818, in Hampstead, ME,[79] **Olive Johnson**.
Children:
350.   i **James A. Shute** b. 4-Jan-1819, Londonderry, NH.[127]

203. **William B. Shute** b. 9-Sep-1796, Londonderry, NH,[178] Occupation: Teacher, Pinkerton Acad., m. Mar-1818 int., in Londonderry, NH,[127] **Sarah Chadwick**, b. 1795, d. 15-Feb-1868, Londonderry, NH,[126] Buried: Forest Hill, Cem., East Derry, NH. William died 17-Sep-1871, Derry, NH,[126] Buried: Forest Hill, Cem., East Derry, NH.
      Pvt. William B. Shute served in Capt. Nathaniel G. Bradley's company of NH Militia in the War of 1812.
Children:
351.   i **Lucy J. Shute** b. 1820, Londonderry, NH, d. 20-Aug-1843, Londonderry, NH,[126] Buried: Forest Hill, Cem., East Derry, NH.
352.   ii **Sarah R. Shute** b. 1824, Londonderry, NH, d. 30-Nov-1848, Londonderry, NH,[126] Buried: Forest Hill, Cem., East Derry, NH.
353.   iii **Elizabeth Ann Shute** b. 1829, Londonderry, NH, d.

28-Apr-1855, Londonderry, NH,[126] Buried: Forest Hill, Cem., East Derry, NH.

354.   iv **John C. Shute** b. 1832, Londonderry, NH, d. 16-May-1846, Londonderry, NH,[126] Buried: Forest Hill, Cem., East Derry, NH.

209. **George Shute** b. 19-Aug-1807, Londonderry, NH,[179] m. 1833, **Sarah Rollins Carleton**, b. 1810, d. 1880. George died May-1894, Malden, MA.[180]

     According to Fitts' History of Newfields, NH, George Shute served as Deacon to the First Church and town Selectman in Derry, NH. In 1882, after the death of his wife, Sarah, he removed to Malden, MA, where he made his home with his two daughters. These unnamed daughters were living in Melrose Highlands in 1899.

Children:

355.   i **George Kimball Shute** b. 1835, d. 18-Jun-1836,[126] Buried: Forest Hill Cem., East Derry, NH.

+ 356.   ii **Henry Lyman Shute** b. 1837.

357.   iii **James Edwin Shute** b. 1845, d. 9-Feb-1847,[126] Buried: Forest Hill Cem., East Derry, NH.

358.   iv **Charles Edwin Shute** b. 1848, d. 22-Dec-1871,[126] Buried: Forest Hill Cem., East Derry, NH.

359.   v **Arthur Lawrence Shute** b. 1852, d. 11-Feb-1854,[126] Buried: Forest Hill Cem., East Derry, NH.

212. **Jacob Randall Jr.** (See marriage to number 183.).

Sixth Generation

223. Daniel Shute Jr. b. 23-Jul-1793, Hingham, Plymouth Co., MA,[181] Occupation: Physician, m. 22-Dec-1816, in Hingham, Plymouth Co., MA,[182] **Hannah Lincoln Cushing**, b. 21-Apr-1794, Hingham, Plymouth Co., MA,[64] (daughter of **Robert Cushing** and **Judith Loring**) d. 6-May-1875, Hingham, Plymouth Co., MA.[183] Daniel died 26-Jun-1838, Hingham, Plymouth Co., MA.[64]

Dr. Daniel Shute graduated from Harvard College in 1812 (A.B.), and received his medical degree in 1815. As a physician in Hingham, MA, Daniel Shute lived on Main Street, opposite the Meeting House, at South Hingham Street.

Children:
+ 360.   i **Daniel Waldo Shute** b. 24-Oct-1817.
  361.   ii **Isaiah Shute** b. 12-Sep-1819, Hingham, Plymouth Co., MA,[64] m. 2-Jan-1879, **Caroline -----**, b. Kittery, ME.
            Isaiah Shute married Mrs. Caroline Smith of Kittery, ME.
+ 362.   iii **Henry Shute** b. 4-Aug-1821.
+ 363.   iv **Edwin Shute** b. 6-Mar-1824.
  364.   v **Hannah Cushing Shute** b. 31-Aug-1826, Hingham, Plymouth Co., MA,[64] m. 28-Apr-1850,[64] **Richardson F. Loring**. Hannah died 31-Dec-1867.[64]
  365.   vi **Walter Shute** b. 28-Oct-1828, Hingham, Plymouth Co., MA,[136] d. 7-Sep-1830, Hingham, Plymouth Co., MA.[64]
  366.   vii **Anna Cushing Shute** b. 28-Oct-1830, Hingham, Plymouth Co., MA,[64] d. 5-Oct-1848, Hingham, Plymouth Co., MA.[64]
  367.   viii **Elizabeth Shute** b. 11-Apr-1833, Hingham, Plymouth Co., MA,[64] d. 26-Jun-1833, Hingham, Plymouth Co., MA.[64]
  368.   ix **Walter Shute** b. 5-Nov-1836, Hingham, Plymouth Co., MA,[136] d. 7-Dec-1853, Hingham, Plymouth Co., MA.[64]

225. Charles Shute b. 20-Apr-1799, Hingham, Plymouth Co., MA,[184] Occupation: Farmer/Capt., m. 18-Jul-1820, in Hingham, Plymouth Co., MA,[64] **Mary Chauncey Cushing**, b. 18-Jul-1799, Hingham, Plymouth Co., MA,[64] (daughter of **Seth Cushing** and **Joanna Cushing**) d. 12-Jan-1827, Hingham, Plymouth Co., MA.[64] Charles died 23-Jan-1863, Hingham, Plymouth Co., MA.[64]

Charles Shute resided at his paternal homestead on the corner of Main and South Pleasant Streets, Hingham, MA.

Children:
+ 369.   i **Betsey Shute** b. 16-Oct-1820.
+ 370.   ii **Charles Shute Jr.** b. 24-Apr-1822.
  371.   iii **Mary Chauncey Shute** b. 10-Feb-1824, Hingham, Plymouth Co., MA,[64] m. 24-Apr-1845,[64] **Thomas Drew**, b. 1819, Worcester, MA, d. 1888, Newton, MA. Mary died 1914.
+ 372.   iv **Elijah Shute** b. 24-Apr-1825.

230. Solomon Shute b. 6-Sep-1801, Malden, Middlesex Co., MA,[94] m. 24-Jan-1833, in Malden, Middlesex Co., MA,[185] **Sarah Faulkner**. Solomon died 29-Aug-1849, Malden, Middlesex Co., MA.[24]

Children:
  373.   i **Sarah Elizabeth Shute** b. 24-May-1835, Malden, Middlesex

Co., MA.[24]

374.   ii **Solomon Shute** b. 11-Sep-1839, Malden, Middlesex Co., MA,[186] m. **Sarah Hawes**.

231. **Joseph Belcher** b. 20-Feb-1782, Chelsea, Suffolk Co., MA,[31] m. 1807, **Nancy Burrill**, b. 1786, (daughter of **Joseph Burrill** and **Sally Belcher**) d. 1849. Joseph died 1850.
        Children:
+ 375.   i **Joseph Belcher** b. 1808.
376.   ii **Warren Belcher** b. 1825, Winthrop, MA,[187] d. aft 1906, Winthrop, MA.[187]

241. **Mary Green Shute** b. 3-Jul-1804, m. **Andrew Morton Jr.**, b. 1805, d. 1842. Mary died 25-Jul-1884.
        Children:
377.   i **Mary Green Morton** b. 1842, d. 1905.

243. **William Shute** b. 30-Jan-1781, Malden, Middlesex Co., MA,[94] m. 31-Jan-1804, in Malden, Middlesex Co., MA,[156] **Mary Watts**, b. cir 1783, Malden, Middlesex Co., MA. William died 16-Nov-1847, Malden, Middlesex Co., MA.[24]
        Children:
+ 378.   i **Henry Shute** b. 27-Jan-1805.
379.   ii **Amos Shute** b. 8-Jan-1807, Malden, Middlesex Co., MA,[94] d. 28-Sep-1807, Malden, Middlesex Co., MA.[24]
380.   iii **Mary Shute** b. 27-Feb-1808, Malden, Middlesex Co., MA,[24] m. 6-Oct-1827 int, in Malden, Middlesex Co., MA,[24] **Ebenezer Neagles**.

245. **Benjamin Sargent Shute** b. Malden, Middlesex Co., MA,[148] m. 28-Mar-1830, in Malden, Middlesex Co., MA,[188] **Sarah -----**, b. Malden, MA.
        Children:
381.   i **Elizabeth Hitchings Shute** b. 17-Feb-1831, Malden, Middlesex Co., MA.[24]
382.   ii **Benjamin Sargent Shute** b. 9-Sep-1832, Malden, Middlesex Co., MA.[94]

246. **Sarah Shute** m. 25-Oct-1802, in Malden, Middlesex Co., MA,[24] **John Burditt**.
        Children:
383.   i **John Burditt** b. 29-Oct-1803, Malden, Middlesex Co., MA.

257. **William Shute** b. 5-Jan-1800, Prospect, ME,[189] m. bef 1826, **Malinda French**, b. 22-Sep-1805, Belfast, Waldo Co., ME,[81] d. 4-Mar-1893.[81] William died 3-Jan-1871, Prospect (now Stockton), Waldo Co., ME.[81]
    William Shute died of consumption.
        Children:
384.   i **William Lewis Shute** b. 27-Jun-1826, Belfast, Waldo Co., ME,[189] m. 26-Sep-1854, in Belfast, Waldo Co., ME,[190] **Evelina Small**. William died 18-Jan-1886.[81]
           William Lewis Shute died of pneumonia.
385.   ii **Mary Elizabeth Shute** b. 19-Sep-1827, Belfast, Waldo

Co., ME,[81] d. 24-Mar-1908.[81]
+ 386.　　iii **Franklin Shute** b. 15-Jan-1830.
+ 387.　　 iv **Alonzo Shute** b. 13-May-1832.
　 388.　　　v **Darius F. Shute** b. 31-May-1834, Belfast, Waldo Co.,
　　　　　　　　 ME,[189] m. (1) 8-Sep-1860, **Lucy H. Aims**, m. (2)
　　　　　　　　 1-Mar-1869, **Fannie E. Boynton**. Darius died 1874.[81]
　 389.　　 vi **Daniel F. Shute** b. 4-Feb-1838, Belfast, Waldo Co.,
　　　　　　　　 ME,[189] m. **Emily I. Farrow**. Daniel died 5-Jul-1895.[81]
　 390.　　vii **Leander P. Shute** b. 12-Mar-1840, Belfast, Waldo Co.,
　　　　　　　　 ME,[189] d. 25-Oct-1862.[81]
　 391.　　viii **Tryposia E. Shute** b. 20-Apr-1842, Belfast, Waldo Co.,
　　　　　　　　 ME,[81] m. 25-Dec-1875, in Searsport, ME,[81] **Robert
　　　　　　　　 Erskine**, b. 19-Jan-1843, Prospect, Waldo Co., ME,[81]
　　　　　　　　 (son of **Alexander Erskine** and **Eliza Thompson**) d.
　　　　　　　　 13-Jan-1932, Prospect, Waldo Co., ME.[81] Tryposia died
　　　　　　　　 3-Jan-1918.[81]
　 392.　　 ix **Hartford Shute** b. 16-Jan-1844, Belfast, Waldo Co.,
　　　　　　　　 ME,[88] d. 30-Mar-1917.[81]

260. Alfred Shute b. 18-Dec-1806, m. 13-Feb-1831, **Nancy Newman
Perkins**, b. 30-Dec-1810, d. 24-Jun-1899. Alfred died 13-Nov-1878.
　　　　　 Children:
　 393.　　　i **Almira Shute** b. 12-Feb-1851, Bangor, ME, m.
　　　　　　　　 14-Feb-1869, **Alonzo Tozier**, b. 23-Apr-1846, d.
　　　　　　　　 9-Sep-1920. Almira died 26-Feb-1927.

263. Samuel Shute Jr. m. **Harriet -----**, b. cir 1805, d.
30-Jun-1857, Prospect, Waldo Co., ME.
　　　　　 Children:
　 394.　　　i **Samuel W. Shute** b. cir 1827, Prospect, Waldo Co., ME,
　　　　　　　　 d. 1843, Prospect, Waldo Co., ME.[81]

264. Zetham French Shute b. 11-Jun-1806, ME, Occupation: Farmer, m.
25-Aug-1830, in Prospect, Waldo Co., ME, **Francis ("Fannie") Boyd
Clifford**, b. 28-Jan-1812, ME,[191] d. 30-Oct-1889, ME. Zetham died
22-May-1880, ME.
　　　　　 Children:
　 395.　　　i **Helen M. Shute** b. 12-Jul-1832, Prospect, ME.[192]
　 396.　　 ii **Mary E. Shute** b. 20-Jun-1834, Prospect, ME,[192]
　　　　　　　　 Occupation: Seamstress, d. aft 1860.
+ 397.　　iii **Francis M. Shute** b. 24-Jan-1836.
　 398.　　 iv **Savilian F. Shute** b. 21-Jun-1841, Prospect, ME.[192]
　 399.　　　v **Zetham Lock Shute** b. 31-Dec-1845, Prospect, ME.[192]
　 400.　　 vi **Samuel Irving Shute** b. 20-Mar-1848, Prospect, ME.[192]
+ 401.　　vii **Albert Alliston Shute** b. 8-Mar-1855.

280. Samuel Shute b. 15-Aug-1813, Malden, Middlesex Co., MA,[94] m.
6-Dec-1838, in Malden, Middlesex Co., MA,[193] **Marianne Bailey**, b.
cir 1817, Malden, Middlesex Co., MA, d. 14-Jan-1899, Malden, Middlesex
Co., MA.[24]
　　　　　 Children:
　 402.　　　i **Maria Antoinette Shute** b. 7-Apr-1840, Malden, Middlesex
　　　　　　　　 Co., MA,[24] d. 15-Jun-1843, Malden, Middlesex Co.,

MA.[194]
+ 403.   ii **Charles Bailey Shute** b. 24-Jan-1843.

285. **Ebenezer Shute Jr.** b. cir 1804, Boston, Suffolk Co., MA,[195]
Occupation: Constable, m. Dec-1828, in Boston, Suffolk Co., MA,
Francis Arrowsmith, b. cir 1808, Boston, Suffolk Co., MA. Ebenezer
died 14-Dec-1875.
      According to his obituary that appeared in the Boston Transcript,
16-Dec-1875, Ebenezer Shute, Jr. was "one of the oldest constables in
Boston." Born in the North-End, Ebenezer Shute first learned the
trade of shipwright. He afterwards made two voyages at sea, but upon
his return, was appointed a Special Officer by Mayor Lyman. From that
time until February, 1875, he was connected with the Police Dept. or
the Courts. He left a son and three daughters.
            Children:
   404.   i **Francis Arrowsmith Shute** b. 17-Jan-1832, Boston,
            Suffolk Co., MA, d. 7-Oct-1836, Boston, Suffolk Co., MA,
            Buried: Copp's Hill, Boston, Suffolk Co., MA.
   405.   ii **Francis Arrowsmith Shute** b. 27-May-1838, Boston,
            Suffolk Co., MA,[2] d. 31-Aug-1838, Boston, Suffolk Co.,
            MA,[2] Buried: Copp's Hill Burial Ground, Boston, MA.

286. **Caleb B. Shute** b. 7-Jul-1806, Boston, Suffolk Co., MA,[196] m.
Jul-1830, **Abigail E. Clough**, b. cir 1808, Boston, Suffolk Co., MA.
Caleb died 4-Apr-1840, Boston, Suffolk Co., MA,[197] Buried: Copp's
Hill Burial Ground, Boston, MA.
      Rev. Caleb B. Shute served a parish in Dunstable, NH. His
daughter, Susan, was once referred to as his "youngest daughter,"
leading one to believe that there were other children.
            Children:
   406.   i **Susan Shute** b. 5-Apr-1836, Boston, Suffolk Co., MA,[2]
            d. 26-Aug-1839, Boston, Suffolk Co., MA,[2] Buried: Copp's
            Hill Burial Ground, Boston, MA.

288. **James M. Shute** b. cir 1813, Boston, Suffolk Co., MA,[198] m. bef
1844, **Mary -----**, b. cir 1819, MA.[199] James died aft 1850,
Somerville, MA?.
            Children:
   407.   i **James M. Shute** b. cir 1837, MA,[199] Occupation:
            Stockbroker, d. 1883, Boston, Suffolk Co., MA.
                  According to the obituary which appeared in the
            17-Aug- 1883 issue of the "Boston Transcript," James M.
            Shute, Jr., a member of the stock exchange, "was about 45
            years old, and has been well known in business circles
            for many years. He commenced business with Horatio
            Harris and Co., auctioneers, and afterwards engaged in
            the Valparaiso trade with the firm of Loring and Shute.
            He was Quartermaster Sergeant of the Fifth Massachusetts
            in their five months campaign, and for the last fifteen
            years, has been on State Street. He leaves a daughter
            and two sons."
   408.   ii **Thomas R. Shute** b. cir 1839, MA.[199]
   409. iii **Mary Shute** b. cir 1841, MA.[199]

410.   iv **Elizabeth Shute** b. cir 1843, MA.[199]
411.   v **Sarah Stetson Shute** b. 14-May-1844, Boston, Suffolk
             Co., MA,[2] d. 14-May-1844, Boston, Suffolk Co., MA,[2]
             Buried: Copp's Hill Burial Ground, Boston, MA.
412.   vi **Susan Stetson Shute** b. 5-Oct-1845, Boston, Suffolk Co.,
             MA,[2] d. 8-May-1846, Boston, Suffolk Co., MA,[2] Buried:
             Copp's Hill Burial Ground, Boston, MA.
413.   vii **Susan Shute** b. cir 1847, MA.[199]
414.   viii **Frank Shute** b. cir 1849, MA.[199]

296. **Stephen Tufts Shute** b. 11-Aug-1818, Malden, Middlesex Co.,
MA,[94] m. 1844, **Rosetta Elvira Stanton**.
             Children:
415.   i **Lucien R. Shute** b. Malden, Middlesex Co., MA.[24]
416.   ii **Charles Sumner Shute** b. Malden, Middlesex Co., MA.[200]

297. **John William Shute** b. 21-Mar-1792, Newmarket, Rockingham Co.,
NH,[201] m. 10-May-1818, in Durham, NH,[202] **Mary Grover**, b.
25-Aug-1794, Durham, NH,[109] (daughter of **Edmund Grover** and
Catherine Bunker) d. bef 14-May-1845. John died 7-Jun-1830, Buried:
Junction Cem., nr. Newmarket, NH.
     Pvt. John William Shute served in a detachment commanded by Capt.
John Hearsey, 4th Reg't, NH Militia, stationed at Portsmouth Plains, 9
thru 27-Sep-1814.
     A master shipbuilder, John W. Shute, in partnership with George
O. Hilton, built the "Nile," from the Newmarket stocks, in 1825.
Joseph Coe furnished materials; Nathaniel Garland worked as an
apprentice blacksmith. In 1828, a John Shute of Newmarket was
credited with the construction of the "Minerva," a square stern,
billet head for Ebenezer Dodge of Salem, MA [see Ray Brighton's "Port
of Portsmouth Ships and the Cotton Trade 1783-1829" (1986)].
             Children:
417.   i **John E. Shute** b. 26-May-1819, Newmarket, Rockingham
             Co., NH,[203] d. aft 12-Nov-1847.
418.   ii **William H. Shute** b. 10-Oct-1821, Newmarket, Rockingham
             Co., NH,[203] d. 2-May-1822, Newmarket, Rockingham Co.,
             NH.[109]
+ 419.   iii **James Gilbert Shute** b. 14-Jul-1823.
420.   iv **Charles Henry Shute** b. 1825, Newmarket, Rockingham Co.,
             NH,[204] d. 17-Feb-1897.
421.   v **Leonard Cheever Shute** b. 1827, Newmarket, Rockingham
             Co., NH,[204] d. aft 12-Nov-1847.

298. **Andrew Breden Shute** b. 21-Mar-1794, Newmarket, Rockingham Co.,
NH,[205] Occupation: Shipbuilder, m. 26-Apr-1818, in Durham, NH,
Catherine Grover, b. 29-Jun-1798, Durham, NH,[109] (daughter of
Edmund Grover and **Catherine Bunker**) d. 12-Mar-1867, Cambridgeport,
MA, Buried: Oak Grove Cem., Gloucester, MA. Andrew died 30-Nov-1842,
Charlestown Twp., MA.
     Sgt. Andrew B. Shute served at Portsmouth (1814) during the War
of 1812. His widow, Catharine, is buried in Oak Grove Cemetery in
Gloucester, MA, as Catharine Shute, despite her second marriage to
William Sabine in East Boston on 6-Jan-1845.

Children:
- 422.   i **Andrew W. Shute** b. 4-May-1819, Newmarket, Rockingham Co., NH,[206] d. 11-Nov-1846.
- 423.   ii **George Shute** b. 4-Feb-1821, Newmarket, Rockingham Co., NH,[203] d. Dec-1902.
- 424.   iii **Nancy Foss Shute** b. cir 1823, Newmarket, Rockingham Co., NH.
- + 425.   iv **Henry Breden Shute** b. 1826.
- 426.   v **Augustus B. Shute** b. cir 1822-32, Newmarket, Rockingham Co., NH.[204]
- 427.   vi **Calvin C. Shute** b. cir 1822-32, Newmarket, Rockingham Co., NH.[204]
- 428.   vii **Edmund W. Shute** b. cir 1822-32, Newmarket, Rockingham Co., NH.[207]
- + 429.   viii **James Lovell Shute** b. Feb-1833.
- 430.   ix **John W. Shute** b. 31-Mar-1835, Newmarket, Rockingham Co., NH.[208]
- 431.   x **Mary Melvina Shute** b. 1838, Newmarket, Rockingham Co., NH, m. ----- **Sanger**. Mary died aft 1912.

300. **Nathaniel Shute** b. 1807,[209] m. 1-Oct-1832, in Exeter, NH,[210] **Susannah Gilman Barker**. Nathaniel died 1886.[211]
Children:
- + 432.   i **Nathaniel Appleton Shute** b. 28-Jun-1833.

303. **George Smith Shute** b. 2-Mar-1827, Exeter Twp., Rockingham Co., NH,[212] Occupation: Clerk/Boston Custom House, m. Mar-1853, **Joanna Simpkins**, d. Feb-1895, Exeter, NH. George died aft 1904, Exeter Twp., Rockingham Co., NH.
    George Smith Shute served as a clerk in the Boston Naval Office for 26 years.
Children:
- 433.   i **Celia E. Shute** b. cir 1853, Exeter, NH.
- + 434.   ii **Henry Augustus Shute** b. 17-Nov-1856.
- 435.   iii **Frank F. Shute** b. Exeter, NH,[213] Occupation: Hotel keeper, d. Lakewood, NJ?.
- 436.   iv **Anne P. Shute** b. Exeter, NH.
- 437.   v **Georgia W. Shute** b. Exeter, NH,[213] Occupation: Latin inst./Albany Acad., d. NY?.
- 438.   vi **Cornelia F. (Keene) Shute** b. Exeter, NH, m. in Exeter, NH, **C. E. Byington**.
- 439.   vii **Edward Ashton Shute** b. 7-Jul-186?, Exeter, NH.[214]

310. **Elizabeth Barker Shute** b. 31-Mar-1811, Sanbornton, NH,[120] m. 11-Jan-1835,[120] **Addison Stevens Rowell**, d. Brentwood, NH. Elizabeth died 25-Apr-1875, Brentwood, NH.[120]
Children:
- 440.   i **Ambrose Edwin Rowell** b. 8-May-1836, Brentwood, NH.[120]
- 441.   ii **Merinda Georgianna Rowell** b. 10-Dec-1838, Brentwood, NH.[120]
- + 442.   iii **John Shute Rowell** b. 7-Mar-1842.
- 443.   iv **Addison Barker Rowell** b. 7-Dec-1849, Brentwood, NH.[120]
- 444.   v **Mary Eliza Rowell** b. 5-Feb-1853, Brentwood, NH,[120] d.

24-Nov-1864, Brentwood, NH.[120]

313. **Thomas Shute** b. 9-Jan-1819, Bridgewater, Grafton Co., NH,[215]
Occupation: Farmer/Lumberman, m. 8-Jun-1843, in Bridgewater, Grafton
Co., NH,[120] **Mary Ann Emerson**, b. 9-Feb-1823, Bridgewater, Grafton
Co., NH, (daughter of **Ebenezer Emerson** and **Sarah Blake**) d.
25-Sep-1908, Oregon City, Clackamus Co., OR, Buried: Mt. View Cem.,
Oregon City, OR. Thomas died 9-Feb-1912, Oregon City, Clackamus Co.,
OR, Buried: Mt. View Cem., Oregon City, OR.
  Thomas and Mary (Emerson) Shute moved to Plymouth, NH, in 1854.
There he served as Selectman (1861-62) and State Representative
(1863-64). A farmer and lumberman, Thomas Shute lived at Shutes Point
at Lower Intervale at Plymouth. He later moved his family into the
Emerson House on Highland Avenue in Plymouth Village.
  In 1872, Thomas Shute and his family removed to Nebraska for a
short time; then on to Kansas (where they had a large farm with a
sod-and-log house); later to California, and finally to Oregon City,
Oregon.
    Children:
+ 445. i **Augusta Sherburn Shute** b. 2-Mar-1847.
+ 446. ii **Ebenezer Emerson Shute** b. 9-Oct-1849.
 447. iii **Celestia Johnson Shute** b. 31-Jan-1854, Bridgewater,
    Grafton Co., NH,[120] d. 2-Jun-1862, Shute's Pt.,
    Plymouth, NH.[120]
+ 448. iv **Frank Thomas Shute** b. 12-Feb-1859.
+ 449. v **Elsie Etta Shute** b. 6-Apr-1863.

314. **Noah Johnson Shute** b. 30-Nov-1821, Bridgewater, Grafton Co.,
NH,[120] Occupation: Farmer, m. 13-Jun-1849,[120] **Sally Shute**, b.
7-Feb-1827, Sanbornton, NH,[120] (daughter of **Noah Shute** and **Mary
(Molly) Smith**). Noah died aft 1879, Sanbornton, NH.[120]
    Children:
 450. i **Clarinda Taylor Shute** b. 7-Jan-1853, Sanbornton,
    Belknap Co., NH.[120]
 451. ii **Marshall Barker Shute** b. 9-Apr-1855, Sanbornton,
    NH.[120]
+ 452. iii **Martha Ella Shute** b. 10-Dec-1859.
 453. iv **Mary Rachel Shute** b. 10-Jun-1862, Sanbornton, NH,[120]
    d. 27-May-1863, Sanbornton, NH.[120]

315. **Ebenezer Shute** b. 19-Jun-1824, Bridgewater, Grafton Co.,
NH,[215] Occupation: Farmer/joiner, m. 19-Mar-1846, in Bridgewater,
Grafton Co., NH,[120] **Julia Ann Emerson**, b. 31-Mar-1826, Plymouth,
Grafton Co., NH, (daughter of **Ebenezer Emerson** and **Sarah Blake**) d.
1907. Ebenezer died 30-Nov-1900, Lakeport, Belknap Co., NH.
    Children:
 454. i **Emma Narcissa Shute** b. 23-May-1847, Plymouth, Grafton
    Co., NH.[120]
+ 455. ii **John Johnson Shute** b. 1-Nov-1849.
+ 456. iii **George Emerson Shute** b. 2-Apr-1852.
 457. iv **Ida Elizabeth Shute** b. 5-Mar-1854, Plymouth, Grafton
    Co., NH,[120] d. 1918, Lakeport, NH.
 458. v **Lyman O. Shute** b. 15-Feb-1857, Plymouth, Grafton Co.,

NH,[215] d. 1919, Lakeport, NH.
459.   vi **Milan (Mihlon) O. Shute** b. 19-Aug-1860, Plymouth, Grafton Co., NH,[215] d. 1918, Lakeport, NH.
460.   vii **Wesley A. Shute** b. 21-Jul-1864, Plymouth, Grafton Co., NH,[215] d. 17-Oct-1865.[120]

318. **Joseph B. Shute** b. 1-Dec-1820, Littleton, NH,[121] m. **Adaline Eastman**, b. 10-Apr-1828, Whitefield, NH, (daughter of **William Eastman** and **Rebecca Gale**) d. 4-Aug-1870, Whitefield, NH. Joseph died 9-Jun-1861, Whitefield, NH.[120]
          Children:
+ 461.   i **Fred A. Shute** b. 5-Feb-1854.

320. **Horace Shute** b. 17-Dec-1829, Littleton, NH,[121] Occupation: Farmer, m. 5-Nov-1850, **Mary Jane Bowman**, b. 17-Nov-1833, Littleton, NH. Horace died aft 1879, Littleton, NH.[120]
     Pvt. Horace Shute served in Co. I, NH Heavy Artillery, Grand Army of the Republic.
          Children:
462.   i **Kate Maria Shute** b. 11-Jan-1855, Littleton, NH.
463.   ii **Mary Jane Shute** b. 3-Apr-1859, Littleton, NH.

321. **Sewell Shute** b. 20-May-1833, Littleton, NH,[121] m. **Mary B. Stoddard**. Sewell died 11-Oct-1884, Waterford, Caledonia Co., VT.
          Children:
464.   i **Charles F. Shute** b. 11-Jun-1861, Waterford, Caledonia Co., VT.[216]
465.   ii **Florence M. Shute** b. 27-Jun-1862, Waterford, Caledonia Co., VT.

327. **Gilman Dudley Shute** b. 18-Jun-1831, Littleton, NH,[121] Occupation: Farmer, m. 1852, **Lucy A. Whiting**, b. 1831, Lyman, d. 1890, Lisbon. Gilman died aft 1879, Littleton, NH.[120]
     Pvt. Gilman Dudley Shute served in Co. I, NH Heavy Artillery, Grand Army of the Republic.
          Children:
466.   i **Ellen M. Shute** b. 1855, Littleton, NH.
+ 467.   ii **Arthur Nathaniel Shute** b. 1857.
468.   iii **Grace L. Shute** b. 1863, Littleton, NH.
469.   iv **Alice M. Shute** b. Littleton, NH.
470.   v **Ambrose B. Shute** b. Littleton, NH.[217]

331. **Sally Shute** (See marriage to number 314.).

333. **Noah Brackett Shute** b. 10-Mar-1834, Sanbornton, NH,[120] m. **Molly (Mary) Smith Morrison**, b. 9-Apr-1831, Sanbornton, NH,[120] (daughter of **Theophilus Rundlet Morrison** and **Betsey Robinson Smith**) d. aft 1881.[120] Noah died aft 1879.[120]
     Noah Brackett Shute retained the family homestead in Sanbornton, NH (1875-1879), but was mainly engaged in the ice business in New York, NY.
          Children:
471.   i **Frank Taylor Shute** b. 12-Dec-1856, Sanbornton, NH,[120]

d. 5-Jun-1875, Sanbornton, NH.[120]
472. ii **Lizzie Barker Shute** b. 20-Nov-1860, Sanbornton, NH.[120]
473. iii **Lucy Morrison Shute** b. 14-Nov-1862, Sanbornton, NH.[120]
474. iv **Nellie May Shute** b. 24-Dec-1864, Sanbornton, NH.[120]
475. v **Hattie Nora Shute** b. 4-Jul-1868, Sanbornton, NH.[120] d.
  10-Aug-1870, Sanbornton, NH.[120]

341. **Charles Shute** b. 4-Nov-1829, Newburyport, Essex Co., MA,[218] m.
Hannah Davenport Jenness, b. 4-Nov-1829, Newburyport, Essex Co., MA,
Buried: Northwood, NH. Charles died 18-Jan-1905, MA, Buried:
Northwood, NH.
   Children:
476. i **Viola R. Shute** b. 23-Apr-1857, Allenstown, Merrimack
  Co., NH.
+ 477. ii **Elmer Shute** b. 11-Aug-1868.
478. iii **Allice B. Shute** b. 1873.
479. iv **Etta Shute**.
480. v **Horace Shute** b. MA.[219]

343. **Rebecca Boardman Shute** b. cir 1809, Londonderry, NH, m.
14-May-1839, in Newburyport, Essex Co., MA,[220] **Amos Pearson, Jr.**,
b. 15-Aug-1783, Newburyport, Essex Co., MA,[221] (son of **Amos Pearson**
and **Mary Coffin**) Occupation: Carpenter, d. aft 1850, Newburyport,
Essex Co., MA?.
   Children:
481. i **Amos Coffin Pearson** b. 6-Feb-1840, Newburyport, Essex
  Co., MA.[221]
482. ii **Henry T. Pearson** b. 23-Apr-1844, Newburyport, Essex
  Co., MA.[222]

344. **Benjamin Shute** b. Mar-1811, Derry, NH,[223] Occupation: Cabinet
Maker, m. 30-May-1833, in Reading, Middlesex Co., MA,[224] **Lois
Smith**, b. 15-May-1812, Lynnfield, Essex Co., MA,[225] (daughter of
William Smith and **Lois Parker**) d. 4-Jul-1868, Lynnfield, Essex
Co., MA.[225] Benjamin died 23-Nov-1849, Lynnfield, Essex Co., MA.[225]
   Children:
483. i **Lois Augusta Shute** b. 27-Aug-1836, Reading, Middlesex
  Co., MA,[224] m. 14-Oct-1858, **Henry Jackson Hart**. Lois
  died 2-Jan-1917.
484. ii **Benjamin Alward Shute** b. 11-Jun-1842, Lynnfield, Essex
  Co., MA,[226] d. 27-Jun-1858.

345. **Eliza Shute** b. 2-Mar-1813, Derry, Rockingham Co., NH,[227] m.
26-Oct-1836, in Derry, Rockingham Co., NH,[228] **Joshua Pillsbury**, b.
18-Mar-1813, Newbury, Essex Co., MA,[229] (son of **Enoch Pillsbury** and
Mary Pillsbury) d. 17-Sep-1887, Athens, Athens Co., OH.[229] Eliza
died 18-Sep-1884, Marietta, Washington Co., OH.
   Children:
+ 485. i **James William Pillsbury** b. 30-Nov-1837.
486. ii **Mary Elizabeth Pillsbury** b. 4-Dec-1839, Deerfield,
  NH,[229] d. 2-Jun-1862, Wheeling, W.VA.
+ 487. iii **George Edwin Pillsbury** b. 13-Dec-1841.
488. iv **Rebekah Pearson Pillsbury** b. 3-Jul-1843, Newburyport,

Essex Co., MA,[229] d. 22-Jul-1844, Newburyport, Essex Co., MA.

489.   v **Prescott Grovernor Pillsbury** b. 13-Jun-1846, Newburyport, Essex Co., MA,[229] m. 16-Feb-1870, in Boston, Suffolk Co., MA,[229] **Isabel McCrillis**, b. Haverhill, MA, d. 14-Mar-1870. Prescott died 6-Nov-1888, Boston, Suffolk Co., MA.

+ 490.   vi **Joshua Plummer Pillsbury** b. 26-Aug-1849.

+ 491.   vii **Ellen (Helen) Maria Pillsbury** b. 19-Feb-1854.

346. **James Shute** b. 17-May-1815, Derry, Rockingham Co., NH,[230] Occupation: Cordwainer/Brickmaker, m. 3-Sep-1837, in MA,[231] **Priscilla Ayers Fiske**, b. 16-Jul-1816, Derry, Rockingham Co., NH,[230] (daughter of **Mark Fiske** and **Eleanor Wilson**) d. 29-Oct-1899, Somerville, Middlesex Co., MA,[232] Buried: 31-Oct-1899, Woodlawn Cem., Everett, MA.[144] James died 1-Jan-1891, Somerville, Middlesex Co., MA,[233] Buried: 4-Jan-1891, Woodlawn Cem., Everett, MA.[144]

    James Shute entered the brickmaking trade most probably through his brother-in-law, Mark Fiske (1814-1869) who, with Gen. James Dana, owned and developed a large part of the northeasterly side of Sommerville, MA. Fiske owned the patent and built the first kiln for the manufacture of bricks with one side glazed or marbelized.

    By 1877, James Shute resided at #18 Temple Street, Winter Hill, North Somerville, MA, in a "white house near the brick store."

    Children:

492.   i **Ellen Priscilla Shute** b. 27-Jun-1838, No. Woburn, MA,[230] m. 29-Aug-1872,[230] **Lucius B. Angier**, b. 1834,[144] Occupation: Coal store owner, d. 1904, Somerville, Middlesex Co., MA.[144] Ellen died 19-Feb-1920, Somerville, Middlesex Co., MA,[234] Buried: 22-Feb-1920, Woodlawn Cem., Everett, MA.[144]

493.   ii **son** b. Oct-1840,[230] d. 1840.

494.   iii **Mary Adelaide Shute** b. 22-May-1842,[230] d. Nov-1842.[235]

495.   iv **Adelaide Shute** b. 13-Sep-1844,[235] m. 11-Jun-1867,[235] **John Bolton**, d. bef 1896. Adelaide died 1-Jul-1934, Somerville, MA,[236] Buried: 3-Jul-1934, Woodlawn Cem., Everett, MA.[144]

496.   v **James Henry Shute** b. 9-Feb-1847,[235] d. 2-Aug-1932, Somerville, MA,[144] Buried: 4-Aug-1932, Woodlawn Cem., Everett, MA.[144]

        James Henry Shute resided at his parents' home, #18 Temple Street, Winter Hill, North Somerville, MA, with his widowed sisters.

+ 497.   vi **Benjamin Franklin Shute** b. 16-May-1851.

348. **Jonathan Boardman Shute** b. cir 1819, Derry, NH,[237] Occupation: Shoemaker, m. 15-Aug-1847, in Lynnfield, MA, **Abigail S. Russell**, b. cir 1827, Lynnfield, MA, (daughter of **Orin Russell** and **Esther Smith**).

    Children:

498.   i **Boardman Plumer Shute** b. 24-Feb-1848, Lynnfield,

MA.[238]

356. **Henry Lyman Shute** b. 1837,[239] m. 1859, **Clara Brown**. Henry died 1910.

         Children:

499.   i **Estelle Louise Shute** b. aft 1859, East Dubuque, IL, m. 1859, **William Marsh Kenyon**.

Seventh Generation

360. **Daniel Waldo Shute** b. 24-Oct-1817, Hingham, Plymouth Co., MA,[240] Occupation: Shoemaker, m. 16-Mar-1843, in Hingham, Plymouth Co., MA,[64] **Hannah Wilder**, b. 11-Jul-1820, Hingham, Plymouth Co., MA,[64] (daughter of **Joseph Wilder** and **Lydia Loring**). Daniel died 12-May-1891.
> Daniel Shute lived on Main Street in Hingham, MA.
> > Children:
+ 500.　　i **Daniel Waldo Shute** b. 29-Apr-1845.
　 501.　　ii **Annie Walter Shute** b. 16-Sep-1855, Hingham, Plymouth Co., MA,[64] d. 1938.

362. **Henry Shute** b. 4-Aug-1821, Hingham, Plymouth Co., MA,[241] m. 16-Nov-1848,[242] **Abigail B. Cushing**, (daughter of **Leonard Cushing** and **Mary C. Whiting**). Henry died 4-Apr-1895.
> > Children:
+ 502.　　i **Henry Leonard Shute** b. 18-Jun-1850.

363. **Edwin Shute** b. 6-Mar-1824, Hingham, Plymouth Co., MA,[243] Occupation: Mason, m. 14-Oct-1849, in Hingham, Plymouth Co., MA,[64] **Cassandana Lane**, b. 21-Apr-1824, Hingham, Plymouth Co., MA,[64] (daughter of **Quincy Lane** and **Elizabeth Hersey**) d. 22-Apr-1869, Taunton, Bristol Co., MA.[64] Edwin died 15-Jan-1870, Hingham, Plymouth Co., MA.[64]
> > Children:
　 503.　　i **Edwin Lincoln Shute** b. 14-Dec-1854, Boston, Suffolk Co., MA.[244]
　 504.　　ii **Quincy Lane Shute** b. 28-Nov-1857, Hingham, Plymouth Co., MA,[244] d. 24-Dec-1860.[64]
　 505.　　iii **Hattie Gordon Shute** b. 9-Feb-1862, Hingham, Plymouth Co., MA.[64]

369. **Betsey Shute** b. 16-Oct-1820, Hingham, Plymouth Co., MA,[64] m. (1) 25-Nov-1845,[64] **Henry Hersey**, b. 1820, d. 1853, Hingham, MA, m. (2) 15-Aug-1858,[64] **Caleb Francis Hersey**. Betsey died 1889.
> > Children by Henry Hersey:
+ 506.　　i **Elizabeth Hersey** b. 1853.

370. **Charles Shute Jr.** b. 24-Apr-1822, Hingham, Plymouth Co., MA,[245] m. (1) 11-Apr-1847, **Elizabeth Wilson**, b. cir 1827, Sharon, CT, d. 1850, Hingham, Plymouth Co., MA,[64] m. (2) 16-Oct-1852, in Belfast, ME, **Elizabeth Jane Wellman**, b. Belfast, ME.
> > Children by Elizabeth Wilson:
　 507.　　i **Mary Cushing Shute** b. 10-Jul-1847, Hingham, Plymouth Co., MA.[64]
　 508.　　ii **Elizabeth Wilson Shute** b. 6-Jan-1849, Hingham, Plymouth Co., MA,[64] m. 28-Nov-1867, in Worcester, MA,[220] **Daniel W. Darling**, b. Charlton, MA.
> > Children by Elizabeth Jane Wellman:
　 509.　　iii **Mary Deborah Shute** b. 26-Aug-1853, Hingham, Plymouth Co., MA,[64] m. **William F. Stone**.
　 510.　　iv **Charles Wellman Shute** b. 7-Aug-1856, Worcester, MA.[245]
　 511.　　v **Arthur Henry Shute** b. 15-Dec-1857.[245]

512.   vi **Abby Brewer Shute** b. 4-May-1860.[64]
513.   vii **William Augustus Shute** b. 20-Oct-1866.[244]

372. Elijah Shute b. 24-Apr-1825, Hingham, Plymouth Co., MA,[244] m. 20-Jun-1853, in Boston, Suffolk Co., MA,[64] **Margarette Harvey Palfrey**, b. 18-Oct-1832, Hopkinton, NH,[64] (daughter of **John Locke Palfrey** and **Damarius Darling**) d. Hingham, Plymouth Co., MA. Elijah died Hingham, Plymouth Co., MA.
      Elijah Shute resided at his paternal homestead on Main Street at South Pleasant Street in Hingham, MA.
            Children:
514.   i **George Henry Shute** b. 2-Aug-1854, Boston, Suffolk Co., MA,[244] d. 24-Feb-1857.[64]
515.   ii **Walter Chauncey Shute** b. 28-Jan-1858, Boston, Suffolk Co., MA,[246] m. **Ellen O. Matson**. Walter died aft 1907, Hingham, Plymouth Co., MA.

375. Joseph Belcher b. 1808, m. 1830, **Serena Coates**, b. 1809, d. 1858. Joseph died 1866.
            Children:
+ 516.   i **Mary Belcher** b. 1832.

378. Henry Shute b. 27-Jan-1805, Malden, Middlesex Co., MA,[247] m. 1-Jun-1828, in Malden, MA, **Tabitha Nichols**, b. 11-Dec-1803, Malden, Middlesex Co., MA,[248] (daughter of **Ebenezer Nichols** and **Esther Sargeant**) d. 28-Aug-1885, Everett, Middlesex Co., MA,[144] Buried: 30-Aug-1885, Woodlawn Cem., Everett, MA.[144] Henry died 2-Oct-1891, Everett, Middlesex Co., MA,[144] Buried: 4-Oct-1891, Woodlawn Cem., Everett, MA.[144]
      Henry and Tabitha Shute made their home at the furthest point in Everett, MA, near the Malden line "in the house next north of Zera Estes' residence on Ferry Street." By 1891, four houses stood on this same lot of land.
            Children:
517.   i **George Henry Shute** b. 21-Mar-1829, Malden, MA,[247] d. 4-Sep-1859, Malden, Middlesex Co., MA,[144] Buried: 6-Sep-1859, Woodlawn Cem., Everett, MA.[144]
518.   ii **William Shute** b. 17-May-1831, Malden, Middlesex Co., MA,[249] Occupation: Leather Manufacturer, m. cir 1856, **Elizabeth M. Kimball**, b. 24-Aug-1836, Lynn, Middlesex Co., MA, d. 1-Nov-1893, Lynn, Middlesex Co., MA,[250] Buried: Pine Grove Cem., Lynn, MA. William died 25-Nov-1891, Lynn, Middlesex Co., MA,[251] Buried: Pine Grove Cem., Lynn, MA.
            William Shute, a prominent morocco leather manufacturer of Lynn, MA, died in that city on 25-Nov-1891. His obituary which appeared in the Boston Transcript, 27-Nov-1891, observed that he had been in the morocco business in Lynn for 35 years. He left a widow, but no children were mentioned.
            William Shute is perhaps best remembered for his bequest of $10,000 to the City of Everett, MA, upon his death in 1891, to establish the Shute Memorial Library.

His gift was later joined by another $10,000 bequest, left by his widow, Elizabeth M. (Kimball) Shute, upon her death in 1893. The City of Everett purchased land for the new library in 1895, but the Shute Memorial Library didn't open until 10-Jun-1920. It has subsequently been renamed.

519.   iii **Eliza Nichols Shute** b. 1-Jan-1834, Malden, Middlesex Co., MA.[24]

520.   iv **Amos Shute** b. 1-Jan-1834, Malden, MA,[144] d. 1-Jan-1834, Malden, MA,[144] Buried: 10-Oct-1860, Woodlawn Cem., Everett, MA.[144]

+ 521.   v **Charles Francis Shute** b. 17-Jun-1838.

522.   vi **Esther Nichols Shute** b. 9-Jan-1842, Malden, Middlesex Co., MA,[24] d. 11-Mar-1843, Malden, Middlesex Co., MA,[252] Buried: 10-Oct-1860, Woodlawn Cem., Everett, MA.[144]

523.   vii **Edward L. Shute** b. 10-Jul-1844, Malden, Middlesex Co., MA,[94] d. 27-Dec-1910, Weston, MA,[144] Buried: 28-Dec-1910, Woodlawn Cem., Everett, MA.[144]

524.   viii **Esther N. Shute** b. 20-Jan-1850, Malden, Middlesex Co., MA.[24]

386. Franklin Shute b. 15-Jan-1830, Belfast, Waldo Co., ME,[189] m. 9-Sep-1855, in Belfast, Waldo Co., ME,[190] **Hannah Jane Beckmore**. Franklin died 24-Jul-1878, Belfast, Waldo Co., ME.[81]
    Children:

525.   i **Frank Edward Shute** b. 19-Jan-1858, Searsport, ME.

387. Alonzo Shute b. 13-May-1832, Belfast, Waldo Co., ME,[253] m. 5-Jul-1855, in Belmont, ME, **Margaret J. Rust**, b. 25-Dec-1835.
    Children:

526.   i **Flora Ella Shute** b. 16-Apr-1856, Belfast, Waldo Co., ME, d. 23-Mar-1857.

527.   ii **Fred Alonzo Shute** b. 4-Jan-1861/62, Belfast, Waldo Co., ME.[254]

+ 528.   iii **Ralph D. Shute** b. 4-Sep-1866.

529.   iv **Vesta Jane Shute** b. 7-Aug-1872, d. 3-Feb-1875.

397. Francis M. Shute b. 24-Jan-1836, Prospect, ME,[192] m. 8-Dec-1853, in Prospect, ME,[192] **Albert Shute**, b. 16-Jan-1830, Prospect, ME,[192] (son of **Leonard Shute** and **Elizabeth Treat**).
    Children:

530.   i **Ezra A. Shute** b. 25-Feb-1856, Prospect, ME.[192]

401. Albert Alliston Shute b. 8-Mar-1855, Prospect, Hancock Co., ME,[192] m. 15-May-1880, in Prospect, Hancock Co., ME, **Celia French Cousens**, b. 26-Jul-1862, ME, (daughter of **James Irving Cousens** and **Edna J. Clewloy**) d. 10-Feb-1931, ME. Albert died 17-Dec-1930, ME.
    Children:

+ 531.   i **James Irving Shute** b. 27-Nov-1886.

403. Charles Bailey Shute b. 24-Jan-1843, Malden, Middlesex Co., MA,[186] Occupation: Physician, m. 28-Nov-1871, in Malden, MA, **Ella**

Robinson Ewens, b. Salem, NH. Charles died 25-Nov-1888.[255]
Dr. Charles Bailey Shute received his undergraduate degree from Harvard in 1865. His daughter, Bertha, married Andrew H. Brown, who later became President of U.S. Rubber Co. Dr. Charles Bailey Shute died of typhoid in 1888.

        Children:
+ 532.   i **George P. Shute** b. 1877.
+ 533.   ii **Bertha Shute**.

419. **James Gilbert Shute** b. 14-Jul-1823, Newmarket, Rockingham Co., NH,[256] m. 1-Oct-1849, **Harriett Newall Horne**, b. 1830, d. 1911. James died 17-Feb-1908, Boston, Suffolk Co., MA.
James Gilbert Shute resided in Jamaica Plains, MA, in 1888. At that time he owned a telescope made by Charles Wesley Tuttle. The two had been boyhood friends and apprenticed to the carpentry trade at the same shop.

        Children:
  534.   i **Ada Marian Shute** b. 17-Oct-1850, Reading, MA, m. 5-Dec-1876, in Boston, Suffolk Co., MA, **Charles Theodore Bauer**, b. 1837, d. 1917. Ada died 27-Jan-1934, Boston, Suffolk Co., MA.

425. **Henry Breden Shute** b. 1826, Newmarket, Rockingham Co., NH,[257] m. 17-Nov-1852, **Adelia Witham**. Henry died 27-Dec-1911, Hanover, MA.
At the age of 85, Henry Breden Shute was one of the oldest residents of Hannover, MA. He had removed to Hannover from Newmarket, NH.

        Children:
  535.   i **Lizzie Adelia Shute** b. 7-May-1854.
  536.   ii **Frances M. Shute** b. 7-May-1858.
  537.   iii **Elizabeth Hale Shute** b. 2-Feb-1861.
+ 538.   iv **Frank Henry Shute** b. 17-Nov-1866.
  539.   v **Kilby Shute** b. MA.[258]
        Kilby Shute headed a bank in Gloucester, MA.

429. **James Lovell Shute** b. Feb-1833, Kennebunk, ME,[259] Occupation: Carpenter/Fish Packaging, m. 6-Feb-1857, in Gloucester, Essex Co., MA, **Sarah Abigail Merchant**, b. 1836, Gloucester, Essex Co., MA, (daughter of **Samuel Merchant** and **Sally Davis**) d. 1927, Gloucester, Essex Co., MA, Buried: Oak Grove Cem., Gloucester, MA. James died 4-Jan-1909, Gloucester, Essex Co., MA, Buried: Oak Grove Cem., Gloucester, MA.
James Lovell Shute was a carpenter by trade. He removed to Gloucester, MA, before he was 20 years old (circa 1851), where he, at first, was in charge of the cemetery owned by the Universalist Church. He even repaired the church's Christopher Wren-style steeple.
James L. Shute later worked for Samuel Merchant in the fish business. With Merchant's son, William T. Merchant, James later became a partner in the business (Shute & Merchant).
With the Merchants, James L. Shute became part-owner in several Gloucester-registered vessels, including the "Hattie N. Gove," "Hattie B. West," "Leonard McKenzie," "Lightfoot," and the "William T.

Merchant."

James L. Shute made his will on 7-Oct-1892. He was to die of a heart-attack suffered while getting off an electric tram. He had lived at #8 Prospect Square in Gloucester, MA, but the estate inventory also revealed that he owned a house and land at 160 Washington St.

Children:

540.   i **James Lovell Shute Jr.** b. 22-Sep-1857, Gloucester, Essex Co., MA,[260] d. 1862, Buried: Oak Grove Cem., Gloucester, MA.

541.   ii **Samuel Merchant Shute** b. 11-Nov-1859, Gloucester, Essex Co., MA,[260] m. **Annie L. Gardiner**, b. 1861, d. 1903. Samuel died 1894, Buried: Oak Grove Cem., Gloucester, MA.

+ 542.   iii **William Thomas Shute** b. 11-Jul-1861.

543.   iv **Abby Merchant Shute** b. 1864, Gloucester, Essex Co., MA, d. 1866.

544.   v **Frances Grover Shute** b. 11-May-1866, Gloucester, Essex Co., MA, d. 1956, Buried: Oak Grove Cem., Gloucester, MA.

545.   vi **Sally Merchant Shute** b. 24-Jul-1868, Gloucester, Essex Co., MA, m. 9-Oct-1891, **Bert Shipman**. Sally died 1952, Buried: Oak Grove Cem., Gloucester, MA.

+ 546.   vii **Ada Marian Shute** b. 14-Oct-1870.

547.   viii **Edward Grover Shute** b. 23-Jul-1873, Gloucester, Essex Co., MA,[260] d. 1883, Buried: Oak Grove Cem., Gloucester, MA.

+ 548.   ix **Robert Thomas Shute** b. 1875.

432. Nathaniel Appleton Shute b. 28-Jun-1833, Fitchburg, MA,[261] Occupation: Banker, m. **Ellen Sophia Holbrook**, b. 15-Feb-1837, Sherborn, MA,[211] (daughter of **Edward Holbrook** and **Lois Bacon Coombes**) d. 16-Feb-1881, Oberlin, OH.[211] Nathaniel died 1-Apr-1900, Bournemouth, England.[211]

Nathaniel Appleton Shute gained notoriety while working for the Granite State Bank in Exeter, NH. To quote from Bell's History of Exeter, NH: "In January, 1873, the cashier, Nathaniel Appleton Shute, after having embezzled a great part of the funds, fled the country." This may, in part, explain his death in England in 1900.

Nathaniel A. Shute's wife, Ellen Holbrook, was descended from Simon Bradstreet and Francis Dudley, both Royal Governors of the Massachusetts Bay Colony, as well as of Thomas Wiggen, a Royal Governor of New Hampshire.

Children:

549.   i **Helen Winifred Shute** b. 3-Nov-1863, Exeter Twp., NH,[262] m. 21-Jun-1900, in Boston, Suffolk Co., MA,[263] **Warren Joseph Moulton**, b. 30-Aug-1865, Sandwich, NH,[262] (son of **Gilman Moulton** and **Lydia Ann Dearborn**) Occupation: Pres., Bangor Theol. Sem., d. aft 1931, Bangor, ME?. Helen died 24-Feb-1931, Bangor, ME.[262]

550.   ii **Mary Appleton Shute** b. 11-Jul-1865, Exeter, Rockingham Co., NH,[264] m. 28-Dec-1904, in Springfield, MA,[265] **Charles Snow Thayer**, b. 4-Aug-1865, Westfield, MA, (son of **Lucius Fowler** and **Martha Ann Harrison**) Occupation:

Librarian, Hartford Sem., d. aft 1941, Hartford, CT?.
Mary died 14-Jun-1940, Hartford, CT.[211]

434. Henry Augustus Shute b. 17-Nov-1856, Exeter, NH,[266]
Occupation: Lawyer/Judge/Author, m. (1) 18-Nov-1885?, **Amelia F.
Weeks**, d. Jan-1895, m. (2) **Ella Kent**. Henry died aft 1904.
      A lawyer and judge, Henry Augustus Shute graduated from Harvard
in 1879. He was also the well-known author of "The Real Diary of a
Real Boy" (published in 1902), "Farming It," and other works.
            Children by Amelia F. Weeks:
+ 551.   i **Richard Everett Shute** b. 17-Oct-1887.
  552.   ii **Nathalie Shute** b. 18-Apr-1893.

442. John Shute Rowell b. 7-Mar-1842, Brentwood, NH,[267] Occupation:
Postal Clerk/Captain, m. 15-Feb-1864, in Exeter, NH,[268] **Roselvina
Belknap**, b. 9-Nov-1831, Exeter, NH, (daughter of **William Augustus
Belknap** and **Ruth Long Poore**) d. aft 1878. John died aft 1881,
Exeter, NH.
            Children:
  553.   i **Arthur B. B. Rowell** b. 17-Jun-1867,[268] d.
                1-Sep-1868.[268]
  554.   ii **John Edward Everet Melvin Rowell** b. 7-Mar-1871, Exeter,
                NH.
  555.   iii **Grace Darling Rowell** b. 7-Feb-1876,[268] d.
                6-Aug-1876.[268]

445. Augusta Sherburn Shute b. 2-Mar-1847, Bridgewater, Grafton Co.,
NH,[120] m. 18-Nov-1869, in Plymouth, NH,[120] **George Augustus Brown**,
b. 23-Apr-1844, (son of **Abraham Brown** and ----- -----) d.
16-Apr-1924.
            Children:
+ 556.   i **Dora Estella Brown** b. 23-Aug-1875.
+ 557.   ii **Flora Estella Brown** b. 23-Aug-1875.
  558.   iii **Melzena Frances Brown** b. 12-Dec-1880, m. 15-Oct-1906,
                Harry H. Ordway.

446. Ebenezer Emerson Shute b. 9-Oct-1849, Bridgewater, Grafton Co.,
NH,[269] m. 19-Oct-1876, in Salem, KS,[120] **Ruth Ella Hodgson**, b.
15-Feb-1856, Greentown, Howard Co., IN, (daughter of **Nathan Hodgson**
and ----- **Reich**) d. 27-Aug-1933, Buried: Orient Cem., Orient, Ferry
Co., WA. Ebenezer died 9-Jul-1917, Boyds, WA, Buried: Orient Cem.,
Orient, WA.
            Children:
  559.   i **Harland Blakely Shute** b. 17-Dec-1877, KS,[270] d. 1954.
+ 560.   ii **Herbert Thomas Shute** b. 8-Aug-1883.
  561.   iii **Fred Delos Shute** b. 10-Oct-1886, Burr Oak, KS, d.
                8-Dec-1909.
  562.   iv **Geneva Lorena Shute** b. 17-Oct-1891, nr. Clackamus,
                Clackamus Co., OR, d. 17-Oct-1909.
  563.   v **Etna Grace Shute** b. 14-Nov-1893, m. 7-Mar-1912, in
                Rockcut, WA, **Frank Chester Soper**, b. 6-Sep-1875.
+ 564.   vi **Fanny Marguerite Shute** b. 7-Jun-1897.

448. Frank Thomas Shute b. 12-Feb-1859, Plymouth, Grafton Co., NH,[215] Occupation: Farmer, m. 27-Nov-1889, in Oregon City, OR, **Mandana Dane**. Frank died 19-Oct-1952, Fales City, OR.
Children:

565.   i **Bernice Aletha Shute** b. 4-Mar-1894, m. 27-Apr-1913, in Oregon City, OR, **Ray Welsh**.

449. Elsie Etta Shute b. 6-Apr-1863, Plymouth, Grafton Co., NH,[120] m. 14-Apr-1880, in Red Cloud, NE, **David H. Cartwright**, d. 14-Aug-192?, Red Cloud, NE?. Elsie died 14-Sep-1915.
Children:

566.   i **Maud Mary Cartwright** b. 12-Apr-1881.
567.   ii **Bell Augusta Cartwright** b. 4-Jan-1883.
568.   iii **Blanche Luella Cartwright** b. 25-Dec-1884.
569.   iv **Jerry Earl Cartwright** b. 27-Aug-1886.
570.   v ----- **Cartwright** b. 24-Apr-1888, d. 25-Nov-18??.
571.   vi **Thomas Cartwright** b. 24-Apr-1888.
572.   vii **Cora Geneva Cartwright** b. 21-Sep-1895.
573. viii **Gertie Melzena Cartwright** b. 21-Sep-1895.
574.   ix **Elsie Celestia Cartwright** b. 9-Feb-1898.
575.   x **Nellie Irene Cartwright** b. 17-Apr-1900.
576.   xi **Bessie Oral Cartwright** b. 5-Mar-1902.
577.   xii **Essie Olive Cartwright** b. 5-Mar-1902.
578. xiii **Lena Fay Cartwright**.
579.   xiv ----- **Cartwright** b. 4-Jul-1906.
580.   xv ----- **Cartwright** b. 4-Dec-1908.

452. Martha Ella Shute b. 10-Dec-1859, Sanbornton, NH,[120] m. **John Franklin Smith**, b. 10-Apr-1851, Loudon, NH,[120] Occupation: Farmer.
Children:

581.   i **Nancy May Smith** b. 16-Apr-1880, Sanbornton, NH.[120]

455. John Johnson Shute b. 1-Nov-1849, Plymouth, Grafton Co., NH,[271] m. **Fannie Dorcas Bentley**, b. Bradford, NH, d. 7-Mar-1927, Claremont. John died 17-Aug-1937, Claremont.
Children:

582.   i **Henry Shute** b. 4-Jan-1878.
583.   ii **Nettie Bell Shute** b. 13-Jan-1879, Contoocock, NH, d. 1958.
584.   iii **Henry Benjamin Shute** b. 31-Jul-1881, Concord, NH, d. 1958.
585.   iv **George Wesley Shute** b. 3-Dec-1882, Concord, NH, Occupation: Teacher, Robinson Sem., d. 1952.
586.   v **Elsie May Shute** b. 12-Oct-1894, Dover, NH, m. **Ora Warren Matthews**, d. Greenfield, MA?.

456. George Emerson Shute b. 2-Apr-1852, Plymouth, Grafton Co., NH,[215] m. 17-May-1883, in Harvard, Neb., **Laura Ann Still**, b. 3-Nov-1861, Annville, PA, d. 27-Mar-1950, Denver, CO. George died 13-Dec-1920, Esbon, KS.
Children:

587.   i **Julia Amelia Shute** b. 16-Feb-1884, m. **William Claude Creider**.

588.   ii **Zacharia Shute** b. 14-Jul-1885, d. 14-Jul-1885.
589.   iii **Grace Lee Shute** b. 1-Aug-1886, m. **Frederick E. McGee**.
590.   iv **Marie Shute** b. 15-Aug-1888, m. **Carl P. Hedge**.
591.   v **Carrie Shute** b. 8-Jun-1890, m. **Lewis E. Ashbaugh**.
592.   vi **Flora D. Shute** b. 12-Aug-1893, m. **William T. Boren**.
593.   vii **Estelle M. Shute** b. 14-Jul-1895, m. **William H. Wodell**.
+ 594.   viii **Ralph Thomas Shute** b. 11-May-1900.

461. **Fred A. Shute** b. 5-Feb-1854, Whitefield, NH, m. 1879, **Lizzie Derby**, b. 8-Sep-1852, Lancaster, NH, d. Jun-1933, Lancaster, NH. Fred died 30-Aug-1946, Lancaster, NH.
          Children:
+ 595.   i **Ralph Darby Shute** b. 19-Jan-1887.

467. **Arthur Nathaniel Shute** b. 1857, Littleton, NH,[217] m. **Adela Dyke**.
          Children:
+ 596.   i **Forrest Arthur Shute** b. 13-Dec-1882.

477. **Elmer Shute** b. 11-Aug-1868, Northwood, NH,[172] m. bef 1888, **Mary S. Goodwin**, b. 7-Mar-1869, d. 30-Apr-1939. Elmer died 5-Mar-1928.
          Children:
+ 597.   i **George Elmer Shute** b. 2-Apr-1888.
598.   ii **Edith May Shute** b. 15-Apr-1889, Newburyport, Essex Co., MA, d. 27-Mar-1977.
599.   iii **Leon Blaisdell Shute** b. 29-Jan-1891, Newburyport, Essex Co., MA,[172] m. **Edith Morse**. Leon died 1962, MA.
+ 600.   iv **Frederick William Shute** b. 18-Oct-1892.
601.   v **Eudora Bertha Shute** b. 13-Jun-1894, Newburyport, Essex Co., MA.
602.   vi **Viola Francis Shute** b. 14-Feb-1896, Newburyport, Essex Co., MA, d. 14-Sep-1965.
603.   vii **Charles Elmer Shute** b. 4-Apr-1898, Newburyport, Essex Co., MA,[172] d. 17-Feb-1974.
604.   viii **Helen Gould Shute** b. 24-Apr-1900, West Newbury, Essex Co., MA.
605.   ix **Mildred Louise Shute** b. 5-Mar-1902, West Newbury, Essex Co., MA, d. 10-Apr-1922.
606.   x **Walter Raymond Shute** b. 19-Jun-1903, West Newbury, Essex Co., MA,[172] m. **Margaret Connors**. Walter died 28-Feb-1970.
607.   xi **Bessie Evelyn Shute** b. 26-Jul-1905, West Newbury, Essex Co., MA.
608.   xii **Horace Jenness Shute** b. 3-Aug-1907, West Newbury, Essex Co., MA,[172] m. **Viola Angelica Messer**. Horace died 2-Jan-1978, CA.

485. **James William Pillsbury** b. 30-Nov-1837, South Deerfield, NH,[229] Occupation: Hotelier/restauranteur, m. 1863, **Elizabeth S. Fetheroe/Favereaux**, b. Montreal, Canada. James died 20-Feb-1887, Marietta, Washington Co., OH.

Children:
609.   i **George L. Pillsbury** b. Sep-1866, Marietta, Washington Co., OH,[229] d. 10-Aug-1896, Athens, Athens Co., OH.

487. **George Edwin Pillsbury** b. 13-Dec-1841, Newburyport, Essex Co., MA,[229] m. 23-Jan-1868, in Harmer, OH,[229] **Elizabeth C. Hall**. George died aft 1898, New York, NY?.
Children:
610.   i **Edwin A. Pillsbury** b. 25-May-1871, Marietta, Washington Co., OH,[229] d. 24-Nov-1888.
611.   ii **Franklin H. Pillsbury** b. 15-Jul-1876, Alleghany City, PA.[229]
612. iii **Evelyn H. Pillsbury** b. 11-Mar-1883, Detroit, MI.[229]
613.   iv **Mary E. Pillsbury** b. 26-Oct-1888, Detroit, MI.[229]

490. **Joshua Plummer Pillsbury** b. 26-Aug-1849, Derry, Rockingham Co., NH,[229] Occupation: Methodist minister, m. 24-Jun-1872,[229] **Harriet Matilda Ross**, b. Marietta, Washington Co., OH. Joshua died 14-Jul-1904, Pueblo, CO.
Children:
614.   i **Joshua P. Pillsbury** b. 7-Dec-1873, Buena Vista, OH.[229]
615.   ii **Amy Ellen Pillsbury** b. 5-Aug-1876, OH.[229]
616. iii **Ross Sumner Pillsbury** b. 18-Jun-1879, Lucasville, OH.[229]
617.   iv **Hattie M. Pillsbury** b. 30-Jul-1881, Lucasville, OH.[229]
618.   v **Frank Edwin Pillsbury** b. 19-Jun-1884, Mt. Sterling, OH.[229]
619.   vi **James William Pillsbury** b. 8-Jan-1888, Newark, OH.[229]
620. vii ----- **Pillsbury** b. 3-Nov-1891, Federal, Clay Co., FL, d. 3-Nov-1891, Federal, Clay Co., FL.

491. **Ellen (Helen) Maria Pillsbury** b. 19-Feb-1854, Derry, Rockingham Co., NH,[229] m. 20-Oct-1874,[229] **Elias C. Needham**, b. Marietta, OH.
Children:
621.   i **P. Grosvenor Needham** b. 15-Oct-1875.
622.   ii **Clarence Needham** b. 15-Apr-1881.
623. iii **Fred C. Needham** b. 29-Mar-1882.
624.   iv **Florence C. Needham** b. 28-Dec-1883.
625.   v **Ellen P. Needham** b. 19-Jan-1886.
626.   vi **Elisabeth Needham** b. 23-Feb-1888.
627. vii **Edward C. Needham** b. 30-Aug-1894.

497. **Benjamin Franklin Shute** b. 16-May-1851, Somerville, Middlesex Co., MA,[272] Occupation: Poultry Trader, m. 28-Apr-1883, in Somerville, Middlesex Co., MA,[273] **Lena Pearson**, b. 18-Feb-1857, Sweden,[274] (daughter of **Nels Pearson** and **Sophia Ericson**) Occupation: Parlor maid, d. 26-Apr-1930, Somerville, Middlesex Co., MA,[275] Buried: 29-Apr-1930, Woodlawn Cem., Everett, MA.[144] Benjamin died 5-Mar-1930, Somerville, Middlesex Co., MA,[276] Buried: 8-Mar-1930, Woodlawn Cem., Everett, MA.[144]
Children:
+ 628.   i **Priscilla Adelaide Shute** b. 4-Feb-1884.
+ 629.   ii **Clara Augusta Shute** b. 28-Feb-1886.

+ 630.   iii **Benjamin Harrison Shute** b. 19-Nov-1888.

631.   iv **James Edwin Shute** b. 12-Sep-1891, Somerville, MA,[274] d. 23-Sep-1893, Medford, MA,[274] Buried: 25-Sep-1893, Woodlawn Cem., Everett, MA.[144]

632.   v **Walter Albert Shute** b. 5-Mar-1893, MA,[274] d. 29-Jul-1893, Medford, MA,[274] Buried: 30-Jul-1893, Woodlawn Cem., Everett, MA.[144]

633.   vi **Frank Wilson Shute** b. 16-Oct-1895, MA,[274] d. 25-Feb-1950, MA,[144] Buried: 28-Feb-1950, Woodlawn Cem., Everett, MA.[144]

Eighth Generation

500. Daniel Waldo Shute b. 29-Apr-1845, Hingham, Plymouth Co., MA,[244] Occupation: Shoemaker, m. 17-Nov-1869, in Hingham, Plymouth Co., MA,[64] **Josephine Souther**, b. 3-Jun-1849, Hingham, Plymouth Co., MA,[64] (daughter of **John Sprague Souther** and **Harriet N. Snow**). Daniel died 18-Oct-1905.
> Children:
> 634. i **Herbert Waldo Shute** b. 7-Aug-1872, Hingham, Plymouth Co., MA,[244] d. cir 1947, Weymouth, MA.
> 635. ii **Hattie Austin Shute** b. 9-Jan-1879, Hingham, Plymouth Co., MA.[64]
> 636. iii **Marion Dayton Shute** b. 29-Nov-1880, Hingham, Plymouth Co., MA.[64]

502. Henry Leonard Shute b. 18-Jun-1850, So. Scituate, MA,[277] Occupation: Public Weigher, m. 14-Oct-1880,[64] **Mary Sumner Martin**, b. Salem, MA. Henry died 17-Jan-1931, Salem, MA.
> Henry Leonard Shute was a public weigher by trade. In 1905, he was a member, Society of the Cincinnati.
> Children:
> + 637. i **Henry Martin Shute** b. 16-Jul-1881.
> 638. ii **William Cushing Shute** b. 10-Jan-1885,[278] d. 2-Jul-1887.
> 639. iii **Mary Shute** b. 8-Jun-1886, m. 1931, **Joseph W. Lincoln**. Mary died 25-Dec-1975.
> + 640. iv **Philip Cushing Shute** b. 12-Nov-1892.

506. Elizabeth Hersey b. 1853, Hingham, MA, m. 1871, **E. L. Ripley**, b. 1831. Elizabeth died 1918.
> Children:
> 641. i **Alice Ripley**.
> 642. ii **Nettie Melville Ripley**.
> 643. iii **Bessie W. Ripley**.

516. Mary Belcher b. 1832, m. 1851, **William Wheatley**, b. 1826, d. 1900. Mary died 1889.
> Children:
> 644. i **Annie D. Wheatley**.
> 645. ii **Mary A. Wheatley**.

521. Charles Francis Shute b. 17-Jun-1838, Malden, Middlesex Co., MA,[94] Occupation: Milk Dealer, m. 30-Dec-1860, **Martha W. Morrison**, b. 6-Feb-1837, Londonderry, Nova Scotia, Canada, (daughter of **Alexander Morrison** and **Margaret McNutt**) d. 2-Jun-1916, Malden, Middlesex Co., MA. Charles died 10-Jul-1914, Malden, Middlesex Co., MA.
> Children:
> 646. i **Charles Sumner Shute** b. 4-Nov-1864, Malden, Middlesex Co., MA, Occupation: Milk Dealer, d. Jul-1933, Buried: 28-Jul-1933, Forest Dale Cem., Malden, MA.
> + 647. ii **Georgie Anna Morrison Shute** b. 24-Apr-1867.
> 648. iii **Grace Edith Shute** b. 4-Jun-1871.

649.   iv **Jennie Ethel Shute** b. 26-Jun-1876, Malden, Middlesex
              Co., MA, d. aft 1956.
                  Jennie E. Shute was elected a teacher in the Malden,
          MA, elementary schools, and taught in Malden continuously
          until her retirement, a total of 46 years.
                  Ms. Shute was a graduate of the Malden public
          schools and Malden High, and received her B.S. degree at
          Salem Normal School, now Salem Teachers College. She had
          also taken courses in English literature at Harvard
          University, was a member of the Harvard Teachers Club,
          and had studied art under the late William Robinson,
          famous Malden artist, and in New York under nationally
          known instructors.
                  After retiring, Ms. Shute continued her residence in
          Malden until 1956 when she went to make her home with her
          niece, Mrs. Russell L. George. She was a member of
          Malden Old and New, of the First Universalist Church, the
          Kings Daughters and the Malden W.S.T.U.

528. **Ralph D. Shute** b. 4-Sep-1866,[254] m. 21-Mar-1888, **Orilla C.
Knight**.
              Children:
  650.   i **Vesta Jane Shute** b. 13-Jun-1889.
  651.   ii **Clyde R. Shute** b. 10-Sep-1890.[279]

531. **James Irving Shute** b. 27-Nov-1886, Prospect, Hancock Co., ME,
m. 14-Oct-1913, in Bucksport, ME, **Jennie Bernice Hooper**, b.
31-Aug-1887, West Sullivan, ME, d. 24-Jul-1967, Braintree, MA, Buried:
Mt. Wollaston Cem., MA. James died 8-Aug-1950, Walliston, MA.
              Children:
+ 652.   i **Elinor Shute**.
+ 653.   ii **Ruth Edna Shute** b. 17-Apr-1916.
+ 654.   iii **James Irving Shute**.
+ 655.   iv **Milton Shute**.
+ 656.   v **Marilyn Bernice Shute**.

532. **George P. Shute** b. 1877,[280] m. **Lulu Schaub**.
              Children:
+ 657.   i **Jean Percival Shute** b. 19-Jul-1912.
  658.   ii **Charles B. Shute** b. MA.[280]

533. **Bertha Shute** m. **Andrew H. Brown**.
              Children:
  659.   i **Alexander S. Brown**.
  660.   ii **Andrew H. Brown Jr.**.

538. **Frank Henry Shute** b. 17-Nov-1866, Gloucester, Essex Co.,
MA,[281] Occupation: Hotel Worker, m. 10-Oct-1912, in Gloucester, Essex
Co., MA, **Annie A. ("Addie") Burnham**, b. 20-Oct-1872, Gloucester,
Essex Co., MA, (daughter of **Elias P. Burnham** and **Annie P. Babson**)
d. 21-Feb-1953. Frank died 4-Mar-1954.
              Children:
  661.   i **Barbara Shute** b. 17-Jul-1914, Gloucester, Essex Co.,

MA, m. divorced, ----- **Friberg**.

542. **William Thomas Shute** b. 11-Jul-1861, Gloucester, Essex Co.,
MA,[282] Occupation: Fish Packaging Business, m. 2-Oct-1884, in
Gloucester, Essex Co., MA, **Marion ("Mattie") Bruce Rust**, b.
5-Mar-1864, Gloucester, Essex Co., MA, (daughter of **George Proctor
Rust** and **Caroline Amelia Bruce**) d. 26-Mar-1943, Gloucester, Essex
Co., MA, Buried: Oak Grove Cem., Gloucester, MA. William died
9-Apr-1920, Gloucester, Essex Co., MA, Buried: Oak Grove Cem.,
Gloucester, MA.

William Thomas Shute succeeded his father as a partner in "Shute
& Merchant" fish business with William T. Merchant. The business at
that time was not doing well and, when William T. Merchant suddenly
died of a heart-attack, William Thomas Shute was left with crippling
debts. He managed to pay back every cent owed. In May, 1907, he sold
the business to Gorton-Pew Fisheries Company, agreeing to stay on in a
salaried position. In October of that year, he arranged to devote
half of his time to the old business and half to "Merchant Box &
Cooperage Company."
  Children:
+ 662.   i **Kenneth Bruce Shute** b. 17-Aug-1886.
+ 663.   ii **Margaret Grover Shute** b. 31-Dec-1894.
+ 664. iii **George Haase Shute** b. 27-Feb-1897.
  665.   iv **James Lovell Shute II.** b. 18-Dec-1900, Gloucester,
          Essex Co., MA,[283] d. 9-Jan-1981.
          Academy Award-winning scriptwriter, James Lovell
          Shute, received his "Oscars" for "A Chance to Live" (Best
          Short Documentary) and "Helen Keller in Her Story" (Best
          Documentary Feature) in 1949 and 1955, respectively.
          Preceding and following these milestones were theatre and
          film credits far to lengthy to list here, but which
          include work under Edmond Jones and Eugene O'Neill at the
          Old Provincetown Playhouse, a year with Ben Hecht and
          Charlie MacArthur during their producing venture at the
          Old Paramount Studios on Long Island, 15 years as Chief
          Scriptwriter and Associate Producer of The March of Time,
          and two years as head of the script department for the
          film section of E.C.A. -- the Marshall Plan -- in France.
          Many of his E.C.A. films were honored by being chosen
          for showing at the Cannes, Edinburgh and Venice film
          festivals.
+ 666.   v **Benjamin Smith Shute** b. 27-Jan-1904.

546. **Ada Marian Shute** b. 14-Oct-1870, Gloucester, Essex Co., MA, m.
18-Oct-1893, in Gloucester, Essex Co., MA, **Alexander James Smith**, b.
24-Sep-1868, Lower Barney's River, Nova Scotia, Can., (son of **David
Fraser Smith** and **Jane Scott Williams**) d. 16-Jun-1944, Weymouth, MA,
Buried: Blue Hills Cem., Braintree, MA. Ada died 26-Aug-1953, Newton,
MA, Buried: Blue Hills Cem., Braintree, MA.
  Children:
  667.   i **Robert Shute Smith** b. 9-Nov-1894, Gloucester, Essex
          Co., MA, m. 11-Aug-1929, **Ruth Warren**. Robert died
          17-Jun-1961.

+ 668.   ii **Katharine Grover Smith** b. 21-Oct-1897.
  669.   iii **Marjorie Bradley Smith** b. 19-Aug-1899, Gloucester, Essex Co., MA, m. 4-Aug-1920, **George Lawrence Arbuckle**, d. 24-May-1941, Buried: Murray's Pt. Cem., Pictou Co., NS. Marjorie died 7-Oct-1985, Buried: Murray's Pt. Cem., Pictou Co., NS.

548. **Robert Thomas Shute** b. 1875, Gloucester, Essex Co., MA,[284] m. **J. Ethel Tarr**, b. 1-Aug-1870, Gloucester, Essex Co., MA, d. 1972, Gloucester, Essex Co., MA. Robert died 9-Apr-1920.
          Children:
  670.   i **Mildred Aline Shute** b. 23-Oct-1908, St. Paul, MN, m. 13-Jan-1942, in Gloucester, MA, **Wilder Smith**, b. 17-Apr-1913, Cambridge, MA, d. cir 1989.

551. **Richard Everett Shute** b. 17-Oct-1887,[285] m. **Doris MacKenzie**. Richard died 1-Oct-1957.
          Children:
+ 671.   i **Henry W. Shute** b. 25-May-1924.
  672.   ii **Richard M. Shute**.

556. **Dora Estella Brown** b. 23-Aug-1875, Webster Co., NE,[120] m. 1-Jul-1905, **Walter Robert Evans**.
          Children:
  673.   i **Irena Augusta Evans** b. Feb-1906.
  674.   ii **Alice Lillian Evans** b. Mar-?.

557. **Flora Estella Brown** b. 23-Aug-1875, Webster Co., NE,[120] m. 12-Oct-1898, **Herbert Francis Carter**. Flora died 8-Jan-1908.
          Children:
  675.   i ----- **Mabel Carter** b. 21-Jun-1900.
  676.   ii **Leroy Brown Carter** b. 28-Jun-1903.
  677.   iii **Francis Shute Carter** b. 28-Mar-1905.

560. **Herbert Thomas Shute** b. 8-Aug-1883, Burr Oak, Jewell Co., KS,[286] m. (1) 21-Dec-1904, in Kent, Sherman Co., OR, **Nellie Mabel Whitney**, b. 12-Aug-1884, Washington Co., KS, (daughter of **James C. Whitney** and **Laura I. Pickering**) d. 6-Oct-1909, Blodgett, Benton Co., OR, Buried: 7-Oct-1909, Blodgett, Benton Co., OR, m. (2) 18-Mar-1911, **Della May Robbins**, b. 29-Oct-1890, The Dalles, OR, (daughter of **Peter Roscoe Robbins** and **Alice May Clark**) d. 29-Apr-1983, Colville, WA, Buried: 2-May-1983, Mountain View Park, Colville, WA. Herbert died 25-Apr-1979, Colville, WA, Buried: 28-Apr-1979, Mountain View Park, Colville, WA.
          Children by Nellie Mabel Whitney:
+ 678.   i **Herbert Richard Shute** b. 6-Feb-1906.
+ 679.   ii **Laurel Sanford Shute** b. 29-Jun-1908.
          Children by Della May Robbins:
  680.   iii **Alice Ruth Shute** b. 30-Dec-1911, Fairview, OR, m. 15-Apr-1932, **Lloyd Elwood Bellmore**, b. 6-Sep-1905, d. 29-Dec-1977, Buried: Highland Cemetery, Colville, WA. Alice died 8-Jun-1968, Buried: Highland Cemetery, Colville, WA.

681.   iv **Mildred Geneva Shute** b. 19-Aug-1914, Fairview, OR, m.
          1-Oct-1933, **David Harold Wilson.**

682.   v **Shirley Lillian Shute** b. 8-Apr-1918, Boyds, Ferry Co.,
          WA, m. (1) 14-Feb-1938, **Robert Clinton Connell**, m. (2)
          1947, **William Rodney Deer.** Shirley died 8-Oct-1983,
          Buried: Masonic Mem. Park, Tumwater, WA.

683.   vi **Delbert Roscoe Shute** b. 25-May-1921, Boyds, Ferry Co.,
          WA, m. (1) 1943, **Erma Davis**, m. (2) 1971, **Frances
          -----.** Delbert died 31-Oct-1971, Buried: Forest Lawn,
          Bremerton, WA.

+ 684.   vii **Darrell Thomas Shute** b. 10-Aug-1928.

564. **Fanny Marguerite Shute** b. 7-Jun-1897, m. 2-Jul-1914, in
Colville, WA, **Gust Robert Hendricks**, b. 1-Feb-1883, Jarthed,
Smoleen, Sweden, d. 22-Jan-1974, Spokane, WA.
          Children:

685.   i **Robert Iver Hendricks** b. 17-Feb-1915, Rockcut, WA, d.
          5-Jan-1972, Spokane, WA, Buried: Spokane, WA.

686.   ii **Harley Albert Hendricks** b. 15-Oct-1916, Rockcut, WA, d.
          15-Oct-1916, Rockcut, WA, Buried: Orient, WA.

687.   iii **Donald Ronald Hendricks** b. 14-Jun-1917, Rockcut, WA, d.
          28-Jul-1917, Rockcut, WA, Buried: Orient, WA.

688.   iv **Kenneth Emerson Hendricks** b. 10-Aug-1919, Spokane, WA,
          m. 28-Jan-1960, in Spokane, Spokane Co., WA, **Ethel
          Kathleen Stiles.**

689.   v **Joy Marguerite Hendricks** b. 27-Jul-1921, Spokane, WA,
          m. 4-Aug-1938, in Rosalia, WA, **Leo Mortensen.** Joy died
          28-Jan-1960, Renton, WA.

690.   vi **Leah Lennea Hendricks** b. 12-Dec-1925, Spokane, WA, m.
          18-Feb-1961, in Delta Junction, AK, **Robert Calvin
          Smith**, b. 3-Jun-1908, Yanceyville, NC, (son of **Robert
          Lawson Smith** and **Annie Elizabeth Burton**) Occupation:
          Steamfitter, d. 30-Sep-1986, Fairbanks, AK.

691.   vii **Raymond Louis Hendricks** b. 5-May-1928, Spokane, WA, m.
          1958, **Cora Richardson.** Raymond died 14-Sep-1973,
          Sacramento, CA.

692.   viii **Bonnie June Hendricks** b. 6-Jun-1929, Spokane, WA, m.
          John H. Larrabee. Bonnie died 10-Aug-1988, Fairbanks,
          AK.

693.   ix **Lowell Eugene Hendricks** b. 28-Dec-1930, Spokane, WA, m.
          5-Aug-1961, in CA, **Yolanda -----.**

694.   x **Larry Dell Hendricks** b. 15-Aug-1938, Spokane, WA, d.
          16-Aug-1938, Spokane, WA.

594. **Ralph Thomas Shute** b. 11-May-1900, m. 14-Apr-1927, **Mary Alice
Wittwer**, b. 11-Sep-1906, Smith, KS.
          Children:

695.   i **Maribelle Lee Shute** b. 14-Sep-1928, m. **Trenton
          Sealock.**

696.   ii **Mildred Mae Shute** b. 19-Jun-1931, m. **Robert A.
          Wallace.**

697.   iii **George Edward Shute** b. 15-Jul-1933, m. **Jaralie Ann
          Davis.**

698.   iv **Pauline Louise Shute** b. 6-Sep-1941, m. **Henry Joseph Maldaner**.

595. **Ralph Darby Shute** b. 19-Jan-1887, Whitefield, NH, m. 1911, **Cora McCutcheon**, b. 28-Dec-1887, Maguadauk, New Brunswick, Canada. Ralph died 19-Feb-1978, Lancaster, NH.
          Children:
+ 699.   i **Kenneth E. Shute** b. 19-Jan-1912.

596. **Forrest Arthur Shute** b. 13-Dec-1882, Lisbon, NH, m. 13-Feb-1914, in San Francisco, CA, **Maria Bessing**, b. 12-Dec-1889, Alsace, France, (daughter of **Louis August Besson** and **Catherine Kolb**) d. 15-Feb-1971, San Francisco, CA, Buried: 18-Feb-1971, Cypress Lawn, Colma, CA. Forrest died 22-Jul-1976, San Francisco, CA, Buried: 25-Jul-1976, Cypress Lawn, Colma, CA.
          Children:
700.   i **Lorraine Shute** b. 15-Nov-1914, San Francisco, CA, m. 13-Nov-1938, **William M. Wright**. Lorraine died 25-Apr-1979.
+ 701.   ii **Forrest Arthur Shute, Jr.** b. 16-Nov-1924.

597. **George Elmer Shute** b. 2-Apr-1888, Newburyport, Essex Co., MA,[172] m. 7-Sep-1909, **Alma Ahern**. George died 5-Mar-1928.
          Children:
702.   i **Eilleen Shute** b. 1-Apr-1910.

600. **Frederick William Shute** b. 18-Oct-1892, Newburyport, Essex Co., MA,[172] m. **Edith Stanley Wilson**, b. 21-Mar-1890, d. 2-Apr-1945, Amesbury, Essex Co., MA. Frederick died 19-Jun-1971, Amesbury, Essex Co., MA.
          Children:
703.   i **Arthur Holmes Shute** b. 13-Dec-1917.[172]
704.   ii **Robert Chapman Shute** b. 5-Feb-1920.[172]
+ 705.   iii **Clifford Wilson Shute** b. 3-May-1922.
706.   iv **Kenneth Henry Shute** b. 4-Mar-1925.[172]
707.   v **Richard Thurlow Shute** b. 26-Feb-1927.[172]
708.   vi **Leonard Merle Shute** b. 9-Mar-1929.[172]

628. **Priscilla Adelaide Shute** b. 4-Feb-1884, Somerville, Middlesex Co., MA,[287] m. 14-Nov-1915, in First Baptist Ch., Miami, Dade Co., FL,[288] **John Henry Ryan, Jr.**, b. 20-Aug-1875, Charlottetown, P.E.I., Canada,[289] Baptized: 23-Jan-1878, Trinity Methodist Church, Charlottetown, (son of **John Henry Ryan** and **Margaret Jane Webster**) Occupation: Hotel engineer, d. 7-Nov-1937, Nassau, Bahamas,[290] Buried: Western Cem., Nassau, Bahamas. Priscilla died 20-Jun-1983, New London, New London Co., CT, Buried: 23-Jun-1983, Starr Burial Ground, Groton, New London.
          Children:
709.   i **John Allen Ryan** b. 24-Apr-1916, Miami, Dade Co., FL,[274] d. 22-Jul-1994, Groton, New London Co., CT, Buried: 28-Jul-1994, Starr Burial Ground, Groton, New London.
+ 710.   ii **Ellen Priscilla Ryan** b. 6-Jul-1918.

711.   iii **Alma Pauline Ryan** b. 5-Oct-1922, Somerville, Middlesex
Co., MA.
        Seaman 3rd Class Alma Ryan joined the WAVES in
November 1943, and was assigned to the Naval Submarine
Medical Research Laboratory (NSMRL), Groton, CT, in
September 1944, after completing indoctrination at Hunter
College in New York, NY, Yeoman School in Stillwater, OK,
and brief duty in Washington, DC. In 1947, she left the
service with the rank of Yeoman 1st Class, but continued
with the NSMRL as a civilian employee, in the newly
created Vision Branch. Upon her retirement in 1986, Ms.
Ryan had the longest service record of any employee -- 39
years with the Vision Branch and 42 years with NSMRL.

629. **Clara Augusta Shute** b. 28-Feb-1886, Melrose, MA,[274] m. (1)
18-Feb-1909,[274] **Clarence Herbert Rumford**, b. 22-Aug-1880, London,
Ont., Canada, Occupation: Waiter, d. Aug-1947, Buried: Belmont, MA, m.
(2) Jun-1951, in Cambridge, MA, **William Sheppard**, d. 1963,
Worcester, MA, Buried: Worcester, MA. Clara died 11-Oct-1960,
Worcester, MA, Buried: 14-Oct-1960, Worcester, MA.
        Children by Clarence Herbert Rumford:
+ 712.   i **Charlotte Helena Rumford** b. 6-Feb-1910.

630. **Benjamin Harrison Shute** b. 19-Nov-1888, Somerville, MA,[274] m.
6-May-1918,[274] **Hazel A. Beverly**, d. 10-May-1962, Pompano Beach, FL.
 Benjamin died 26-May-1956, Belmont, MA, Buried: Belmont Cem.,
Belmont, MA.
        Children:
+ 713.   i **Richard Harrison Shute** b. 25-Mar-1938.

Ninth Generation

637. **Henry Martin Shute** b. 16-Jul-1881,[278] m. 16-Jul-1912, **Harriet Farrar**. Henry died 16-Dec-1952.

Children:

714.   i **Henry Farrar Shute** b. 5-Aug-1914, m. 21-Jun-1940, ----- -----. Henry died cir 1960.

640. **Philip Cushing Shute** b. 12-Nov-1892,[278] m. (1) 7-Jun-1917, **Gladys Ethyl Keith**, m. (2) 1930, **Agnes Smyth Kelsey**. Philip died 7-Sep-1971.

Children by Gladys Ethyl Keith:

715.   i **Gladys Martin Shute** b. 19-Oct-1917.

+ 716.   ii **Philip Keith Shute** b. 6-Dec-1919.

717.   iii **George Bernard Shute** b. 19-Sep-1923, d. 20-Dec-1944, Germany (Battle of the Bulge),[144] Buried: 1-Apr-1949, Woodlawn Cem., later to Hingham Cem., MA.

647. **Georgie Anna Morrison Shute** b. 24-Apr-1867, Malden, Middlesex Co., MA, m. **Frank Warren Keith**, b. Nov-1864, MA, (son of **James Monroe Keith** and **Adeline Wetherbee**). Georgie Buried: 24-Sep-1919, Malden, Middlesex Co., MA.

Children:

+ 718.   i **Marion Shute Keith** b. 21-Sep-1893.

652. **Elinor Shute** m. (1) ----- **Kenney**, m. (2) **Lawrence Nelson**.

Children by ----- Kenney:

+ 719.   i **Jean Constance Kenney**.

Children by Lawrence Nelson:

720.   ii **Jeffrey O. Nelson**.

653. **Ruth Edna Shute** b. 17-Apr-1916, Hammond St., Bangor, ME, Baptized: Wollaston, MA, m. 3-Sep-1939, in St. Mary's Ch., W. Quincy, MA, **Francis Martell**, b. 9-May-1916, W. Quincy, MA, Baptized: St. Mary's Ch., W. Quincy, MA, (son of **Napoleon A. Martell** and **Elizabeth Shepard**).

Children:

+ 721.   i **Lois Ann Martell** b. 22-Nov-1941.

+ 722.   ii **Kenneth Alan Martell** b. 6-Mar-1944.

723.   iii **Cynthia Louise Martell** b. 24-Aug-1946, Quincy, MA.

654. **James Irving Shute** m. ----- -----.

Children:

724.   i **James Nevil Shute**.

725.   ii **Kevin David Shute**.

726.   iii **Richard Alan Shute**.

727.   iv **Maura Catherine Shute** m. **Robert Stuart Nichols**.

655. **Milton Shute** m. ----- -----.

Children:

+ 728.   i **Barbara Jeanne Shute**.

729.   ii **Gary Milton Shute**.

656. Marilyn Bernice Shute m. **Everett Irving Miller.**
    Children:
 730. i **Pamela Jean Miller** m. **Martin Foley.**
 731. ii **Nanci Lee Miller** m. **Steven Sawyer.**
 732. iii **Susan Gail Miller** m. **Richard McHugh.**
 733. iv **Daniel Scott Miller.**
 734. v **Gregory Alan Miller.**

657. Jean Percival Shute b. 19-Jul-1912, Montreal, Quebec,
Canada,[291] Occupation: U.S. Army, m. 9-Jun-1956, in Dayton, OH,
Francis (Nan) Winifred Rice, b. 18-May-1914, Niles, MI. Jean died
7-Aug-1981, MD, Buried: Arlington Nat. Cem., Ft. Myer, VA.
    Children:
 735. i **Jean Derby Shute** b. 17-May-1957, Washington, DC.[291]

662. Kenneth Bruce Shute b. 17-Aug-1886, Gloucester, Essex Co.,
MA,[292] Occupation: B&M Railroad/U.S. Army, m. 6-Jun-1928, in
Gloucester, Essex Co., MA, **Anna Sponagle**, b. 29-Oct-1902,
Gloucester, Essex Co., MA, (daughter of **Stephen Sponagle** and **Anne
Morrison**) d. Jun-1989, Chelmsford, MA, Buried: Oak Grove Cem.,
Gloucester, MA. Kenneth died 7-Apr-1941, Gloucester, Essex Co., MA,
Buried: Oak Grove Cem., Gloucester, MA.
   A graduate of Amherst College, Kenneth Bruce Shute was initially
employed by the Boston & Maine (B&M) Railway. At the start of World
War I, he went to Officers Candidate School in Plattsburgh, NY; was
commissioned as a 2nd Lt. of Artillery, and saw action in France.
After the war, he was chosen to activate and command a battalion of
75mm Artillery in the MA Nat. Guard. He died as his battalion was
being activated for World War II.
    Children:
+ 736. i **Ann Bruce Shute** b. 22-Aug-1929.
+ 737. ii **Margaret Rust Shute** b. 12-May-1932.

663. Margaret Grover Shute b. 31-Dec-1894, Gloucester, Essex Co.,
MA, m. 15-Sep-1918, in Gloucester, Essex Co., MA, **Philip Oliver
Palmstrom**, b. 4-Jul-1893, Philadelphia, PA, (son of **Nils Palmstrom**
and **Anna Thulin**) Occupation: Commercial Artist, d. 18-Mar-1945,
Needham, Norfolk Co., MA, Buried: Mt. Auburn Cem., Cambridge, MA.
Margaret died 10-Oct-1977, Needham, Norfolk Co., MA, Buried:
13-Oct-1977, Mt. Auburn Cem., Cambridge, MA.
    Children:
+ 738. i **Norman Bruce Palmstrom** b. 1-Jun-1921.
 739. ii **William Nils Palmstrom** b. 29-Oct-1922, Needham, Norfolk
     Co., MA, Baptized: Cong. Ch., Needham, MA, Occupation:
     Graphic Artist, m. (1) 10-Mar-1946, **Norma Cravens**, m.
     (2) 10-Aug-1982, **Patricia Mae Foster**, b. 26-Jan-1939,
     Morrisville, VT, Baptized: N. Wolcott, VT.
+ 740. iii **David Shute Palmstrom** b. 8-Jan-1924.

664. George Haase Shute b. 27-Feb-1897, Gloucester, Essex Co.,
MA,[293] Occupation: Insurance Adjuster, m. **Marion Stoddard**, b.
29-Jun-1898, Gloucester, Essex Co., MA, d. 16-Nov-1992, Manchester,
NH. George died 28-Apr-1968, Manchester, NH, Buried: Manchester, NH.

George Haase Shute served as a signalman in the U.S. Navy during World War I.

Children:
741.   i **Marilyn S. Shute** b. 25-Apr-1927, Gloucester, Essex Co., MA, d. 8-Jul-1993, Derry, NH.
+ 742.   ii **Carol B. Shute** b. 5-Dec-1937.

666. **Benjamin Smith Shute** b. 27-Jan-1904, Gloucester, Essex Co., MA,[294] Occupation: U. S. Army, m. (1) 25-Dec-1928, in Gloucester, Essex Co., MA, **Barbara Newman Winchester**, b. 28-Aug-1905, Gloucester, Essex Co., MA, (daughter of **Henry Winchester** and **May Lamson Brewer**) d. 15-Jun-1973, Dewitt Army Hosp., Ft. Belvoir, VA, Buried: Arlington Nat. Cem., Ft. Myer, VA, m. (2) 16-Jun-1977, in Boston, MA, **Louise D'Ercole**, b. 3-Apr-1916, Springfield, MA, (daughter of **Camillo D'Ercole** and **Maria Guglielmotte**).
     Col. (U.S. Army Ret.) Benjamin Smith Shute graduated from the U.S. Military Academy in 1928. In World War II, he served in Europe as Corps Engineer with the 18th Airborne Corps. He saw action in Belgium, France and Germany. After the war he was assigned to the Occupational Forces in Japan. He retired in 1958. Col. Shute has received numerous decorations for his wartime and peacetime services.
Children by Barbara Newman Winchester:
743.   i **David Winchester Shute** b. 6-Dec-1929, Washington, DC,[295] m. May-1951, **Janet Carol Cahoon**. David died 28-May-1952, Korea.
             Lt. (U.S. Army) David Winchester Shute was killed in action in Korea.
+ 744.   ii **Alan Henry Shute** b. 6-Feb-1932.

668. **Katharine Grover Smith** b. 21-Oct-1897, Gloucester, Essex Co., MA, m. 7-Sep-1921, in Boston, Suffolk Co., MA, **Clarence Flaig Woodman**, b. 10-Jun-1895, East Cambridge, Suffolk Co., MA, (son of **Clarence Albert Woodman** and **Rose Flora Flaig**) d. 5-Sep-1975, Waltham, Middlesex Co., MA, Buried: Mt. Auburn Cem., Cambridge, MA. Katharine died 2-Nov-1990, Buried: Oak Grove Cem., Gloucester, MA. Clarence:
     Sgt. Clarence Flaig Woodman served in World War I.
Children:
745.   i **Barbara Shute Woodman** b. 1-Jul-1922, Newton, MA, m. Jul-1960, divorced, **Peter H. Wyden**.
746.   ii **William Clarence Woodman** b. 29-Jan-1927, Newton, MA, d. 5-Feb-1927, Newton, MA, Buried: Mt. Auburn Cem., Cambridge, MA.
+ 747.   iii **Virginia Woodman** b. 14-May-1929.
748.   iv **Richard Ellis Woodman** b. 2-Aug-1931, Newton, MA, m. 10-Nov-1956, **Paula Dresser**.

671. **Henry W. Shute** b. 25-May-1924, Exeter, Rockingham Co., NH,[296] Occupation: Lawyer, m. ----- -----.
     Henry W. Shute is a lawyer in Exeter, NH.
Children:
749.   i **Woodworth Shute**.

678. **Herbert Richard Shute** b. 6-Feb-1906, Kent, Sherman Co., OR, m.
(1) 22-Nov-1930, divorced 1944, **Fern Ethyl Rosina Nelson**, b.
4-Aug-1909, Coeur D'Alene, ID, (daughter of **Frank Owen Nelson** and
Minnie Adell Knickerbocker) m. (2) cir 1945, **Violet Plum**. Herbert
died Mar-1986, Spokane, WA, Buried: Spokane, WA.
> Children by Fern Ethyl Rosina Nelson:
+ 750.   i **Stanley Richard Shute** b. 24-Jul-1933.
+ 751.   ii **Kenneth Dale Shute** b. 24-Jul-1933.

679. **Laurel Sanford Shute** b. 29-Jun-1908, Blodgett, Benton Co., OR,
m. 25-Jun-1929, in Black Diamond, King Co., WA, **Fannie Louise
Simmons**, b. 25-Mar-1911, Basin, MT, (daughter of **Al Simmons** and
Edith Hankins) d. 27-Nov-1986, Kennewick, Benton Co., WA, Buried:
29-Nov-1986, Desert Lawn Mem. Park, Kennewick, WA. Laurel died
11-Jan-1993, Buried: Desert Lawn Mem. Park, Kennewick, WA.
> Children:
+ 752.   i **Laurel Herbert Shute** b. 7-Aug-1930.
+ 753.   ii **Dean Alva Shute** b. 23-Jan-1935.
+ 754. iii **Janice Louise Shute** b. 4-Aug-1936.

684. **Darrell Thomas Shute** b. 10-Aug-1928, Barstow, Ferry Co., WA, m.
19-Jul-1949, in Barstow, WA, **Karen Ann Wang**, b. 18-Feb-1933, The
Dalles, OR, (daughter of **Alfred Ingemar Wang** and **Blanche May
Vaughan**).
> Children:
+ 755.   i **Donald Thomas Shute** b. 8-Feb-1950.
+ 756.   ii **Christine Kay Shute** b. 1-Mar-1952.
  757. iii **Michael Lloyd Shute** b. 16-Dec-1954, Spokane, Spokane
           Co., WA, d. 3-Jul-1972.
+ 758.   iv **Vicki Lynn Shute** b. 11-Feb-1957.
+ 759.   v **Sandra Ann Shute** b. 11-Jan-1966.

699. **Kenneth E. Shute** b. 19-Jan-1912, Lancaster, NH, m. **Eileen Ross
Gadd**, b. 18-Feb-1912, W. Newbury, MA, (daughter of **Samuel Gadd** and
Bertha Ross) d. 5-Jun-1981, Concord, NH.
> Children:
+ 760.   i **Barbara Eileen Shute** b. 6-Dec-1936.
+ 761.   ii **Thomas Ralph Shute** b. 3-Jul-1939.
+ 762. iii **Nancy Kaye Shute** b. 30-Aug-1943.
+ 763.   iv **Jonathan Kenneth Shute** b. 28-Oct-1949.

701. **Forrest Arthur Shute, Jr.** b. 16-Nov-1924, Petaluma, CA, m.
29-Aug-1944, in San Francisco, CA, **Patricia Anna Earl**, b.
23-Mar-1926, Stockton, CA, (daughter of **Duncan Douglas Earl** and
Eileen Cecilia Belew). Forrest died 4-Mar-1991, Mt. Zion Hosp., San
Francisco, CA, Buried: 10-Mar-1991, Golden Gate Nat. Cem., San Bruno,
CA.
> Children:
  764.   i **Douglas Arthur Shute** b. 20-Apr-1945, Merced, Merced
           Co., CA.
+ 765.   ii **Forrest Earl Shute** b. 12-Jul-1948.
  766. iii **Deborah Sue Shute** b. 6-Dec-1950, San Francisco, CA, m.

15-Dec-1973, **Darrel Ferguson**.
767.   iv **Jerald Brian Shute** b. 14-Jul-1953, San Francisco, CA,
            d. 2-Jul-1958, San Francisco, CA.
768.   v **Stephen Kenneth Shute** b. 11-May-1964, San Francisco,
            CA.

705. **Clifford Wilson Shute** b. 3-May-1922, Newburyport, Essex Co.,
MA,[172] m. 20-Oct-1945, in Georgetown, Essex Co., MA, **Mary Catherine
O'Donnell**, b. 30-Mar-1924, Beverly, Essex Co., MA.
            Children:
769.   i **Dennis James Shute** b. 24-Jul-1946, Amesbury, Essex Co.,
            MA.[297]
770.   ii **Edith Catherine Shute** b. 24-Jul-1948, Amesbury, Essex
            Co., MA, m. **John J. Tirone, Jr.**.
771.   iii **William Frederick Shute** b. 30-Aug-1953, Amesbury, Essex
            Co., MA.[172]
772.   iv **Philip Allan Shute** b. 30-Aug-1953, Amesbury, Essex Co.,
            MA.[297]

710. **Ellen Priscilla Ryan** b. 6-Jul-1918, Miami, Dade Co., FL, m.
10-Jul-1944, in Webster Groves, St. Louis Co., MO, **Raymond Eugene
Flint**, b. 30-May-1913, Webster Groves, St. Louis Co., MO,[298] (son of
John Clark Flint and **Anna Louise Corpening**) Occupation: Civil
engineer, d. 2-Jan-1994, Oakland, St. Louis Co., MO,[299] Buried:
6-Jan-1994, Oak Hill Cem., Kirkwood, St. Louis Co.
            Children:
+ 773.   i **Priscilla Anne Flint** b. 8-Jul-1947.
+ 774.   ii **Kathleen Louise Flint** b. 17-Mar-1952.
  775.   iii **Clark Henry Flint** b. 25-Jul-1956, St. Louis, St. Louis
            Co., MO,[298] Occupation: Writer.
                 Clark H. Flint received his B.A. from Washington
            University in St. Louis in December, 1977. A freelance
            writer/editor, he has lived in the Chicago area since
            1979.

712. **Charlotte Helena Rumford** b. 6-Feb-1910, Somerville, MA,[274]
Occupation: Telephone worker, m. 13-Oct-1931, in New York, NY,
divorced 1945, **George Griffing Chapman**, b. 1908, Omaha, NE, (son of
George B. Chapman and **Elizabeth G----**) Occupation: Salesman, d.
1970, Harrisburg, PA. Charlotte died 15-Aug-1990, Lexington, MA,
Buried: Shawsheen Cem., Bedford, MA.
            Children:
+ 776.   i **Claire Elizabeth Chapman** b. 30-Oct-1937.

713. **Richard Harrison Shute** b. 25-Mar-1938, MA, Occupation: Horse
Shoer & Trainer, m. (1) 1959, in Scottsdale, AZ, divorced 1965, **Verna
Cain**, b. 23-Mar-1942, Delta, CO, (daughter of **Verne Cain** and **Lois
Thomas**) Occupation: Accountant, m. (2) 1970, **Marilee Johnson**.
            Children by Verna Cain:
+ 777.   i **Peggy Sue Shute** b. 7-Apr-1961.
+ 778.   ii **Rose Marie Shute** b. 22-Jul-1962.
+ 779.   iii **Desa Rae Shute** b. 4-Aug-1963.

Tenth Generation

716. Philip Keith Shute b. 6-Dec-1919, m. 20-Feb-1943, **Elizabeth Jean Glassford**, b. Canada.

Philip Keith Shute served in WWII as a commissioned Air Force Navigator. He retired from the Volunteer Reserve as a Lt. Colonel. He entered into his family business as Public Weigher of goods on the Hingham, MA, waterfront, but expanded it into a marine surveyor and consulting firm to deep-water ships. Now retired, Philip K. Shute has passed the business along to his son, marking five generations in an ongoing, family operation.

A resident of Hingham, MA, and Ft. Myers, FL, Philip K. Shute has been on the standing committee, and served as secretary, of the Society of the Cincinnati since 1958.

       Children:
+ 780.   i **Philip Edward Shute** b. 15-Jun-1946.
+ 781.   ii **Elizabeth Shute** b. 8-Sep-1948.
  782. iii **Virginia Shute** b. 13-Mar-1951.
  783.   iv **Stephanie Shute** b. 23-Sep-1952, m. 27-Jun-1987, **Stephen G. Kelsch**.

718. Marion Shute Keith b. 21-Sep-1893, Malden, Middlesex Co., MA, m. 24-Apr-1917, in Malden, Middlesex Co., MA, **Russell Lowell George**, b. 21-Jun-1889, Newbury, Orange Co., VT, (son of **Edmund Harriman George** and **Jane E. Ham**) d. 11-Oct-1963, Boston, Suffolk Co., MA, Buried: 15-Oct-1963, Malden, Middlesex Co., MA. Marion died 25-Sep-1979, Hanover, MA.
       Children:
+ 784.   i **Priscilla Keith George** b. 11-Sep-1920.
  785.   ii **Richard Keith George** b. 16-Oct-1923, Whitman, MA.

719. Jean Constance Kenney m. **Robert Joseph Thomson**.
       Children:
  786.   i **Steven R. Thomson**.
  787.   ii **James R. Thomson**.
  788. iii **Richard S. Thomson**.
  789.   iv **John K. Thomson**.

721. Lois Ann Martell b. 22-Nov-1941, Quincy, MA, Baptized: Emmanuel Episcopal Ch., Braintree, MA, m. 9-Jun-1962, **Sumner E. Svedeman**, b. 4-May-1936, Baptized: Milton, MA, (son of **Stuart Nils Svedeman** and **Mabel Pierce**).
       Children:
  790.   i **Donna Lee Svedeman** b. 21-Dec-1963, Forest Hills, NY.
  791.   ii **James Bradley Svedeman** b. 28-Apr-1965, Cincinnati, OH.
  792. iii **Lauri Jean Svedeman** b. 31-Jan-1969, Cincinnati, OH.
  793.   iv **Eric Matthew Svedeman** b. 26-Feb-1970, Cincinnati, OH.

722. Kenneth Alan Martell b. 6-Mar-1944, Quincy, MA, Baptized: Emmanuel Episcopal Ch., Braintree, MA, m. 19-Aug-1967, in Montreal, Quebec, Canada, **Diane Marshall**, b. 14-Aug-1945, Montreal, Quebec, Canada, (daughter of **Eric E. Marshall** and **Joyce Anne Gidney**).

Children:
794.   i **Erica Anne Martell** b. 5-Sep-1974, Bad Hersfeld, Germany.
795.   ii **Alexander Gidney Martell** b. 6-Nov-1978, Newport, RI.

728. **Barbara Jeanne Shute** m. **Wayne Morrison**.
Children:
796.   i **Mary Jane Morrison** m. (1) ----- **Luckenbach**, m. (2) **Jeff Gutzler**.

736. **Ann Bruce Shute** b. 22-Aug-1929, Gloucester, Essex Co., MA, m. 29-Oct-1958, in Holbrook, AZ, **Emory James Pickens**, b. 20-May-1933, Rankin, Upton Co., TX.
Children:
+ 797.   i **James Bruce Pickens** b. 18-May-1963.
798.   ii **Elizabeth Anne Pickens** b. 9-Jul-1965, Phoenix, Maricopa Co., AZ.

737. **Margaret Rust Shute** b. 12-May-1932, Gloucester, Essex Co., MA, Baptized: Jun-1932, St. Ann's Ch., Gloucester, Essex Co., MA, m. 2-Jun-1956, in Gloucester, Essex Co., MA, **John Richard Tousignant**, b. 5-Apr-1929, Boston, Suffolk Co., MA, Baptized: May-1929, St. James's Ch., Medford, MA, (son of **Denis Peter Tousignant** and **Helen Burnett Purcell**).
Children:
+ 799.   i **David Bruce Tousignant** b. 13-Mar-1960.
800.   ii **Beth Anne Tousignant** b. 24-Mar-1961, Gloucester, Essex Co., MA.
801.   iii **Stephen John Tousignant** b. 7-Aug-1964, Lowell, Middlesex Co., MA.

738. **Norman Bruce Palmstrom** b. 1-Jun-1921, Mattapan, Suffolk Co., MA, Occupation: Commercial artist, m. 2-Jul-1947, in Brookline, Suffolk Co., MA, **Eleanor O'Shea**, b. 25-Nov-1924, Watertown, MA, (daughter of **George G. O'Shea** and **Ida McCarthy**). Norman died 13-Jun-1992, Boston, Suffolk Co., MA.
Children:
802.   i **Kathe Marie Palmstrom** b. 1-Jan-1949, Needham, MA, m. 27-Jun-1975, in Marshfield, MA, **Joseph E. Donlan**, b. 3-Feb-1944, Roslinda, MA, (son of **Walter Donlan** and **Vincenzina Roscio**).
+ 803.   ii **Michelle Palmstrom** b. 10-May-1950.
+ 804.   iii **Moira Palmstrom** b. 17-Jun-1952.
+ 805.   iv **Mark Palmstrom** b. 18-May-1953.
+ 806.   v **Eric Palmstrom** b. 26-Jan-1955.
807.   vi **Jonathan Bruce Palmstrom** b. 9-Apr-1965, Boston, Suffolk Co., MA, m. 30-Apr-1994, in Cohasset, MA, **Brenna Veroni**, b. 24-Oct-1966, Pawtucket, RI, (daughter of **Robert Veroni** and **Carol Oliver**).

740. **David Shute Palmstrom** b. 8-Jan-1924, Needham, Norfolk Co., MA, Occupation: Physician, m. 20-Jun-1947, in St. Paul's Episc. Ch., Canton, OH, **Jane Marchbank Robertson**, b. 13-May-1923, Chicago, Cook

Co., IL, Baptized: 14-Jun-1925, Second Ch., Dorchester, MA, (daughter of **Walter Harrison Robertson** and **Helen Carpenter Goodell**).

> Children:
> 808. i **Linda Bruce Palmstrom** b. 14-Sep-1949, Burlington, Chittenden Co., VT, m. 27-Aug-1989, **Douglas Lipman**, b. 23-Dec-1946, (son of **Paul Lipman** and **Virginia -----**).
> + 809. ii **Margaret Ellen Palmstrom** b. 29-Mar-1952.
> 810. iii **Mary Jane Palmstrom** b. 30-Dec-1953, Ravenna, Portage Co., OH.
> 811. iv **John Erik Palmstrom** b. 10-Feb-1956, Ravenna, Portage Co., OH, d. 11-Apr-1994.
> 812. v **Nancy Sue Palmstrom** b. 23-Nov-1960, Ravenna, Portage Co., OH.

742. **Carol B. Shute** b. 5-Dec-1937, Manchester, NH, Baptized: Grace Episc. Ch., Manchester, NH, m. 20-Aug-1960, **Robert L. Quigley**, b. 2-Jun-1929, Manchester, NH, Baptized: St. Joseph Cath., Manchester, NH, (son of **Henry J. Quigley** and **Alice Minton**) d. 10-Nov-1994, Manchester, NH.

> Children:
> + 813. i **Deborah Ann Quigley** b. 10-Feb-1962.
> 814. ii **Shawna Jane Quigley** b. 30-Jun-1964, Manchester, NH.

744. **Alan Henry Shute** b. 6-Feb-1932, Louisville, KY,[300] m. 11-Jun-1954, in Ryland Meth. Ch., Washington, DC, **Maxine ("Mac") Elizabeth Benhoff**, b. 24-Sep-1933, Washington, DC, (daughter of **William Henry Benhoff Jr.** and **Elizabeth Slayton Foster**).

Alan Henry Shute received his B.A. from American University in Washington, D.C., in 1954. In 1987, he retired from the Defense Intelligence Agency, after 33 years' service to the federal government.

> Children:
> + 815. i **Bonnie Leigh Shute** b. 7-Jun-1956.
> + 816. ii **Robin Kay Shute** b. 21-Jan-1959.
> + 817. iii **Terry Lynne Shute** b. 24-May-1960.

747. **Virginia Woodman** b. 14-May-1929, Newton, MA, m. 28-Jul-1951, in Auburndale, Middlesex Co., MA, **Charles Frederick Cordes**, b. 10-Aug-1929, Delaware Co., PA, (son of **Oscar Carl Clemens Cordes** and **Mary Louise Caten**).

Virginia (Woodman) Cordes graduated from Lasell Jr. College in 1949. Charles:

2d Lt. Charles Frederick Cordes served in the Korean War at Wright-Patterson Air Force Base, 1951-1953, after graduating MIT in 1951. Now retired, Cordes was with the Lukens Steel Company for 39 years.

> Children:
> 818. i **Bradford Charles Cordes** b. 15-Jul-1952, Dayton, OH, d. 28-Oct-1978, Buried: Oakwood Cem., Syracuse, NY.
> + 819. ii **John Frederick Cordes** b. 20-Sep-1955.
> 820. iii **Katherine Louise Cordes** b. 5-Nov-1956, Bryn Mawr, PA, m. 20-Aug-1988, **Robert John Lorenz**.
> Katherine (Cordes) Lorenz graduated from Lehigh

University in 1978, and has a M.S. in Pharmaceutical
Quality Assurances from Temple University. She currently
works with Smithkline Beecham in pharmaceutical
technologies.

750. **Stanley Richard Shute** b. 24-Jul-1933, Spokane, WA, m. (1)
22-Nov-1952, in Coeur D'Alene, ID, **Elizabeth Margaret Briggle**, b.
12-Oct-1935, Spokane Bridge, WA, (daughter of **Lester Charles Briggle**
and **Robina Crawford**) m. (2) **Sally Sue Scott**, m. (3) **Florence H.
Thomason**.
> Children by Elizabeth Margaret Briggle:
  821.   i **Richard Charles Shute** b. 28-Jun-1953, Spokane, Spokane
            Co., WA, m. 9-Nov-1979, **Jean Justice**.
+ 822.   ii **Laura Adele Shute** b. 23-Nov-1954.
+ 823.   iii **Rexward Shute** b. 2-Apr-1957.

751. **Kenneth Dale Shute** b. 24-Jul-1933, Spokane, WA, m. 17-Aug-1956,
in Spokane, WA, **Carol Kay Lavonne Yden**, b. 9-Oct-1936, Spokane, WA,
(daughter of **Martin A. Yden** and **Ester N. Johnson**).
> Children:
  824.   i **Russell Allan Shute** b. 28-Jan-1958, Spokane, WA.
+ 825.   ii **Steven Glen Shute** b. 9-Jun-1960.
+ 826.   iii **Stuart Owen Shute** b. 20-May-1962.

752. **Laurel Herbert Shute** b. 7-Aug-1930, Black Diamond, King Co.,
WA, m. Sep-1954, in Spokane, Spokane Co., WA, **Joy Erna Litzenberger**,
b. 21-Apr-1931, Latah, Spokane Co., WA, (daughter of **Aaron
Litzenberger** and ----- -----). Laurel died 27-Mar-1988, Kennewick,
Benton Co., WA, Buried: Desert Lawn Mem. Park, Kennewick, WA.
> Children:
+ 827.   i **Melanie Ann Shute** b. 6-Mar-1959.

753. **Dean Alva Shute** b. 23-Jan-1935, Seattle, King Co., WA, m.
31-Oct-1954, in Kennewick, Benton Co., WA, **Margaret L. Wright**, b.
28-Jul-1935, Yakima, Yakima Co., WA, Baptized: Yakima, Yakima Co., WA,
(daughter of **Wilbur A. Wright** and ----- **Swope**).
    Dean Alva Shute is with the Washington State Department of
Corrections, currently Supervisor of Security at Maple Lane
(institution for young male juveniles); instructor on non-violent
crisis intervention for the Department of Criminal Justice.
> Children:
+ 828.   i **Cheryl Lynn Shute** b. 6-Oct-1955.
  829.   ii **Thomas Dean Shute** b. 29-Mar-1958, Yakima, Yakima Co.,
            WA, m. 17-Oct-1987, in Tumwater, Thurston Co., WA, **Linda
            Scott**, b. 4-Sep-1948, PA, (daughter of **Ed Scott** and
            ----- -----).
+ 830.   iii **Douglas Brian Shute** b. 6-May-1961.

754. **Janice Louise Shute** b. 4-Aug-1936, Seattle, King Co., WA, m.
17-Aug-1955, in Kennewick, Benton Co., WA, **Ingval John Sunford**, b.
19-Feb-1930, Forks, Philips Co., MT, (son of **Thomas Sunford** and
Randi Fjeldheim).
> Children:

+ 831.   i **Scott Alan Sunford** b. 10-Jan-1959.
  832.   ii **Robert Dean Sunford** b. 4-Dec-1960, Kennewick, Benton
          Co., WA, m. 19-Dec-1981, in Kennewick, Benton Co., WA,
          divorced 1982, **Cheryl Schlosser**.

755. **Donald Thomas Shute** b. 8-Feb-1950, Colville, Stevens Co., WA,
m. Dec-1974, **Deann Elizabeth Jones**, (daughter of **Heber Jones** and
Jessie -----).
          Children:
  833.   i **Evan Thomas Shute** b. 30-May-1979, Spokane, Spokane Co.,
          WA.
  834.   ii **Erin Elizabeth Shute** b. 24-Jun-1983, Hillsboro, OR.

756. **Christine Kay Shute** b. 1-Mar-1952, Spokane, Spokane Co., WA, m.
Sep-1981, **Keith Alan Martenson**, (son of **Alvin Martenson** and
Lorraine -----).
          Children:
  835.   i **Anja Christine Martenson** b. 24-Mar-1985, Everett,
          Snohemish Co., WA.
  836.   ii **Kayley Ann Martenson** b. 17-Jun-1988.

758. **Vicki Lynn Shute** b. 11-Feb-1957, Spokane, Spokane Co., WA, m.
Feb-1974, **Leslie Paul Baker**, b. Mar-1956, (son of **Ronald Baker** and
----- -----).
          Children:
  837.   i **Michael Paul Baker** b. 5-Sep-1974, Colville, EA.
  838.   ii **Justin Douglas Baker** b. 27-Jan-1977, Ft. Carson,
          Colorado Springs, CO.

759. **Sandra Ann Shute** b. 11-Jan-1966, Seattle, King Co., WA, m.
May-1987, **Patrick Andrew Walsh**, b. 8-Nov-1966, Seattle, King Co.,
WA, (son of **Michael Walsh** and **Carolyn -----**).
          Children:
  839.   i **Caitlyn Marie Walsh** b. 16-Jun-1990, Honolulu, HI.
  840.   ii **Karalee Christine Walsh** b. 27-Sep-1992, Colville, WA.

760. **Barbara Eileen Shute** b. 6-Dec-1936, Haverhill, MA, m.
28-Oct-1966, in Washington, DC, **Alfred Holland Lowrey**, b.
1-Sep-1940, Chicago, Cook Co., IL, (son of **Ernest Rupert Lowrey** and
Eleanor Victoria Cederstrom).
          Children:
  841.   i **Kirsten Andrea Lowrey** b. 12-May-1968, Washington, DC.
  842.   ii **Jefferson Ralph Lowrey** b. 17-Jul-1969, Washington, DC.

761. **Thomas Ralph Shute** b. 3-Jul-1939, Haverhill, MA, m.
13-Aug-1966, in Milton, DE, **Carole Ann Pepper**, b. 13-Apr-1943,
Milton, DE, (daughter of **Foster Pepper** and **Edith Reed**).
          Children:
  843.   i **Dana Jean Shute** b. 19-Dec-1968, Silver Spring, MD.
  844.   ii **David Allen Shute** b. 17-Jul-1970, Washington, DC.

762. **Nancy Kaye Shute** b. 30-Aug-1943, Haverhill, MA, m. 2-Dec-1961,
in Concord, NH, **Mark D. Whitman**, b. 24-May-1944, Plymouth, Plymouth

Co., MA, (son of **Paul Whitman** and **C. Louise Molnar**).
          Children:
  845.   i **Mark D. Whitman Jr.** b. 8-Jul-1962, Concord, NH, m.
          14-Aug-1993, **Debra Downing**.
+ 846.   ii **Adrian K. Whitman** b. 27-Jul-1963.
  847.   iii **Deborah B. Whitman** b. 11-Jun-1969, Laconia, NH.

763. **Jonathan Kenneth Shute** b. 28-Oct-1949, Concord, NH, m.
11-Aug-1979, in Halifax, Nova Scotia, Canada, **Penny Maureen Reid**, b.
2-Jul-1956, Saskatoon, Sask., Canada, (daughter of **Melville Reid** and
Marilyn Johnson).
          Children:
  848.   i **Katherine Eileen Reid-Shute** b. 7-May-1980, Halifax, NS,
          Canada.
  849.   ii **Jonathan Morley Reid-Shute** b. 9-Oct-1982, Halifax, NS,
          Canada.

765. **Forrest Earl Shute** b. 12-Jul-1948, San Francisco, CA, m.
28-Mar-1978, in St. Helena, CA, **Carole Poertner**, b. 21-Dec-1946,
Martinez, CA, (daughter of **Norman Poertner** and ----- **Barnett**).
          Children:
  850.   i **Anna Lorraine Shute** b. 2-Feb-1980, Santa Rosa, CA.

773. **Priscilla Anne Flint** b. 8-Jul-1947, St. Louis, St. Louis Co.,
MO, Occupation: SEC Registered Sales Asst, m. (1) 9-Aug-1969, in
Kirkwood, St. Louis Co., MO, divorced 1981, **Floyd Arnold Rauch Jr.**,
b. Nixa, MO, (son of **Floyd Arnold Rauch Sr.** and ----- **Peterson**)
Occupation: Postman, m. (2) 9-Feb-1986, in Kirkwood, St. Louis Co.,
MO, divorced 1995, **Charles Thurza**, b. Hungary, (son of **Georg
Thurza** and **Rosalia** -----).
          Children by Floyd Arnold Rauch Jr.:
  851.   i **John Christopher Rauch** b. 4-May-1971, Ellsworth, KS.
  852.   ii **Brian Flint Rauch** b. 13-Jun-1974, Camp Pendleton, CA.
  853.   iii **Keith Arnold Rauch** b. 8-Mar-1979, Camp Pendleton, CA.

774. **Kathleen Louise Flint** b. 17-Mar-1952, St. Louis, St. Louis Co.,
MO, Occupation: Arts Administrator, m. 3-Aug-1974, in University City,
St. Louis Co., MO, **Dennis F. Moran**, b. 6-Oct-1951, (son of **Robert
Moran** and **Irma** -----) Occupation: Mechanical engineer.
          Children:
  854.   i **Erin Flint Moran** b. 30-Apr-1979.
  855.   ii **Paula Flint Moran** b. 25-Mar-1982.

776. **Claire Elizabeth Chapman** b. 30-Oct-1937, Harrisburg, PA,
Baptized: Harrisburg, PA, Occupation: School Dist. Secretary, m.
8-Jun-1957, in Belmont, MA, divorced 1990, **Alden Page French**, b.
25-Jul-1934, Cambridge, MA, (son of **Earl K. French** and **Marion
Dwight**) Occupation: Police officer.
          Children:
  856.   i **David James French** b. 13-Aug-1958, Concord, MA.
  857.   ii **Diane Elizabeth French** b. 18-May-1963, Concord, MA, m.
          13-Aug-1994, in 1st Ch. Christ, Bedford, MA, **Richard
          Thomas Ceraolo**.

+ 858.   iii **Timothy Andrew French** b. 28-Aug-1964.
+ 859.   iv **Jeffrey Page French** b. 12-May-1967.

777. **Peggy Sue Shute** b. 7-Apr-1961, Jerseyville, IL, m. (1) -----
Vance, m. (2) **Steve Prinke**, m. (3) **Frank Anaya**.
              Children by ----- Vance:
   860.   i **Kenneth Charles Vance** b. 21-Oct-1976, Douglas, AZ.
              Children by Frank Anaya:
   861.   ii **Chelsea Marie Anaya** b. 8-Aug-1992, Yuma, AZ.

778. **Rose Marie Shute** b. 22-Jul-1962, Tucson, AZ, m. ----- **Regan**.
              Children:
   862.   i **Tyler Lee Regan** b. 3-Jun-1992, Yuma, AZ.
   863.   ii **Tayler Louise Regan** b. 11-Apr-1994, Yuma, AZ.

779. **Desa Rae Shute** b. 4-Aug-1963, Douglas, AZ, m. ----- **Sears**.
              Children:
   864.   i **Jamie Lynn Sears** b. 11-Apr-1992, Yuma, AZ.
   865.   ii **Catherine Lee Ann Sears** b. 26-Jun-1994, Yuma, AZ.

Eleventh Generation

780. Philip Edward Shute b. 15-Jun-1946, m. 26-Jun-1971, **Jane Paul**.

        Children:
- 866.   i **Philip George Shute** b. 3-Sep-1976.
- 867.   ii **Russell Lincoln Shute** b. 1-Apr-1979.

781. Elizabeth Shute b. 8-Sep-1948, m. 6-Aug-1977, **Wiley Zimeon Cozait**, b. 2-Dec-1949.

        Children:
- 868.   i **Emily Smyth Cozait** b. 17-May-1981.
- 869.   ii **Benjamin Shute Cozait** b. 17-Jul-1984.

784. Priscilla Keith George b. 11-Sep-1920, Melrose, MA, m. (1) Mar-1945, in San Francisco, CA, divorced, **William Bruce Kincannon**, b. 1920, d. 1986, San Jose, CA, Buried: Riverside, San Bernadino, CA, m. (2) 24-Jun-1967, **William Wesley Price**.

        Children by William Bruce Kincannon:
- + 870.   i **William Bruce Kincannon, Jr.** b. 7-Nov-1947.

797. James Bruce Pickens b. 18-May-1963, Phoenix, Maricopa Co., AZ, m. 6-Jul-1983, in Las Vegas, NV, **Machelle Diane Glassburn**, b. 6-May-1962, Williams, Coconino Co., AZ, (daughter of **McNeil Glassburn** and **Carolyn Canty**).

        Children:
- 871.   i **Justin James Pickens** b. 4-Jun-1984, Dothan, Houston Co., AL.
- 872.   ii **Jared Neil Pickens** b. 10-Dec-1990, N. Charleston, Charleston Co., SC.

799. David Bruce Tousignant b. 13-Mar-1960, Boston, Suffolk Co., MA, Baptized: Apr-1960, St. James's Ch., Medford, MA, m. 2-Jan-1988, **Tina Marie Hanes**, b. 22-Apr-1964, Highland, IL, Baptized: Jun-1964, Edwardsville, IL, (daughter of **Jerry Hanes** and **Betsy Allen**).

        Children:
- 873.   i **Nicholas Alan Tousignant** b. 22-Sep-1989, Boston, Suffolk Co., MA.
- 874.   ii **Katie Blossom Tousignant** b. 21-Jul-1992, Nashua, Hillcrest Co., NH.

803. Michelle Palmstrom b. 10-May-1950, Needham, MA, m. (1) **Michael Norris**, m. (2) 10-May-1982, in Burlington, VT, **Robert Donlan**, b. 20-Jul-1943, Roslinda, MA, (son of **Walter Donlan** and **Vincenzina Roscio**).

        Children by Michael Norris:
- 875.   i **Sarah Norris** b. 27-Mar-1973, Northampton, MA.

804. Moira Palmstrom b. 17-Jun-1952, Needham, MA, m. 7-Jul-1984, in Newton, MA, **Lemuel Steven Lanier**, b. 19-Feb-1953, Buffalo, NY, (son of **Lemuel Lanier** and **Fayette Smith**).

        Children:
- 876.   i **Joshua A. Lanier** b. 12-Nov-1984, Newton, MA.

877.   ii **Nathaniel C. Lanier** b. 19-Jan-1987, Newton, MA.

805. **Mark Palmstrom** b. 18-May-1953, Needham, MA, m. 9-Jul-1978, in East Boston, Suffolk Co., MA, **Andrea Marie Saulnier**, b. 30-Sep-1954, Boston, Suffolk Co., MA, (daughter of **Joseph Henri Saulnier** and **Dorothea Geraldine Musi**).
           Children:
878.   i **Noelle Caitin Palmstrom** b. 20-Dec-1983, Boston, Suffolk Co., MA.
879.   ii **Danielle Nicole Palmstrom** b. 20-Dec-1983, Boston, Suffolk Co., MA.
880.   iii **Gabrielle Marie Palmstrom** b. 4-Dec-1985, Boston, Suffolk Co., MA.

806. **Eric Palmstrom** b. 26-Jan-1955, Needham, MA, m. 28-Feb-1982, in Boston, Suffolk Co., MA, **Judith Anne Barry**, b. 18-Apr-1957, Milton, MA, Baptized: 16-Jun-1957, Dorchester, MA, (daughter of **John Joseph Barry** and **Mary D. Robertson**).
           Children:
881.   i **Craig Barry** b. 24-Jul-1986, Plymouth, Plymouth Co., MA.
882.   ii **Kyle Barry** b. 25-Sep-1989, Plymouth, Plymouth Co., MA.

809. **Margaret Ellen Palmstrom** b. 29-Mar-1952, Kaefertal, Mannheim, Germany, m. 2-Feb-1974, in Bowling Green, OH, **Samuel Clifford Tussing**, b. 10-Sep-1947, (son of **Glen H. Tussing Sr.** and **Guadalupe -----**).
           Children:
883.   i **Susan Rae Tussing** b. 24-May-1981, Ravenna, Portage Co., OH.
884.   ii **Andrew Glen Tussing** b. 14-Aug-1984, Ravenna, Portage Co., OH.

813. **Deborah Ann Quigley** b. 10-Feb-1962, Manchester, NH, m. 19-Sep-1987, **William James Buck**, b. 13-Mar-1961, Honesdale, PA.
           Children:
885.   i **Kaitlyn Eileen Buck** b. 15-Aug-1990, Morristown, NJ.
886.   ii **Kylie Megan Buck** b. 18-Jul-1992, Manchester, NH.

815. **Bonnie Leigh Shute** b. 7-Jun-1956, Washington, DC,[301] Occupation: Legal Administrator, m. 13-Oct-1984, **Daniel Alan Reifsnyder**.
           Children:
887.   i **Claire Evans Reifsnyder** b. 16-Feb-1987.
888.   ii **Benjamin Shute Reifsnyder** b. 25-Jun-1991.

816. **Robin Kay Shute** b. 21-Jan-1959, Washington, DC,[301] Occupation: Teacher, m. 21-Jun-1980, **Stephen Grey Judy**.
           Children:
889.   i **Rachel Elizabeth Judy** b. 30-May-1984.
890.   ii **Megan Leigh Judy** b. 17-Oct-1989.
891.   iii **Nicholas Stephen Judy** b. 18-May-1993.

817. **Terry Lynne Shute** b. 24-May-1960, Washington, DC,[301]

Occupation: Claims Representative, m. 15-Aug-1987, **David van den Arend**.

        Children:
892.   i **Alan Russell van den Arend** b. 6-Jul-1988.
893.   ii **Lauren Ella van den Arend** b. 28-Mar-1991.

819. **John Frederick Cordes** b. 20-Sep-1955, Waltham, MA, m. 19-Jun-1982, **Sharon Raymond Lynch**, b. 12-Jul-1959, Aldan, Delaware Co., PA, (daughter of **E. Raymond Lynch** and **Virginia Muench**).
    John Frederick Cordes graduated from Bucknell University in 1978. Licensed C.P.A. from the PA State Board of Accounting, 1985. Received his M.S. in Taxation from Drexel University, 1988. Rotarian of the Year, Central Chester County Rotary Club, and past officer; President of the Gundaker Foundation, Treasurer of the United Way Board of Directors in Chester County, PA.

        Children:
894.   i **Kyle Frederick Cordes** b. 11-Jan-1986, Bryn Mawr, Montgomery Co., PA.
895.   ii **Kevin Raymond Cordes** b. 17-Jul-1989, West Chester, Chester Co., PA.

822. **Laura Adele Shute** b. 23-Nov-1954, Spokane, Spokane Co., WA, m. 4-Dec-1976, **Delmar Joseph Boscacci**.

        Children:
896.   i **Elizabeth Ann Boscacci** b. 19-Jan-1980.
897.   ii **Dominique Rose Boscacci** b. 20-Aug-1984.

823. **Rexward Shute** b. 2-Apr-1957, Spokane, Spokane Co., WA, m. 17-Aug-1985, **Darlene Wood Holt**.

        Children:
898.   i **Cameron Nelson Shute** b. 20-Oct-1991.
899.   ii **Connor Phillips Shute** b. 10-Mar-1993.

825. **Steven Glen Shute** b. 9-Jun-1960, Kennewick, Benton Co., WA, m. 31-Mar-1979, in Wapato, **Karla Jo Riggan**, b. 3-Nov-1961, Brewster, WA, (daughter of **George Edward Riggan** and **Dorothy Lautenschlager**).

        Children:
900.   i **Stephani Beth Shute** b. 13-Sep-1979, The Dalles, Wasco Co., OR.
901.   ii **Kristin Kay Shute** b. 12-Jul-1982, The Dalles, Wasco Co., OR.

826. **Stuart Owen Shute** b. 20-May-1962, Pasco, Franklin Co., WA, m. 5-Aug-1988, **Candi Francis Davidson**, b. 14-May-1968, Yakima, WA, (daughter of **Dale D. Davidson** and **Sue Ann Catron**).

        Children:
902.   i **Atheona Lee Shute** b. 21-Aug-1987, Yakima, WA.
903.   ii **Nathan Dale Shute** b. 11-Jul-1990, Yakima, WA.

827. **Melanie Ann Shute** b. 6-Mar-1959, Kennewick, Benton Co., WA, m. 27-Jun-1982, **Richard Boehler**.

        Children:
904.   i **LaRissa Nicole Boehler** b. 2-Nov-1982, Billings, MT.

905.   ii **Richard Laurel Boehler** b. 2-Nov-1982, Billings, MT.

828. **Cheryl Lynn Shute** b. 6-Oct-1955, Yakima, Yakima Co., WA, m. (1) 14-Feb-1976, **Richard G. Moore**, m. (2) 8-Aug-1987, **Daniel Colin Ghere**.
          Children by Richard G. Moore:
906.   i **Lindsey Anne Moore** b. 20-Apr-1977, Coupeville Island, WA.
          Children by Daniel Colin Ghere:
907.   ii **Kelsey Frances Ghere** b. 7-Sep-1987, Chehalis, Lewis Co., WA.
908.   iii **Lacy Ann Ghere** b. 8-May-1989, Centralia, Lewis Co., WA.

830. **Douglas Brian Shute** b. 6-May-1961, Yakima, Yakima Co., WA, m. 3-Jul-1982, in Chehalis, Lewis Co., WA, **Vicki Sue Haston**, b. 14-Jan-1963, Chehalis, Lewis Co., WA, (daughter of ----- **Haston** and ----- **Orr**).
          Children:
909.   i **Andrea Loretta Shute** b. 23-Dec-1982, Centralia, Lewis Co., WA.
910.   ii **Thomas Alva Shute** b. 1-Jun-1987, Centralia, Lewis Co., WA.

831. **Scott Alan Sunford** b. 10-Jan-1959, Kennewick, Benton Co., WA, m. 30-Sep-1976, **Deborah L. Anderson**, b. 7-Jan-1958, (daughter of **Don Anderson** and **Donna** -----).
          Children:
911.   i **Melissa Thyme Sunford** b. 30-Apr-1977, Kennewick, Benton Co., WA.
912.   ii **Jeffrey Alan Sunford** b. 5-Dec-1979, Kennewick, Benton Co., WA.
913.   iii **Scott Ingval Johan Sunford** b. 19-Jul-1981, Kennewick, Benton Co., WA.

846. **Adrian K. Whitman** b. 27-Jul-1963, Concord, NH, m. 31-Mar-1984, **Carol Wheeler**.
          Children:
914.   i **Justin K. Whitman** b. 27-Apr-1985, Laconia, NH.
915.   ii **Timothy A. Whitman** b. 5-Jun-1986, Laconia, NH.
916.   iii **Isaiah B. Whitman** b. 4-Nov-1987, Laconia, NH.

858. **Timothy Andrew French** b. 28-Aug-1964, Concord, MA, m. Jun-1988, in St. Joseph's, Somerville, MA, **Patricia Ann Kirkland**.
          Children:
917.   i **Timothy Andrew French, Jr.** b. 15-Nov-1990, Boston, Suffolk Co., MA.
918.   ii **Mary Kate French** b. 4-Feb-1992, Boston, Suffolk Co., MA.

859. **Jeffrey Page French** b. 12-May-1967, Concord, MA, m. 10-Feb-1990, in Bedford, MA, separated, **Kristen White**.
          Children:
919.   i **Christopher Page French** b. 20-Apr-1990, Cambridge, MA.

920.   ii **Alexandria Payton French** b. 23-Feb-1992, Concord, MA.

Twelfth Generation

870. **William Bruce Kincannon, Jr.** b. 7-Nov-1947, San Bernadino, CA,
m. **Donna Louise Lindeman**, b. 29-Jun-1951, Heidelberg, Germany.
        Children:
  921.   i **Paul Michael Kincannon** b. 31-Dec-1975, Carmichael, CA.
  922.   ii **David Bryan Kincannon** b. 7-Sep-1978, Carmichael, CA.

1 See also: Savage's Gen. Dict.; VR/Boston; Copps Hill Burials; Gen. Dict. of ME & NH; Chamberlain's Gen. Recs. Early Settlers of Malden, MA; Will of R. Shute; Holbrook's Boston Beginnings; Dir. Ancestral Heads of NE Families

2 Whitmore's Graveyards of Boston, Vol. 1 (1878).

3 Inscriptions from Copp's Hill Burial Ground, Boston, by Old North Chapter, DAR Boston, 1936-37. 79

4 Bridgman, Memorials of the Dead in Boston, 1852. 5

5 Whitmore's Graveyards of Boston, Vol. 1 (1878) [d. 12-Feb-1665, aged 1 week]

6 Appleton's Boston Births, Marriages & Deaths 1630-1699

7 See also: VR/Boston; Copps Hills Burials; NEHGS; Holbrook's Boston Beginnings; Gen. Dict. of ME & NH.

8 VR/Boston, MA

9 Bridgman, Memorials of the Dead in Boston, 1852. 16

10 Noyes, Libby & Davis'Gen. Dict. of ME & NH

11 Suffolk Co. Probate Rec. #2998; Ltrs. of Admin. 23-Oct-1706; inv. 20-Nov-1706

12 McGlennen's Boston Marriages 1700-1809 [Samuel Willard]

13 McGlennen's Boston Marriages 1700-1809 [Cotton Mather]

14 McGlennen's Boston Marriages 1700-1809 [Benjamin Colman]

15 Appelton's Boston Births, Marriages & Deaths 1630-1699

16 McGlennen's Boston Marriages 1700-1809 [Mr. Ebenezer Pemberton]

17 Wyman's Charlestown Genealogies 706

18 Savage's Gen. Dict.

19 Bridgman, Memorials of the Dead in Boston, 1852. 17

20 VR/Boston, MA. See also: VR/Malden & Chelsea, MA; Corey's Hist. of Malden; Fitts' Hist. of Newfields, NH; NEHGS; Copps Hill Burials; Chamberlain's Gen. Recs. Early Settlers of Malden, MA; Freeman's Almanacs; Savage's Gen. Dict.

21 Wyman's Charlestown Genealogies 443

22 VR/Boston, MA [Cotton Mather]

23 See also: Appleton's Narrative; Freeman's Freeman Genealogy (1875); Thwing's Crooked & Narrow Sts. of Boston; Will of R. Shute; Gen. Dict. ME & NH.

24 VR/Malden, MA

25 VR/Malden, MA. See also: Fitts' Hist. of Newfields, NH.

26 Second Church Records, Book 4 (MA Hist. Soc.)

27 McGlennen's Boston Marriages 1700-1809

28 VR/Malden & Boston, MA. See also: Chamberlain's Early Settlers of Malden, MA ; Fitts' Hist. of Newfields, NH.

29 Second Church Records, Book 4 (MA Hist. Soc.).

30 VR/Malden, MA. See also: VR/Chelsea, MA; Corey's Hist. of Malden, MA; Fitts' Hist. of Newfields, NH; NEHGS.

31 VR/Chelsea, MA

32 Wyman's Charlestown Genealogies

33 Appleton's Boston Births, Marriages & Deaths 1630-1699; NEHGS, Oct. 1985 [b. 19-Dec-1683].

34 NEHGS, Vol. 34, p. 94 [Rev. Cotton Mather] records hus. as Joseph Rice. McGlennen's Boston Marriages 1700-1809 records same marriage to John Blue.

35 VR/Boston [Mr. Samuel Miles]

36 Wyman's Charlestown Genealogies 983

37 McGlennen's Boston Marriages 1700-1809 [Rev. Cotton Mather]

38 VR/Charlestown, MA; Wyman's Charlestown Genealogies 706

39 Savage's Gen. Dict. 250

40 Bridgman's Epitaphs from Copp's Hill Burial Ground

41 VR/Charlestown, MA

42 VR/Boston, MA [Mr. Wm. Welsted]; Anc. & Hon. Artillery Co. claims 20-Sep-1728]

43 Roberts' Anc. & Hon. Artillery Co. of MA.

44 Bridgman's Epitaphs from Copp's Hill Burial Ground 26

45 VR/Malden, MA. See also: Chamberlain's Gen. Recs. Early Settlers of Malden; Corey's Hist. of Malden, MA; NEHGS; Fitts' Hist. of Newfields, NH; DAR Lineage Book.

[46] VR/Malden, MA [Rev. D. Parsons]

[47] VR/Malden, MA; grave stone reads 30-Sep-1780

[48] VR/Malden, MA. See also: NEHGS; Chamberlain's Gen. Recs. Early Settlers of Malden, MA.

[49] VR/Malden, MA [Rev. Joseph Emerson]

[50] VR/Malden, MA. See also: Chamberlain's Gen. Recs. Early Settlers of Malden, MA; Corey's Hist. of Malden, MA; Fitts' Hist. of Newfields, NH.

[51] Appleton's Boston Births, Marriages & Deaths 1700-1780

[52] Appleton's Boston Births, Marriages & Deaths 1700-1780 [William Welsted]

[53] McGlennen's Boston Marriages 1700-1809 [Rev. Mr. John Webb]

[54] Wyman's Charlestown Genealogies VR/Chelsea, MA 1002

[55] VR/Malden, MA. See also: VR/Newbury, MA; Fitts' Hist. of Newfields, NH; Gen. Dict. ME & NH; Appleton's Narrative; NEHGS; Rockingham Co., NH, Registry of Deeds.

[56] McGlennen's Boston Marriages 1700-1809, Vol. 1 [Mr. Charles Chauncy]

[57] VR/Newbury, MA 721

[58] VR/Newbury, MA 449

[59] See also: NH Probate Recs.; g.s., Hilton Burial Ground; Will of M. Shute; Estate settlements of M. Shute; Estate settlements of Elizabeth Shute.

[60] VR/Newbury, MA. See also: VR/Malden, MA; Fitt's Hist. of Newfields, NH; NEHGS.

[61] VR/Newbury, MA

[62] VR/Malden, MA. See also: NEHGS; Chamberlain's Gen. Recs. Early Settlers of Malden, MA; Corey's Hist. of Malden, MA.

[63] VR/Malden, MA. See also: Corey's Hist. of Malden, MA; MA Soc. of the Cincinnati; Columbian Centinel (1802, 1825), Hist. of Hingham (1893); NEHGS.

[64] Hist. of Hingham, MA (1893)

[65] Cutter's Gen. Memoirs (1910) 251

[66] Sibley's Harvard Graduates; Hist. of Hingham, MA (1893)

67 Sibley's Harvard Graduates; Columbia Centinel of 11-Sep-1802 [30-Aug-1802].

68 VR/Malden, MA. See also: VR/Chelsea, MA; U.S. Census 1790 Malden, MA; Chamberlain's Gen. Recs. Early Settlers of Malden, MA; Corey's Hist. of Malden, MA; DAR Lineage Book; Columbian Centinel (1796, 1804, 1813); NEHGS.

69 VR/Malden, MA ["wid. formerly wf. of James Howard"]

70 McGlennen's Boston Marriages 1700-1809 [Rev. Samuel Stillman]

71 VR/Malden, MA. See also: Fitts' Hist. of Newfields, NH; Chamberlain's Gen. Recs. Early Settlers in Malden, MA.

72 Abtracts of Rev. War Pension Files [1820; sol. was aged 64] 3128

73 VR/Chelsea, MA; VR/Malden, MA. See also: Chamberlain's Gen. Recs. Early Settlers in Malden, MA; Fitts' Hist. of Newfields, NH.

74 VR/Malden, MA. See also: U.S. Census 1790, Malden, MA; Chamberlain's Gen. Recs. Early Settlers in Malden, MA; Corey's Hist. of Malden, MA; NEHGS.

75 VR/Malden, MA [Rev. P. Thacher]

76 VR/Malden, MA. See also: U.S. Census 1790; Chamberlain's Gen. Recs. Early Settlers in Malden, MA.

77 VR/Malden, MA. See also: VR/Chelsea, MA; VR/Belfast & Stockton Springs, ME; Chamberlain's Gen. Recs. Early Settlers in Malden, MA; Bangor (ME) Daily News.

78 VR/Chelsea, MA [Rev. P. Payson]

79 Youngs' VR from Maine Newspapers 1785-1820 539

80 Youngs' VR from Maine Newspapers 1785-1820; Columbia Centinel of 4-Feb-1807 [d. in Prospect, ME, aged 78]. 539

81 VR/Stockton, ME

82 VR/Chelsea, MA VR/Stockton, ME [10-Jan-1764]

83 Maine Families in 1790, Vol.3 124

84 Maine Families in 1790, Vol.3

85 Maine Families in 1790, Vol.3 125

86 VR/Stockton, ME. See also: VR/Malden & Chelsea, MA; VR/Belfast, ME; Columbian Centinel (1800).

87 Maine Families in 1790, Vol.3 25

88 VR/Stockton Springs, ME.

89 VR/Malden, MA. See also: NEHGS; Chamberlain's Gen. Recs. Early Settlers in Malden, MA.

90 McGlennen's Boston Marriages 1700-1809 VR/Malden, MA [Rev. E. Willis]

91 VR/Malden, MA; VR/Roxbury, MA [int. 17-Feb-1793]

92 VR/Malden, MA. See also: U.S. Census 1790, Malden, MA; NEHGS: Chamberlain's Gen. Recs. Early Settlers in Malden, MA.

93 VR/Malden, MA [Rev. E. Willis]

94 VR/Malden, MA. See also: Chamberlain's Gen. Recs. Early Settlers in Malden, MA.

95 VR/Malden, MA. See also: U.S. Census 1790 Malden, MA; Chamberlain's Gen. Recs. Early Settlers in Malden, MA.

96 VR/Malden, MA. See also: Chamberlain's Gen. Recs. Early Settlers in Malden, MA; U.S. Census 1790 Malden, MA.

97 Sibley's Harvard Graduates

98 Sibley's Harvard Graduates, Vol. 8 225

99 Sibley's Harvard Graduates, Vol. 8 220

100 MA Hist. Soc., 2d ser., Vol. 16, p.117, "Suffolk Reg's of Probate"

101 Sibley's Harvard Graduates, Vol. 8 228

102 MA Loyalists

103 MA Loyalists 15

104 VR/Newbury, MA. See also: Fitts' Hist. of Newfields, NH; NH Probate Recs. #5641 (1791) & #6404 (1797); Will of M. Shute; Estate settlements of M. Shute; Rockingham Co., NH, Reg. of Deeds.

105 NH Probate records #5641

106 See also: Fitts' Hist. of Newfields, NH; NH Probate Recs. #5641 (1791) & #6404 (1797).

107 VR/Newbury, MA. See also: Fitts' Hist. of Newfields, NH; NH Probate Recs. #5640 (1791); Rockingham Co., NH, Reg. of Deeds; Jewett's Hist. & Gen. of Jewetts in America; Will of M. Shute.

108 VR/Newbury, MA VR/Newmarket, NH

109 VR/Newmarket, NH

110 VR/Newbury, MA. See also: Fitts' Hist. of Newfields, NH; NH Gazette (26-Mar-1800); g.s. Junction Cem.; Will of M. Shute.

111 Maine Families in 1790, Vol.3 317

112 "Narrative of Mrs. Shute's Captivity" in Farmer's Collections (1822), vol.1 116

113 See also: VR/Newbury, MA; Fitts' Hist. of Newfields, NH.

114 VR/Newmarket, NH. See also: VR/Newbury, MA; Fitts' Hist. of Newfields, NH; NEHGS; NH Gen. Rec. Vol. 6 (1909-10).

115 VR/Newmarket, NH. See also: VR/Newbury, MA; Fitts' Hist. of Newfields, NH.

116 VR/Exeter, NH. Youngs' VR from Maine Newspapers 1785-1820 [15-Oct-1817]

117 See also: VR/Newbury, MA; Hist. of Littleton, NH; Hist. of Sanbornton, NH.

118 Runnels' Hist. of Sanbornton (1881) 707

119 Runnels's Hist. of Sanbornton (1881)

120 Runnels' Hist. of Sanbornton (1881)

121 Runnels' Hist. of Sanbornton (1881); see also Hist. of Littleton, NH.

122 See also: U.S. Census 1800; Fitts' Hist. of Newfields, NH; NH Gen. Rec., Vol. 6 (1909).

123 VR/Topsfield, MA [Chute, Joseph, s. Michael bp. "at Newbury"]

124 NH Gen. Record, Vol.6 135

125 See also: VR/Newburyport, MA & Londonderry, NH; Fitts' Hist. of Newfields, NH; g.s. Forest Hill Cem.; U.S. Census 1790 Londonderry, NH; NH Gen. Rec., Vol. 6 (1909); Rev. War pension file.

126 Willey's Book of Nutfield

127 VR/Londonderry, NH

128 VR/Londonderry, NH. See also: VR/Newburyport, MA; VR/Newmarket, NH; Fitts' Hist. of Newfields, NH; g.s., E. Derry Cem.

129 Willey's Book of Nutfield; VR/Londonderry, NH 175

130 Willey's Book of Nutfield [11-Jun-1842]

131 Bell's History of Exeter (1888); VR/Newmarket, NH

132 Bell's History of Exeter (1888)

133 Hist. of Hingham, MA (1893). See also: VR/Salem, MA; MA Soc. of the Cincinnati; DAR Lineage Book.

134 Hist. of Hingham, MA (1893) 147

135 Hist. of Hingham, MA (1893); VR/Salem, MA

136 Hist. of Hingham, MA (1893). See also: VR/Salem, MA.

137 VR/Malden, MA. See also: VR/Lynn, MA; U.S. Census 1790 Lynn, MA.

138 VR/Malden, MA [Rev. J. Roby]; VR/Lynn, MA

139 VR/Lynn, MA

140 VR/Lynn, MA. See also: VR/Malden, MA; U.S. Census 1790 Lynn, MA.

141 VR/Chelsea, MA. See also: Chamberlain's Gen. Recs. Early Settlers in Malden, MA; Columbian Centinel (1831, 1834).

142 McGlennan's Boston Marriages 1700-1809 [Rev. Samuel Stillman]

143 McGlennan's Boston Marriages 1700-1809

144 Woodlawn Cem. record

145 VR/Malden, MA. See also: Chamberlain's Gen. Recs. Early Settlers in Malden, MA; Middlesex Co. Probate Rec. #20374.

146 VR/Malden, MA [Rev. E. Nelson]

147 VR/Malden, MA [Ch. of Jacob, Jr.]. See also: Chamberlain's Gen. Recs. Early Settlers in Malden, MA.

148 See also: VR/Malden, MA; Chamberlain's Gen. Recs. Early Settlers in Malden, MA.

149 VR/Malden, Ma

150 VR/Malden, MA [Rev. E. Willis]; VR/Charlestown, MA [3-Aug-1794 int.]

151 Wyman's Charlestown Genealogies 87

152 VR/Stockton, ME. See also: VR/Malden, MA; VR/Belfast, ME.

153 1860 Fed. Census, Stockton, ME.

154 Maine Families in 1790, Vol.3 103

155 VR/Malden, MA. See also: U.S. Census 1790 Malden, MA; Chamberlain's Gen. Recs. Early Settlers in Malden, MA; Middlesex Co. Probate Rec. #20372.

156 VR/Malden, MA [Rev. A. Green]

157 VR/Malden, MA ["wid. of George"]

158 See also: VR/Malden, MA; Chamberlain's Gen. Recs. Early Settlers in Malden, MA; U.S. Census 1790 Malden, MA.

159 VR/Malden, MA. See also: Chamberlain's Gen. Recs. Early Settlers in Malden, MA; Columbian Centinel (1837).

160 VR/Malden, MA [Rev. C. Sawyer]

161 VR/Malden, MA [Rev. A. Briggs]

162 VR/Malden, MA [g.s. 10-Jun-1833]

163 See also: VR/Malden & Boston, MA; Copps Hill Epitaphs; Boston Transcript obit (16-Dec-1875); Columbian Centinel (20-Feb-1836).

164 See also: VR/Boston & Malden, MA; Copps Hill Epitaphs.

165 See also: VR/Newbury, MA; Fitts' Hist. of Newfields, NH; Rockingham Co., NH, Reg. of Deeds; NH Probate Recs.; Ltrs. of M. M. (Shute) Sanger (1912).

166 See also: Fitts' Hist. of Newfields, NH; g.s. Junction Cem.

167 g.s. inscr.

168 VR/Newmarket, NH. See also: VR/Newbury, MA; VR/Exeter, NH; VR/Kennebunk, ME; U.S. Census 1820; Fitts' Hist. of Newfields, NH; NEHGS, Vol. 95; Hist. of Kennebunk, ME.

169 VR/Newmarket, NH. See also: Hist. of Rockingham Co., NH; Hist. of Exeter, NH (1888).

170 Bell's History of Exeter (1888).

171 See also: Hist. of Plymouth, MA; Hist. of Littleton, NH; Hist. of Sanbornton, NH.

172 See also: VR/Newburyport, MA; Ltrs. of Edith (Shute) Tirone.

173 VR/Newburyport, MA

174 VR/Newmarket, NH; NH Record of Birth. See also: VR/Rowley & Lynnfield, MA; VR/Londonderry, NH; U.S. Census 1790 Londonderry, NH; NH Gen. Rec., Vol. 6 (1909); Fitts' Hist. of Newfields, NH.

175 U.S. Census 1850 Newburyport, Essex Co., MA; MA Rec. of Death [aged 79 yrs, 2 mos, 22 days]

176 MA Rec. of Death.

177 VR/Londonderry, NH. See also: Fitts' Hist. of Newfields, NH; U.S. Census 1790 Londonderry, NH; NH Probate Recs.

178 VR/Londonderry, NH. See also: U.S. Census 1790 Londonderry, NH; Willey's Book of Nutfield, NH.

179 VR/Londonderry, NH. See also: U.S. Census 1790 Londonderry, NH; Fitts' Hist. of Newfields, NH; NH Probate Recs.; DAR Lineage Book; g.s. Forest Hill Cem.

180 Fitt's Hist. of Newfields, NH

181 Hist. of Hingham, MA (1893). See also: Columbian Centinel (7-Dec-1816); MA Soc. of the Cincinnati.

182 Youngs' VR from Maine Newspapers 1785-1820 [18-Dec-1816]; Hist. of Hingham, MA 539

183 Hist. of Hingham, MA

184 Hist. of Hingham, MA (1893). See also: VR/Worcester, MA; DAR Lineage Book; Columbian Centinel (5-Aug-1820, 17-Jan-1827).

185 VR/Malden, MA [Rev. A. W. McClure]

186 VR/Malden, MA. See also: Chamberlain's Gen. Recs. Early Settlers in Malden, MA; 1880 Soundex MA.

187 NEHGS, Vol. 60, p. 361.

188 VR/Malden, MA [E. Buck, J.P.]

189 VR/Stockton Springs, ME. See also: VR/Belfast, ME.

190 VR/Belfast, ME

191 DAR Magazine, Mar., 1959, p. 235.

192 VR/Stockton Springs, ME

193 VR/Malden, MA [Rev. J. M. Driver]

194 VR/Malden, MA ["scalding"]

195 See also: VR/Boston & Malden, MA; Boston Transcript obit (16-Dec-1875); Copps Hills Epitaphs; Columbian Centinel (20-Dec-1828, 19-Oct-1836, 5-Sep-1838).

196 See also: VR/Boston, MA; Copps Hill Epitaphs; Columbian Centinel (24-Jul-1830, 7-Sep-1839, 8-Apr-1840).

197 Columbia Centinel of 8-Apr-1840 [Sat., aged 34]

198 1850 Fed. Cen. MA. See also: VR/Boston & Malden, MA; Copps Hill Epitaphs.

199 1850 Fed. Cen. MA.

200 VR/Malden, MA.

201 VR/Newmarket, NH. See also: Fitts' Hist. of Newfields, NH; Hist. of Durham, NH; NH Gen. Rec., Vol. 6 (1909); Rockingham Co., NH, Reg. of Deeds, Vol. 232 (1820); g.s., Junction Cem.

202 VR/Newmarket, NH; NH Gen. Record, Vol. 4 [4-May-1818; Marriages by Rev. John Osborne of Lee, NH]

203 VR/Newmarket, NH. See also: Fitts' Hist. of Newfields, NH; Hist. of Durham, NH.

204 See also: Fitts' Hist. of Newfields, NH; Hist. of Durham, NH.

205 VR/Newmarket, NH. See also: VR/Dover, NH; Fitts' Hist. of Newfields, NH; Hist. of Durham, NH; Ltrs. of M. M. (Shute) Sanger (1912); NH Gen. Rec., Vol. 6 (1909); Pension office correspondence; MA death cert.

206 VR/Newmarket, NH. See also: Fitts' Hist. of Newfields, NH; Hist. of Durham, NH; Rockingham Co., NH, Probate Recs.; Ltrs. of Margery P. Brooke.

207 See also: Fitts' Hist. of Newfields, NH; Hist. of Durham, NH; Ltrs. of M. M. (Shute) Sanger (1912).

208 NH Gen. Rec., Vol. 6 (1909-1910).

209 See also: NEHGS, Vol. 95; Columbian Centinel (10-Oct-1832).

210 VR/Exeter, NH

211 NEHGS, Vol. 95 (1941).

212 Bell's History of Exeter (1888). See also: "Real Diary of a Real Boy"; Hist. of Rockingham Co., NH.

213 See also: "Real Diary of a Real Boy."

214 Shute's Real Dairy of a Real Boy (1902).

215 Runnels' Hist. of Sanbornton (1881); see also Hist. of Plymouth, NH.

216 See also: Hist. of Littleton, NH

217 See also: Hist. of Littleton, NH.

218 See also: VR/Newburyport, MA; 1880 Soundex MA; Ltrs. of Edith (Shute) Tirone.

219 See also: 1880 Soundex MA; Ltrs. of Edith (Shute) Tirone.

220 IGI/MA

221 U.S. Census 1850 Newburyport, Essex Co., MA; VR/Newburyport, MA.

222 U.S. Census 1850 Newburyport, Essex Co., MA; VR/Newburyport, MA

223 See also: VR/Reading & Lynnfield, MA; Essex Co. Probate Recs.;
g.s., Lynnfield & Ipswich, MA.

224 VR/Reading, MA

225 VR/Lynnfield, MA

226 VR/Lynnfield, MA. See also: VR/Reading, MA; g.s., Lynnfield &
Ipswich, MA.

227 g.s. inscription, Marietta, OH

228 NH Marriage rec.

229 Pilsbury's Pillsbury Family (1898)

230 Pierce's Fiske Genealogy (1896) 195

231 Pierce's Fiske Genealogy (1896) VR/Charlestown, MA [18-Aug-1838
int.] 195

232 MA Record of Death B.F. Shute family bible

233 MA Record of Death Pierce's Fiske Genealogy (1896) B.F. Shute
family bible

234 MA Cert. of Death; B. F. Shute family bible rec.; Woodlawn Cem.
record.

235 Pierce's Fiske Genealogy (1896) 196

236 B.F. Shute family bible Woodlawn Cem. record

237 See also: VR/Rowley & Lynnfield, MA; VR/Newmarket & Londonderry,
NH.

238 VR/Lynnfield, MA. See also: VR/Rowley, MA; VR/Newmarket &
Londonderry, NH.

239 See also: DAR Lineage Book III

240 Hist. of Hingham, MA (1893). See also: MA Soc. of the
Cincinnati; Cushing Family Genealogy.

241 Hist. of Hingham, MA (1893). See also: VR/Scituate, MA.

242 Hist. of Hingham, MA (1893); VR/Scituate, MA [int. 15-Oct-1848]

243 Hist. of Hingham, MA (1893). See also: Hist. of Plymouth, MA.

244 Hist. of Hingham, MA (1893).

245 Hist. of Hingham, MA (1893). See also: "Hingham in the Civil War."

246 Hist. of Hingham, MA (1893). See also: Mayflower Soc. Index.

247 VR/Chelsea & Malden, MA. See also: Chamberlain's Gen. Recs. Early Settlers in Malden, MA.

248 VR/Chelsea, MA [26-Dec-1805] VR/Malden, MA

249 VR/Malden, MA. See also: Chamberlain's Gen. Recs. Early Settlers in Malden, MA; Boston Transcript obit (27-Nov-1891).

250 Everett Hist. Soc.'s "The Shute Family of Everett"

251 Everett Hist. Soc.'s "The Shute Family of Everett."

252 Woodlawn Cem. record VR/Malden, MA

253 VR/Stockton Springs, ME. See also: VR/Belfast, ME; "The Rust Family."

254 VR/Belfast, ME. See also: "The Rust Family."

255 Index to Boston Transcript Obituaries 1875-1899

256 VR/Newmarket, NH. See also: Fitts' Hist. of Newfields, NH; Hist. of Durham, NH; Newmarket, NH, town records.

257 See also: Fitts' Hist. of Newfields, NH; Hist. of Durham, NH; VR/Gloucester, MA; SAR Nat. Reg.; Boston Transcript obit (28-Dec-1911).

258 See also: VR/Gloucester, MA; Ltrs. of Mildred (Shute) Smith.

259 See also: VR/Gloucester, MA; 1880 Soundex MA; g.s. Oak Grove Cem.; Will of J. L. Shute; Marr. cert. of J. L. Shute; MA death cert. of Wm. T. Shute.

260 VR/Gloucester, MA. See also: g.s., Oak Grove Cem.

261 See also: VR/Exeter, NH; Abridged Comp. of Amer. Gen.; NEHGS, Vol. 95.

262 NEHGS, Vol. 85 (1931).

263 Virkus' Abrgd. Comp. Am. Gen., Vol. 6; NEHGS, Vol. 85 (1931).

264 NEHGS, Vol. 95 (1941) 79

265 Virkus' Abrgd. Comp. Am. Gen., Vol. 1; NEHGS, Vol. 95 (1941). 263

266 See also: VR/Exeter, NH; Hist. of Rockingham Co., NH; "Real Diary of a Real Boy."

267 Poore's Gen. of John Poore (1881); Runnels' Hist. of Sanbornton (1881) [born 7-Mar-1841]

268 Poore's Gen. of John Poore (1881)

269 See also: Hist. of Plymouth, NH; Hist. of Sanbornton, NH; Ltrs. of Lillian Shute of Markville, MN.

270 See also: Ltrs. of Darrell Thomas Shute & Margaret Wright Shute; Runnels' Hist. of Sanbornton (1881).

271 Runnels' Hist. of Sanbornton (1881); see also Hist. of Plymouth, NH.

272 Pierce's Fiske Genealogy (1896) MA Record of Birth

273 MA Record of Marriage [Rev. W. E. Merriman of Somerville] B.F. Shute family bible

274 B.F. Shute family bible

275 MA Cert. of Death B.F. Shute family bible Woodlawn Cem. record

276 Woodlawn Cem. record B.F. Shute family bible

277 Hist. of Hingham, MA (1893). See also: VR/Scituate, MA; MA Soc. of the Cincinnati.

278 See also: VR/Scituate, MA; MA Soc. of the Cincinnati.

279 See also: VR/Belfast, ME; "The Rust Family."

280 See also: VR/Malden, MA; 1880 Soundex MA; Malden Evening News (5-Nov-1938); Nan Rice Shute's "Rice Trails."

281 VR/Gloucester, MA. See also: F.H.S. Marr. cert.; SAR Nat. Reg.; Ltrs. of Barbara (Shute) Friberg; Barbara Shute Friberg birth cert.

282 VR/Gloucester, MA. See also: W. T. Shute death cert.; g.s., Oak Grove Cem.; James Lovell Shute 2nd recollections; Benjamin Smith Shute recollections & family records.

283 See also: VR/Gloucester, MA; J. L. Shute 2nd. fam. recs.

284 See also: VR/Gloucester, MA; Ltrs. of Mildred Aline (Shute) Smith.

285 See also: Hist. of Rockingham Co., NH.

286 See also: Ltrs. of Darrel Thomas Shute & Margaret Wright Shute.

287 MA Record of Birth; B. F. Shute family bible rec.

288 B.F. Shute family bible; FL marriage lic. [John A. Wray]

289 VR/Charlottetown, P.E.I.; U.S. passport.

290 Headstone, Nassau, Bahamas; U.S. foreign service report of death.

291 See also: Nan Rice Shute's "Rice Trails."

292 See also: VR/Gloucester, MA; K. B. Shute fam. recs.; g.s., Oak Grove Cem.

293 See also: VR/Gloucester, MA; G. H. Shute fam. recs.

294 See also: VR/Gloucester, MA; B. S. Shute fam. recs.; VR/Springfield, MA.

295 See also: B. S. Shute fam. recs.

296 See also: Ltr. of Henry W. Shute.

297 See also: Ltrs. of Edith (Shute) Tirone.

298 MO birth cert.

299 MO death cert.

300 See also: A. H. Shute fam. recs. & certs.; M. E. (Benhoff) Shute fam. recs. & certs.

301 VR/Washington, DC

Descendants of William & Hopestill Shute

The following register report was generated utilizing Brothers Keeper 5.1 software, designed and developed by John Steed. Brothers Keeper software is available through him at 6907 Childsdale Road, Rockford, MI 49341.

Footnote citations, as well as an index to this report, follow immediately.

Each person in the direct family line is numbered in the order of their appearance in the register report (example: 1 - William, 2 - John, 3 - Abigail, etc.). Lowercase roman numerals are used to indicate the number of children and birth order in the family. When the record of a given person is expanded on a subsequent page (or pages) a plus sign will appear to the left of their cardinal number (example: + 7, + 19, +34), and that additional information will be found by turning ahead to that same cardinal number. If no further information is available on an individual, no plus sign appears to the left of their cardinal number.

1. **William Shute** b. cir 1633?, England?, Occupation: Mariner, m. 1-Jul-1659, in Boston, Suffolk Co., MA,[1] **Hopestill Viall**, b. 14-Aug-1639, Boston, Suffolk Co., MA,[1] Baptized: 9-May-1641, First Church, Boston, Suffolk Co., MA,[2] (daughter of **John Viall** and **Mary -----**) d. aft 1700, Charlestown, MA?. William died cir 1668.

William Shute, mariner, first appears in Boston records on 1-Jul-1659, the date of his marriage to Hopestill Viall, daughter of the Boston vintner, John Viall. On 1-Dec-1662, William Shute's father-in-law signed an indenture between himself and William Shute, for a house and land in Boston's North End at the corner of present-day Hanover and Battery Streets. The lot measured 44 feet at the front, by 246 feet on the NE side, by 48 feet at the rear, by 265 feet on the SE side, along Battery Alley. Added to this was the use and title of a four-foot wide passageway offering access and drainage to the sea at low water mark. On 9-Feb-1664, John Viall formally deeded this property to William Shute.

Neither an exact birth nor death date is known for William Shute. Thomas Wyman's 1879 work, "The Genealogies and Estates of Charlestown," claimed that William's wife, Hopestill Shute, remarried to a Mr. Pitts. Indeed, Boston records reveal that a William and Hopestill Pitts conceived their first child in 1669. This would infer that Hopestill's first husband, William Shute, died circa 1668. Among published Suffolk County deeds, however, the first reference to a property abutting "the Land of the late William Shute," does not appear until 7-Jun-1678. William Shute's son and namesake, William Shute, did not become the ward of Deacon Obadiah Gill until October 1683. And to further complicate the picture, Wyman recorded that the administration of William Shute's estate was not granted to his son-in-law, John Soley, until 10-Sep-1685.

One plausible explanation is offered if William Shute perished at sea. If no body was found, and no witness survived or stepped forward to attest to his death, William Shute could not have been declared dead for seven years. Technically, then, the land of William Shute would not be described as the land of the "late" William Shute until 1675/76. In addition, William's widow, Hopestill, could not have legally remarried until her first husband was declared dead. As a result, her union with Pitts was premature and therefore irregular, and possibly the reason for Wyman's description of William Shute's widow as Hopestill "Pitts."

Hopestill (Viall) Shute and William Pitts had three children, each born in Boston: Mary (b. Feb-1669/70), Elizabeth (b. 5-Jul-1671) and John Pitts (b. 28-Aug-1674). Hopestill Pitts died sometime after 1700, the year Wyman records Hopestill "Pitts" serving as a witness to a deed from Soley to Phipps.

     Children:
   2.   i **John Shute** b. 7-Mar-1660/61, Boston, Suffolk Co., MA.[3]
+ 3.   ii **Abigail Shute** b. 13-Aug-1662.
+ 4. iii **William Shute** b. 28-Aug-1665.

Second Generation

3. **Abigail Shute** b. 13-Aug-1662, Boston, Suffolk Co., MA,[3] Baptized: 9-Jan-1687,[4] m. (1) bef 1683, **John Soley**, Occupation: Navigator/mariner, d. 16-Sep-1696,[5] m. (2) 1697, in Charlestown, MA, **Jeffery Gray**, d. cir 1706. Abigail died aft 1724. John:

In 1688, Charlestown mariner, John Soley, was Master of the "Swallow," a plantation-built pink of 50 tons. On 25- Aug-1689, the "Swallow" entered Boston harbor after returning from Nevis and St. Christophers, carrying "36 hhds., 1 butt, 1 ter., 7 kkns., and 4 bar. of sugar, 9 hhds. and 5 kkns. of molasses, and 1 kkn. of lime-juice," according to Massachusetts shipping records.

In 1691, John Soley bought a house and wharf in Charlestown from Andrew Belcher, a mariner and merchant- trader, and also the father of the Hon. Jonathan Belcher, future Royal Governor of the Province of Massachusetts Bay, Governor of New Jersey, etc.

                    Children by John Soley:

  5.   i **Abigail Soley** b. 29-Apr-1683, Charlestown, MA,[6] d. 29-Sep-1684, Charlestown, MA.[6]

  6.   ii **Mary Soley** b. 12-Feb-1687, Charlestown, MA,[6] m. 9-Jan-1704/05, in Charlestown, MA,[7] **Nicholas Rowland**, d. aft 1706. Mary died aft 1705.

+ 7.   iii **John Soley** b. 13-Sep-1690.

+ 8.   iv **Abigail Soley** b. 17-Jun-1692.

+ 9.   v **Margaret Soley** b. 21-Jul-1694.

                    Children by Jeffery Gray:

 10.   vi **William Gray** b. 5-Sep-1702, Charlestown, MA,[6] d. 5-Sep-1702, Charlestown, MA.[6]

4. **William Shute** b. 28-Aug-1665, Boston, Suffolk Co., MA,[3] Occupation: Carver, m. 19-May-1690, in Boston, Suffolk Co., MA,[8] **Martha Budd**, b. 19-Jun-1671, Boston, MA, (daughter of **Edward Budd** and **Dorothy -----**) d. 8-Jan-1721/22, Boston, MA,[9] Buried: Copp's Hill Burial Ground, Boston, MA. William died aft Apr-1724, Boston, Suffolk Co., MA?.

At the October 1683 term of the Inferior Court of Pleas, held at Boston, William Shute was made the ward of Obadiah Gill (1650-1700), a deacon of the North Church, and son of the Boston mariner, John Gill (d. 1671). At the time, William Shute was 18 years old. Four years later, in 1687, William Shute first appeared on the Boston tax rolls, and in 1695, William Shute was included in a list of inhabitants in Boston.

William Shute, like his father-in-law, Edward Budd, was a ship's carver by trade. On 3-Apr-1695, William Shute testified at Boston's Inferior Court of Common Pleas on behalf of his first cousin, Edward Budd, who was suing Ralph Sadler, a Boston mariner, for fees due from carving the taffrail of his new ship (built by Ralph Chapman, shipwright). Shute and George Robinson swore they had "taken a view of a certain Tafrill made by Mr. Edward Budd for the use of Capt. Sadler [and] doo judge it to be worth the money the said Budd has valued it at [of] five pounds fifteen shillings." The court found for Budd.

In January 1699/1700, William Shute was paid for his carving work on Joseph Buckley's (his first-cousin's husband) sloop, "Swallow." On 23-Oct-1706, William Shute, carver, co-signed a 600 pound surety with Michael Shute's widow, Mary (Rainsford) Shute, for letters of administration on her husband's estate. The bond was witnessed by Thomas Maccarty, son of William's uncle Richard Shute's partner, Thaddeus Maccarty.

William and Martha (Budd) Shute lived in a house on the north side of Battery Alley (now Battery Street) in Boston's North End. In August 1717, William Shute and his neighbors (Josiah Langdon, Lydia Shute [signing for her husband, Richard Shute], William Gill and John Langdon) petitioned the Selectmen of Boston to widen Battery Alley to eleven feet. The selectmen agreed to the project on 31-Aug-1717, which also seemingly redirected the street to the northeast between Shute's home and his neighbor William Gill.

In April 1724, Battery Alley and William Shute were once again before the selectmen. Shute's neighbor, Mr. Parkman had successfully diverted waste water runoff from Ship Street from his property into the alley directly. The selectmen ordered that a four-foot wide strip of Parkman's land, abutting William Shute's property, "Be keept clear for carrying off the wast water out of Ship Street & Battery alley to the Sea to Low water mark, In order to Prevent the Said nusance for the future, and that the Said four feet be paved at the charg of the Town." [See the published Records of Boston Selectmen, 1716 to 1736.]

William's wife, Martha, died on 8-Jan-1721/22 and was buried at Copp's Hill Burial Ground. A death date is not known for William Shute who may have survived as late as 21- Apr-1742, the date a "committee appointed to run the line between the North Battery Ground and Mr. Parkman's land" referred to the properties of "messrs. Parkman & Shute" [See the published Records of Boston Selectmen, 1736-1742].

Children:

11.	i	**Abigail Shute** b. 31-Jul-1691, Boston, Suffolk Co., MA,[3] d. 27-Sep-1692, Boston, Suffolk Co., MA.[2]
12.	ii	**William Shute** b. 22-Mar-1693, Boston, Suffolk Co., MA,[3] m. 26-Nov-1725, in Boston, MA,[10] **Elizabeth Allison.**
+ 13.	iii	**Martha Shute** b. cir 1694.
14.	iv	**Richard Shute** b. 12-Aug-1696, Boston, Suffolk Co., MA.[3]
15.	v	**Elizabeth Shute** b. 18-Sep-1697, Boston, Suffolk Co., MA.[3]
16.	vi	**Mary Shute** b. 1-Mar-1699, Boston, Suffolk Co., MA.[3]
17.	vii	**John Shute** b. 3-Aug-1700, Boston, Suffolk Co., MA.[11]
18.	viii	**Abigail Shute** b. 9-Aug-1703, Boston, Suffolk Co., MA.[11]

Third Generation

7. **John Soley** b. 13-Sep-1690, Charlestown, MA,[6] m. 3-Jul-1716,[5] **Dorcas Coffin**, b. 22-Jul-1693, Nantucket, MA, (daughter of **Nathaniel Coffin** and **Damaris Gayer**) d. 8-May-1778, Charlestown, MA.[5] John died 1735.[5]

        Children:
+ 19.   i **Mary Soley**.
+ 20.   ii **Dorcas Soley** b. 28-Aug-1719.
+ 21.   iii **John Soley** b. 5-Jun-1722.
+ 22.   iv **Abigail Soley** b. 26-May-1724.
+ 23.   v **Lydia Soley** b. 3-May-1726.
   24.   vi **Matthew Soley** b. 21-Apr-1728, Charlestown, MA.[5]

8. **Abigail Soley** b. 17-Jun-1692, Charlestown, MA,[6] m. (1) 26-Oct-1710, in Charlestown, MA,[7] **John Rainer**, b. 15-Oct-1687, Charlestown, MA,[6] (son of **John Rainer** and **Abigail Hathorne**) d. bef 28-Nov-1721,[6] m. (2) 19-Aug-1728, in Charlestown, MA,[6] **John Tucker**.

        Children by John Rainer:
   25.   i **Abigail Rainer** b. 15-Aug-1711, Charlestown, MA,[6] d. 28-Nov-1721, Charlestown, MA.[12]
+ 26.   ii **John Rainer** b. 4-Jul-1714.
   27.   iii **Thomas Rainer** b. 12-Apr-1715, Charlestown, MA.[6]

9. **Margaret Soley** b. 21-Jul-1694, Charlestown, MA,[6] m. cir 1715, **Thomas Taylor**, b. Charlestown, MA, Baptized: 24 (5) 1693, Charlestown, MA,[5] (son of **John Taylor** and **Katharine Johnson**) Occupation: Shipwright, d. 25-Aug-1740, Charlestown, MA.[5] Margaret died 14-Feb-1766, Charlestown, MA.[5]

        Children:
+ 28.   i **Margaret Taylor** b. 15-Nov-1716.
+ 29.   ii **Abigail Taylor** b. 9-Jul-1719.
   30.   iii **Katharine Taylor** b. 19-Feb-1721/22, Charlestown, MA.[5]
   31.   iv **Thomas Taylor** b. 28-Aug-1724, Charlestown, MA,[5] d. aft 1748.
+ 32.   v **Sarah Taylor** b. 15-Feb-1726/27.
   33.   vi **Mary Taylor** b. 15-Mar-1728/29, Charlestown, MA.[5]
+ 34.   vii **John Taylor** b. 28-Apr-1731.
   35. viii **Dorcas Taylor** b. 17-May-1733, Charlestown, MA,[5] d. 1762, Buried: 2-Nov-1762.[5]
   36.   ix **William Taylor** b. 12-Sep-1735, Charlestown, MA,[5] m. 1-Oct-1761, in Charlestown, MA,[5] **Ruth Austin**, b. 20-Feb-1739/40, Charlestown, MA,[5] (daughter of **Thomas Austin** and **Ruth Frothingham**). William died 1762.[5]

13. **Martha Shute** b. cir 1694, Boston, Suffolk Co., MA?, m. (1) 17-Dec-1712, in Boston, Suffolk Co., MA,[13] **Edward Burbeck**, d. bef 1738, Boston, Suffolk Co., MA?, m. (2) 7-Dec-1738, in Boston, Suffolk Co., MA,[2] **Ebenezer White**.

    Martha Shute, the presumed daughter of William and Martha (Budd) Shute, is not to be found in Boston birth records. Her marriage, however, is recorded in Boston town records. Given her name and approximate age, as well as the "gap" in Martha (Budd) Shute's recorded childbirths, she has been included as a child of William and Martha (Budd) Shute.

Children by Edward Burbeck:

37.   i **Martha Burbeck** b. 12-Feb-1714, Boston, Suffolk Co., MA,[2] m. 13-Aug-1733, in Boston, Suffolk Co., MA,[2] **Edward Tuttle**.

+ 38.   ii **William Burbeck** b. 22-Jul-1716.

+ 39. iii **Edward Burbeck** b. 18-Dec-1723.

Fourth Generation

19. **Mary Soley** Baptized: 1-Sep-1717, Charlestown, MA,[5] m. 6-Jan-1736/37, in Charlestown, MA,[5] **Nathaniel Gorham**, Occupation: Captain. Mary died 12-May-1800, Boston, Suffolk Co., MA.[5]
> Children:
+ 40.   i **Nathaniel Gorham** b. May-1738.
  41.   ii **Mary Gorham** b. 24-Feb-1739/40, Charlestown, MA,[5] m. 1763,[5] **Paul Coffin**, Occupation: Rev.
  42.   iii **John Gorham** b. 1742, Charlestown, MA,[5] d. 1761.[5]
  43.   iv **Elizabeth Gorham** b. 14-Jul-1745, Charlestown, MA.[5]
  44.   v **Stephen Gorham** b. 19-Apr-1747, Charlestown, MA.[5]

20. **Dorcas Soley** b. 28-Aug-1719, Charlestown, MA,[5] m. (1) **John Leppington**, Occupation: Captain, m. (2) **John Austin**.
> Children by John Leppington:
  45.   i **John Leppington** b. 23-Feb-1742/43, Charlestown, MA.[5]
  46.   ii **Elizabeth Leppington** b. 3-Jan-1744/45, Charlestown, MA,[5] d. 9-May-1810, Charlestown, MA.[5]
  47.   iii **Rebecca Leppington** b. 5-Feb-1745/46, Charlestown, MA.[5]
  48.   iv **Joshua Leppington** b. 24-Dec-1748, Charlestown, MA.[5]
  49.   v **Samuel Leppington** b. 1-Aug-1750, Charlestown, MA.[5]
  50.   vi **Rebecca Leppington** Baptized: 28-Jul-1751, Charlestown, MA.[5]

21. **John Soley** b. 5-Jun-1722, Charlestown, MA,[5] m. 11-Oct-1759, in Charlestown, MA,[14] **Hannah Cary**, b. 5-Jan-1729/30, Charlestown, MA,[5] (daughter of **Samuel Cary** and **Mary Martyn**) d. 12-Feb-1798, Billerica, MA.[5] John died 18-Nov-1801, Billerica, MA.[5]
> Children:
  51.   i **John Soley** b. 20-May-1761, Charlestown, MA,[6] d. 6-Sep-1761, Charlestown, MA.[6]
  52.   ii **Hannah Soley** b. 5-Jun-1762, Charlestown, MA,[6] m. (1) **William G. Maccarty**, (son of **Thaddeus Maccarty** and **Mary Gatcomb**) d. 13-Aug-1791, Charlestown, MA,[5] m. (2) 16-May-1796, in Billerica, MA,[15] **Nathan Adams**, b. cir 1760, Charlestown, MA, Occupation: Merchant/tanner, d. 11-Sep-1830, Charlestown, MA.[5] Hannah died 26-Jan-1842.[5]
  53.   iii **Mary Soley** b. 17-Oct-1763, Charlestown, MA,[6] d. 24-Nov-1763, Charlestown, MA.[6]
+ 54.   iv **John Soley** b. 1-Feb-1765.
  55.   v **Samuel Soley** b. 13-Aug-1766, Charlestown, MA,[5] m. 24-Jan-1797, in Charlestown, MA,[5] **Elizabeth Larkin**. Samuel died Jan-1830, NY.[5]
  56.   vi **Nathaniel Soley** Baptized: 7-Aug-1768, Charlestown, MA.[5]
  57.   vii **Mary Soley** Baptized: 13-Aug-1769, Old South Church.[5]
  58.   viii **Mary Soley** Baptized: 13-Oct-1771, Old South Church,[5] m. **Thomas Kettell**.

22. **Abigail Soley** b. 26-May-1724, Charlestown, MA,[5] m. (1) 29-May-1744, in Charlestown, MA,[16] **John Asbury**, b. 29-May-1723,

Charlestown, MA,[5] (son of **John Asbury** and **Anne Blunt**) Occupation:
Founder, d. bef 1748, m. (2) 1754, in Charlestown, MA,[5] **John
Codman**. Abigail died aft 1761.
Children by John Asbury:
59.   i **John Asbury** b. 22-Oct-1745, Charlestown, MA,[5] d.
15-Mar-1748, Charlestown, MA.[5]

23. **Lydia Soley** b. 3-May-1726, Charlestown, MA,[5] m. (1) 4-Dec-1746,
in Charlestown, MA,[5] **John Stevens**, b. 29-Aug-1723, Charlestown,
MA,[5] (son of **John Stevens** and **Abigail Wyer**) d. 1748, m. (2)
26-Apr-1753, in Haverhill, MA, **Stephen Greenleaf**, b. 16-Apr-1694,[5]
(son of **Tristram Greenleaf** and ----- -----) d. cir 1755, m. (3)
Caleb Call. Lydia died aft 1775, Rockingham Co., NH.[17]
Children by John Stevens:
+ 60.   i **John Stevens** b. 26-Feb-1747/48.

26. **John Rainer** b. 4-Jul-1714, Charlestown, MA,[6] Occupation:
Cooper, m. 23-Feb-1737/38, in Charlestown, MA,[5] **Anne Rand**, d. aft
1775. John died 20-Nov-1760, Charlestown, MA.[5]
Children:
61.   i **John Rainer** b. 15-Jan-1738/39, Charlestown, MA,[5] d.
17-Aug-1761, Charlestown, MA.[5]
+ 62.   ii **Thomas Rainer** b. 10-Nov-1740.
63.   iii **Abigail Rainer** b. 28-Apr-1744, Charlestown, MA,[5] d.
17-Nov-1764, Charlestown, MA,[5] Buried: 19-Nov-1764,
Charlestown, MA.
+ 64.   iv **James Rainer** b. 4-Nov-1745.
65.   v **Anne Rainer** b. 5-Dec-1747, Charlestown, MA,[5] d. aft
1789.
66.   vi **Elizabeth Rainer** b. 30-Nov-1750, Charlestown, MA,[5] d.
21-Apr-1754, Charlestown, MA.[5]
67.   vii **Isaac Rainer** b. 28-Mar-1753, Charlestown, MA,[5]
Occupation: Hatter, d. 1778.[5]
68.   viii **Hannah Rainer** b. 13-Oct-1758, Charlestown, MA.[5]

28. **Margaret Taylor** b. 15-Nov-1716, Charlestown, MA,[5] m.
2-Feb-1738/39, in Charlestown, MA,[5] **Green Shepard**, Occupation:
Mariner.
Children:
69.   i **Thomas Green** b. 18-Aug-1740, Charlestown, MA.[5]
70.   ii **Mary Green** b. 10-Nov-1742, Charlestown, MA.[5]

29. **Abigail Taylor** b. 9-Jul-1719, Charlestown, MA,[5] m. **John Ernest
Pitcher**, Occupation: Sugar-boiler, d. 5-Sep-1780, Marlborough, MA.[5]
Abigail died bef 1755.
Children:
71.   i **John Ernest Pitcher** b. 8-May-1742, Charlestown, MA.[5]
72.   ii **Abigail Pitcher** b. 26-Jan-1743/44, Charlestown, MA.[5]
73.   iii **David Pitcher** b. 9-Dec-1745, Charlestown, MA.[5]
74.   iv **Thomas Pitcher** b. 1-Mar-1747, Charlestown, MA.[5]
75.   v **Jacob Pitcher** b. 3-Aug-1750, Charlestown, MA.[5]
76.   vi **Sarah Pitcher**.

32. **Sarah Taylor** b. 15-Feb-1726/27, Charlestown, MA,[5] m. 3-Oct-1745, in Charlestown, MA,[5] **Thomas Mardlen Jr.**, b. 25-Aug-1721, Charlestown, MA, (son of **Thomas Mardlen** and **Abigail Adams**) Occupation: Shipwright, d. 1756. Sarah died 9-May-1752, Charlestown, MA.[5]

               Children:
- 77.   i   **Sarah Mardlen** Baptized: 31-Aug-1746, Charlestown, MA.[5]
- 78.   ii   **Abigail Mardlen** Baptized: 24-Apr-1748, Charlestown, MA.[5]
- 79. iii   **----- Mardlen** b. 23-Apr-1752, Charlestown, MA,[5] d. 23-Apr-1752, Charlestown, MA.

34. **John Taylor** b. 28-Apr-1731, Charlestown, MA,[5] Occupation: Mariner, m. 15-Jul-1755, in Charlestown, MA,[5] **Sarah Mardlen**, b. 29-Sep-1730, Charlestown, MA,[5] (daughter of **Thomas Mardlen** and **Abigail Adams**) d. aft 1789. John died bef 1777.

               Children:
- 80.   i   **Thomas Taylor** b. 21-Feb-1756, Charlestown, MA.[5]
- 81.   ii   **Thomas Taylor** b. 30-Aug-1757, Charlestown, MA.[5]
- 82. iii   **Sarah Taylor** b. 12-Mar-1760, Charlestown, MA,[5] m. **Thomas Smith**.
- 83.   iv   **Abigail Taylor** Baptized: 13-Dec-1761, Charlestown, MA.[5]
- 84.   v   **William Taylor** Baptized: 4-Dec-1763, Charlestown, MA.[5]
- 85.   vi   **Margaret Taylor** Baptized: 23-Nov-1766, Charlestown, MA,[5] m. **Cotton Center**.
- 86. vii   **Hannah Taylor** Baptized: 9-Sep-1770, Charlestown, MA,[5] m. **Rowland Center**.

38. **William Burbeck** b. 22-Jul-1716, Boston, Suffolk Co., MA,[2] Occupation: Woodcarver/Colonel, m. (1) 3-Sep-1737, in Boston, Suffolk Co., MA,[2] **Abigail Tuttle**, d. bef 1748, Boston, Suffolk Co., MA, m. (2) 7-Oct-1749, in Boston, Suffolk Co., MA,[2] **Jerusha Glover**, b. 3-Dec-1722, Dorchester, MA, (daughter of **John Glover** and **Susannah Ellison**) d. 27-Jul-1777, Boston, Suffolk Co., MA,[9] Buried: Copp's Hill Burial Ground, Boston, MA. William died 22-Jul-1785, Boston, Suffolk Co., MA,[18] Buried: Copp's Hill Burial Ground, Boston, MA.[9]

    William Burbeck, a woodcarver by trade, made a study of gunnery and pyrotechnics. He created the fireworks used in the celebration of the Stamp Act. In 1769, he was second officer, or gunner, at Castle William, and at the close of 1775, he succeeded Col. Gridley in command of the Massachusetts Artillery. After the war, he was again stationed at Castle William, albeit under a new flag.

    William and Jerusha (Glover) Burbeck had nine children.

               Children by Abigail Tuttle:
-   87.   i   **Abigail Burbeck**.
- + 88.   ii   **Edward Burbeck** b. cir 1738.
               Children by Jerusha Glover:
-   89. iii   **William Burbeck** Baptized: 15-Mar-1749/50, Christ Church, Boston, MA.[19]
-   90.   iv   **Jerusha Burbeck** Baptized: 16-Jun-1751, Christ Church, Boston, MA.[19]

91. v **Mary Burbeck** Baptized: 19-Apr-1753, Christ Church, Boston, MA.[19]

92. vi **Henry Burbeck** b. 8-Jun-1754, Boston, Suffolk Co., MA,[20] Occupation: Brigadier general, d. 2-Oct-1848, New London, New London Co., CT.[20]

    Henry Burbeck served with distinction in the Revolutionary War. In 1776 he was a lieutenant and participated in the battles of Brandywine and Germantown, and spent that winter at Valley Forge. He was part of the general retreat through New Jersey, and present at the battle of Monmouth. In 1777, he was made a captain in the artillery, and continued in active service until the close of the war, when he received the brevet of major.

    In 1786, Burbeck again entered the service as a captain in the artillery, and served under Gen. Anthony Wayne in the Indian war on the western frontier. After several promotions he received the rank of colonel in the artillery, and in 1813, during the War of 1812, the brevet of brigadier- general. In 1815, aged 59, he was mustered out of service.

93. vii **John Burbeck** Baptized: 12-Oct-1755, Christ Church, Boston, MA.[19]

+ 94. viii **Joseph Burbeck**.

95. ix **Thomas Burbeck** Baptized: 27-Aug-1758, Christ Church, Boston, MA.[19]

96. x **Mary Burbeck** Baptized: 11-Jul-1762, Christ Church, Boston, MA.[19]

97. xi **Susannah Burbeck** Baptized: 18-Apr-1765, Christ Church, Boston, MA.[19]

39. **Edward Burbeck** b. 18-Dec-1723, Boston, Suffolk Co., MA,[2] m. **Ann** -----.

    Children:

98. i **William Burbeck** Baptized: 16-Jul-1748, Christ Church, Boston, MA.[19]

99. ii **Martha Burbeck** Baptized: 2-Apr-1750/51, Christ Church, Boston, MA.[19]

Fifth Generation

40. **Nathaniel Gorham** b. May-1738, Charlestown, MA, Baptized: 21-May-1738, Charlestown, MA,[5] Occupation: Merchant/State Senator, m. 6-Sep-1763, in Charlestown, MA,[5] **Rebecca Call**, b. cir 1743, Charlestown, MA, d. 18-Nov-1812, Charlestown, MA.[5] Nathaniel died 11-Jun-1796, Charlestown, MA.[5]

Nathaniel Gorham, great-grandson of William Shute's daughter, Abigail (Shute) Soley, was described by Wyman in "Charlestown Genealogies and Estates" as: "One of the most eminent men ever resident in town; merchant; served apprenticeship with Nathaniel Coffin, at New London, CT; representative to General Court, and Speaker of the House; delegate to Provincial Congress, 1774-5; member of the Board of War, 1778-1781; delegate to State Constitutional Convention, 1779; State Senator; member of the Governor's Council; Judge of the C. C. P.; delegate to Continental Congress two terms, and its President in 1786; in 1787 a delegate in convention which framed the Constitution of the United States, where he took high rank, and sometimes presided in the absence of Washington; took refuge at Lunenburg, when Charlestown was burnt, 1775, but returned soon after."

Children:
- 100.   i **Nathaniel Gorham** b. 25-Oct-1763, Charlestown, MA.
- 101.   ii **Rebecca Gorham** b. 20-Mar-1765, Charlestown, MA.
- 102. iii **Mary Gorham** b. 7-Dec-1767, Charlestown, MA.
- 103.   iv **Elizabeth Gorham** b. 21-Jul-1769, Charlestown, MA.
- 104.   v **Ann Gorham** Baptized: 3-Mar-1771, Charlestown, MA.
- 105.   vi **John Gorham** Baptized: 22-Nov-1772, Charlestown, MA.
- 106. vii **Benjamin Gorham** b. 13-Feb-1775, Charlestown, MA.
- 107. viii **Stephen Gorham** b. cir 1776, Charlestown, MA, d. 22-Jun-1849, Charlestown, MA.
- 108.   ix **Lydia Gorham** b. Charlestown, MA.

54. **John Soley** b. 1-Feb-1765, Charlestown, MA,[6] Occupation: Counsellor/judge, m. 28-Nov-1804, **Rebecca Tyng Henley**. John died aft 1789.

Children:
- 109.   i **Catharine H. Soley**.
- 110.   ii **Mary R. Soley**.
- 111. iii **John J. Soley**.
- 112.   iv **Hannah L. C. Soley**.
- 113.   v **James R. Soley**.

60. **John Stevens** b. 26-Feb-1747/48, Boston, Suffolk Co., MA,[5] m. 23-Jun-1769, in Charlestown, MA,[5] **Sarah Wood**. John died 31-Dec-1792, Concord, NH.[5]

Children:
- 114.   i **Grace Stevens** b. 26-Mar-1770, Charlestown, MA.[5]

62. **Thomas Rainer** b. 10-Nov-1740, Charlestown, MA,[5] Occupation: Baker, m. 10-Nov-1763, in Charlestown, MA,[5] **Abigail Stone**, b. cir 1747, d. 27-Feb-1792, Reading, MA.[5] Thomas died 17-Oct-1804, Reading, MA,[5] Buried: Reading, MA.

Children:

115.   i **John Rainer** b. 8-Mar-1764, Charlestown, MA,[5] d. 5-Jul-1765, Charlestown, MA,[5] Buried: 6-Jul-1765, Charlestown, MA.

116.   ii **Abigail Rainer** b. 3-Jun-1765, Charlestown, MA,[5] m. **James Emerson Jr.**.

117.   iii **John Rainer** b. 9-Sep-1766, Charlestown, MA,[5] Occupation: Baker, m. 1789,[5] **Mary Eaton**, b. Reading, MA. John died 1833, Charlestown, MA.[5]

118.   iv **Anne Rainer** Baptized: 25-Dec-1768, Charlestown, MA,[5] m. **Thomas Bryant**, Occupation: Bricklayer. Anne died aft 1812.

119.   v **Sarah Rainer** Baptized: 12-May-1771, Charlestown, MA,[5] d. bef 1800.

120.   vi **Thomas Rainer** Baptized: 2-May-1773, Charlestown, MA.[5]

121.   vii **Thomas Rainer** b. 14-Apr-1775, Charlestown, MA,[5] d. 20-May-1777, Reading, MA.

122. viii **Thomas Rainer** d. aft 1800.

123.   ix **Jacob Stone Rainer**.

64. James Rainer b. 4-Nov-1745, Charlestown, MA,[5] Occupation: Cooper, m. 2-Oct-1773 int, in Charlestown, MA,[5] **Katharine Bispham**. James died 1783.[5]

        Children:

124.   i **James Rainer** b. cir 1775, Charlestown, MA, d. 11-Feb-1793, Charlestown, MA.[5]

125.   ii **Katharine Rainer** m. **Thomas Edmands**.

126.   iii **Elizabeth Rainer** b. cir 1777, Charlestown, MA, d. 2-Jul-1797, Charlestown, MA.[5]

127.   iv **John Rainer** b. 1779, Newburyport, Essex Co., MA, d. 4-Jul-1856, Boston, Suffolk Co., MA.[5]

88. Edward Burbeck b. cir 1738, Boston, Suffolk Co., MA, Occupation: Woodcarver/Captain, m. 23-Mar-1761, in Boston, Suffolk Co., MA,[21] **Jane Milk**, b. 16-Sep-1739, (daughter of **John Milk** and **Jane Brown**). Edward died 23-Jun-1782, Newburyport, Essex Co., MA.

    Edward Burbeck, like his father before him trained as a woodcarver but was also adept with artillery. He served as a captain of artillery, 1775, and, by tradition, was one of the "Boston Tea Party." He removed to Newburyport, MA, where he was killed in his house by a stroke of lightning.

        Children:

128.   i **Jane Burbeck** Baptized: 11-Oct-1761, Christ Church, Boston, MA.[19]

129.   ii **Abigail Burbeck** Baptized: 2-Sep-1764, Christ Church, Boston, MA.[19]

130.   iii **William Burbeck** b. 3-Aug-1771, m. **Thankful Weston**. William died 27-Apr, Battle Creek, MI.

94. Joseph Burbeck Baptized: 21-Nov-1756, Christ Church, Boston, MA,[19] m. **Elizabeth -----**, b. cir 1762, d. 10-Dec-1815,[9] Buried: Copp's Hill Burial Ground, Boston, MA. Joseph died 26-Mar-1820,[9] Buried: Copp's Hill Burial Ground, Boston, MA.

        Children:

131.   i **Joseph Burbeck** b. cir 1784, d. 13-Nov-1811,[9] Buried:
        Copp's Hill Burial Ground, Boston, MA.
132.   ii **Henry Burbeck** b. cir 1794, d. 27-May-1820,[9] Buried:
        Copp's Hill Burial Ground, Boston, MA.

[1] Pope's Pioneers of Mass. (1965)

[2] VR/Boston, MA

[3] Appleton's Boston Births, Marriages & Deaths 1630-1699

[4] Wyman's Charlestown Genealogies; Savage's Gen. Dict.

[5] Wyman's Charlestown Genealogies

[6] VR/Charlestown, MA

[7] VR/Charlestown, MA [Rev. Mr. Simon Bradstreet]

[8] Appelton's Boston Births, Marriages & Deaths [Samuel Sewall Esq.]

[9] Whitmore's Graveyards of Boston, Vol. 1 (1878).

[10] McGlennan's Boston Marriages 1700-1809 [Mr. Samuel Miles]

[11] Appleton's Boston Births, Marriages & Deaths 1700-1780

[12] VR/Charlestown, MA ["dau. of widow Abigail Raynor" smallpox]

[13] VR/Boston, MA [Rev. Mr. Samuel Miles]

[14] VR/Charlestown, MA [Rev. Thomas Prentice]

[15] Wyman's Charlestown Genealogies; VR/Charlestown, MA [24-Apr-1796 int.]

[16] VR/Charlestown, MA [Rev. Mr. Hull Abbot]

[17] Wyman's Charlestown Genealogies 444

[18] Bridgman's Memorials of the Dead in Boston (1852)

[19] NEHGS, Vol. 100.

[20] Appleton's Cyc. of Amer. Biog.

[21] VR/Boston, MA [Rev. Andrew Elliot]

Appendix A.

Will of Richard Shute (1631-1703)

In the Name of God Amen. I Richard Shute of Boston in the county of Suffolk within Her Majesty's Province of the Massachusetts Bay in New England, Mariner, being Sick and weak in Body, & drawing near the Gates of Death; Yet through the mercy and goodness of Almighty God, of Sound and perfect memory and understanding, praised be his name therefore, I do make and ordain this my present Will, to be my very last and onely Will and Testament in manner and forme following. --

That is to say, First and principally I humbly and heartily bequeath my precious Soul into the hands of God my Creator, hopeing and Trusting in the alone merit and mediation of Jesus Christ my Redeemer to have my Sins pardoned, and my person accepted. And my body I commit unto the Earth, decently to be interred at the discretion of my Executors or Such of them as shall at the time of my decease be present, as I shall herein after appoint. And I do hereby revoke and make utterly void and of none Effect all other Wills and Wills by me formerly made, whether by Word or writeing. And as to that Portion of Worldly Goods and Estate, which God of his mercy has given unto me, I do give and dispose of the same in manner and forme as is in these presents particularly mentioned and expressed.

Imp'es: Thereby appoint that my just Debts and funeral charges be paid and defreyed within convenient time after my decease.

Item: Whereas at the time of my Marriage with my present Wife Katherine Shute I made her a Joynter of Ten pounds per annum dureing her natural life after my decease, and for Security of the payment of said Sum, I made over my Farme at Maulden as [?] said contract or Agreement between us may appear I do now to clear my said Farme hereby give and bequeath unto my said beloved Wife Katherine Shute the full Sum of Twelve pounds currant money of New England per annum to be paid unto her my said Wife, by my Executors or Some of them as I shall hereafter appoint, quarterly, viz Three pounds at the end of every three months Successively from the time of my decease dureing the natural life of my said Wife, on condition she quitt the Engagement I gave her of my aforesaid Farme, And also I give unto my said Wife my best bed and furniture to the same belonging, to be improved by her dureing her natural life, and one Silver Spoon forever.

Item: My Will is that no Division of my Farme, parts of Vessells or money be made until after my said Wife's decease.

Item: I give unto my Son Michael Shute my Silver Tankard, and unto my Son Richard Shute my Silver Bekor, and unto my daughter Joanna Buckley my Silver Porringer.

Item: My Mind and Will is, that all my household Goods and Utensills whatsoever, be equally divided unto and among my said Three children immediately after my decease, to each of them part and part alike (excepting what is before bequeathed).

Item: I do hereby give & bequeath unto my Grandaughters Elizabeth Nicholls and Hannah Mountfort (the daughters of my said Daughter Joanna Buckley) to each of them the Sum of Twenty five pounds, viz Fifty pounds money to both of them, and to my other Twelve Grandchildren, viz my Son Michael's Five Daughters, my Son Richard's four children, and my Daughter Joanna Buckley's Three Sons, to each of the said Twelve Grandchildren Forty Shillings in money, and to my Kinsman William Shute, Three pounds in money, all which Legacies are to be paid after my said Wife's decease, which Sums and Legacies being paid, my Will is that all the remaining part of my Estate, That is to say my Farme at Maulden, parts of Vessells and all other Lands and Estate whatsoever, not by me heretofore given or bequeathed, let the same be in any part or place whatsoever, be equally divided between and among my said Sons, Michael Shute and Richard, and my Daughters Joanna Buckley, to each of them part and part alike, to remain to the use of them, their heires and Assignes forever, and that no Division of said Estate be made so long as my Wife shall live. And I do hereby ordain and nominate my Three children, viz Michael Shute, Richard Shute and Joanna Buckley, Widow of Joseph Buckley, late of Boston, Merchant, deceased, Executors of this my Last Will and Testament, and because my said Sons are Seafareing men, and are often abroad I do appoint my said Daughter Joanna Buckley to Act as Sole Executor in their Absence, and to pay all Debts and Legacies and receive all Debts and dues, and make Sale of what may be sold, by herselfe, or with one or both of my other Executors if present to make any Division in Order to the Fulfillment of this my present Will, She my said daughter at any time when demanded rendring an accompt of her proceedings to my other Executors. And I desire all my said children loveingly to Agree & Accord one with the other.

In witness and Testimony whereof, and that all things in this my present Will and Testament are according to my true Intent, Mind and meaning I have hereunto set my hand and Seal the Eleventh day of September Anno Dno One Thousand Seven hundred and three, In the second year of her Majesty's Reign. [signed] Richard Shute.

Signed, Sealed, published and declared by Richard Shute that the within and above written is his Last Will & Testament in presence of us, John Barnard, John Atwood, S. Knight.

Appendix B.

Will of Richard Shute (1666-1742)

In the Name of God, Amen. I Richard Shute of Boston in the county of Suffolk, and Province of the Massachusetts Bay in New England, Mariner, being Weak in Body But of Sound Mind, and Reflecting on the Uncertainty of this Life and the Certainty of Death Do therefore make and Ordain this my Present last will and Testament, in manner and Form Following. That is to Say first and principally I commend my Soul into the Hands of Almighty God hoping thro[ugh] the merritt and Intercession of my Saviour Jesus Christ to have Pardon and free Remission of all my Sins, and Inherit Everlasting Life, and my Body I Submit to the Earth, from whence it was taken, to be decently Interred, at the Discretion of my Executor hereafter Named.

Item: I will that all my Just Debts and funerall Charges Shall be paid as soon as conveniently may be after my Decease. --

Item: I Give and bequeath unto my Son John Shute five Shillings, he being already possessed of the greatest Part of his Grandfather's Estate. --

Item: I give and bequeath to my sons Michaell & Nathan Shute and my Daughter Lydia Maxwell five Shillings Each (having given them their Portions before). --

Item: I give and bequeath all the Remainder of my Estate to my Daughter Mary Shute after my Just Debt and funeral Charges are paid and the foregoing Legacies. --

Lastly I Reverse and make Void all other wills heretofore made, and Appoint my Trusty Friend Mr. Enoch Freeman to be my Sole Executor of this my last will and Testament. In Witness whereof I have hereunto Set my Hand and Seal this Sixteenth Day of April Anno Domini One thousand Seven hundred and thirty Six. -- [signed] Ricd Shute.

Signed, Sealed, published and declared in Presence of us. [signed] John Roberts, Nath'l Greenwood, Joseph Snelling

Appendix C.

Will of Michael Shute (1707-1784)

In th Name of God Amen, I Micahel Shute of the Town of Newmarket in the State of Newhampshire and County of Rockingham, Trader, being thro the goodness of God, of Perfect Mind, and Memory, do make an ordain this my last Will and Testament; First of all I give and Recommend my Soul into the Hand of allmighty God, that gave it, and my Body I Recommend to the Earth, to be Buried in decent Christian Burial, at the discretion of my Executor; and Touching such worldly Estate wherewith it has Pleased God to bless me in this life, I give, demise, and dispose of the same in the Following manner and Form. --

my Will is that all my Debts and Funeral Charges be paid speedily after my decease by my Executor hereafter Named. --

Item: I give and bequeath to my Well beloved Wife Elizabeth Shute, all the Land that I now posess in Newmarket that I bought of Joseph Hall Esq. late of Newmarket deceased & Hubartus Mattoon of Salem in the State of Massichusetts Bay & County of Essex, together with my Mansion House and Barns, during her Natural Life or my Widdows -- and if in case she choses to Marry again, my Will is that she my said Wife Shall forever Quit to my Executor or my Heirs Her Right of Dower in my Estate, upon Receiving from my said Executor or my Heirs the Sum of Fifteen Pounds Lawful money or equal to Forty five Ounces of Silver per Annum during her Natural Life; and further more my will is that she my said Wife, shall have Twelve Cord of Wood per Year during her Natural Life or my Widdow, the aforesaid wood I mean shall be cut, (and hall'd at her own cost and Charge) on fifteen Acres of my Land which I bought of Samuel Gilman Esq. late of Exeter deceased, adjourning to Col. Peter Gilman, Land, Extending the Whole wealth of my Land from Jonathan Colcord, Land, to the Heirs of Theophilis Rundlets, deceased, Land, and likewise Sufficient Fenceing Stuff on said Land to keep the fenceing on her said Land, in Repair during her Natural Life, or Widdowhood -- and further I give unto my said Wife, the One half of all the Household Furniture that we no[w] enjoy together, also two Cows, six Sheep, one Sorre[l], one Chaise, to be at her own disposel forever & further I give unto my said Wife the One third Part of all the Money that shall be found due to me more then what I owe, to be at her own disposel forever. --

Item: I give unto my Son Michael Shute the Sum of Ten Pounds Lawful money to be paid by my Executor at the Expiration of four years after my Decease. --

Item: I give unto my three Daughters, Sarah, Anna, & Mary Shute the whole Improvement or Income of my Farm at Stratham which I bought of John Clark, during the Term of four years from the Twentieth day of October next after the date hereof, I hereby Reserving the wood on said Farm during the aforesaid Term of four years from the aforesaid Twentieth Day of October next, Excepting such as Pines & Birches to Repair the fenceing with. --

Item: I have given unto my Son Thomas Shute, a deed of Forty Acres of Land in the Town of Sanbornton in the State of New Hampshire & County of Strafford, which he now Posesses. --

Item: I give unto my two Sons Joseph & Benjamin Shute & to their Heirs forever, the One Half (in Quantity and Quality) of two Hundred Acres of Land in the aforesaid Town of Sanbornton, which I bought of Daniel Sanborn Esq. of said Sanbornton. --

Item: I give unto my Son Walter Shute a Certain piece of Land Situate and being in Newmarket which I bought of Henry Wiggin as appears by his deed bearing date the Eleventh day of May Anno Domini 1774. --

Item: I give unto my Son John Shute my Large Bible after the decease of my said Wife Elizabeth Shute or after her Widdowhood, and also I give to my said Son John Shute my Watch. --

Item: I give unto my Son William Shute & to his Heirs forever the One half of the Mansion House & Land where he now lives, which I bought of Abraham Libbey by a deed dated the first day of June 1770. --

Item: I give unto my Children hereafter Named, William Shute, John Shute, Walter Shute, Thomas Shute, Joseph Shute, Benjamin Shute, Lydia Wiggins, Elizabeth Shute, Sarah Shute, Anna Shute and Mary Shute, all my Land in Newmarket, which I bought of Joseph Hall Esq. & Hubartus Mattoon aforesaid together with my Mansion House & Barns, that I have given unto my Wife Elizabeth aforesaid during her natural Life or Widdowhood, and after her decease or her Widdowhood to be equally divided among them the aforesaid William, John, Walter, Thomas, Joseph, Benjamin, Lydia, Elizabeth, Sarah, Anna & Mary, for Quantity & Quality, and if in case she my said Wife shall Choose to Marry again, then my Will is tht my aforesaid Children William, John, Walter, Thomas, Joseph, Benjamin, Lydia, Elizabeth, Sarah, Anna & Mary shall pay or cause to be paid unto my said Wife Elizabeth Shute each one his or her proportion of fifteen Pounds Lawful money or equal to forty-five ounces of Silver per Annum during her Natural Life -- and further I give unto my aforesaid Children, William, John, Walter, Thomas, Joseph, Benjamin, Lydia, Elizabeth, Sarah, Anna & Mary all my Farm including the Buildings, thereon in Stratham which I bought of John Clark aforesaid to be equally divided in Quantity & Quality among them the aforesaid William, John, Walter, Thomas, Joseph, Benjamin, Lydia, Elizabeth, Sarah, Anna & Mary as Soon as it shall come into their Posession, which will be at the Expiration of the aforesaid Term of four years from the Twentieth day of October next, wherein I have already given the Improvement & Income of the Farm during the aforesaid Term, unto my three Daughters, Sarah, Anna & Mary Shute. --

Item: I give unto my four Daughters, Elizabeth, Sarah, Anna & Mary Shute, all the other Half of my Household Furniture.

And further I give unto my Six Sons, William Shute, John Shute, Walter Shute, Thomas Shute, Joseph Shute, Benjamin Shute, and to their Heirs forever, Thirty one Acres of Land in Newmarket being part of the forty six Acre Lot I bot of Samuel Gilman Esq. deceased aforesaid, and the fifteen Acres being the Other part of the aforesaid Forty Six Acres Lot, after the decease of my said Wife Elizabeth Shute (or Widdowhood) (to be equally divided in Quantity & Quallity [sic] among them --

And further more I give unto my Six Sons, William, John , Walter, Thomas, Joseph & Benjamin, and their Heirs forever, all my Personal Estate not before given away to be equally divided among them, after my Debts are discharged & Legacys Paid. --

And further I give unto my three Sons, William, John & Walter Shute my Pew in Stratham Meeting house after the decease of my Said Wife. --

Lastly, I do make and [...] Constitute my Son, John Shute, Sole Executor of this my last Will and Testament, and do hereby utterly disallow, Revoke, and disannul all and every other former Testament, Wills, Legacies, bequests and Executors, by me in any wise before Named Wills and bequeathed [...] Ratifying and Confirming this and no other, to be my Last Will & Testament. In Witness whereof I have hereunto Set my hand & Seal this first day of September in the year of our Lord One Thousand Seven hundred & Seventy Eight. Signed, Sealed, published pronounced and declared by the said Michael Shute as his last Will & Testament in the Presence of us, Who in his Presence and in the Presence of each other, have here unto Subscribed our Names -- [signed] Moses Edgerly, Josiah Adams, William Coffin

Appendix D.

Will of Benjamin Shute (1759-1847)

In the name of God, Amen. I, Benjamin Shute of Derry in the county of Rockingham and State of New Hampshire, Husbandman, being weak in body, but of sound and perfect memory, blessed be Almighty God, for the same, do make and publish this my last will and testament in manner and form following, that is to say:

First: I give and bequeath to the chilren of my son Jonathan Shute, whose names are Mary Page, Rebeckah Pearson, Benjamin Shute, Eliza Pilsbury, James Shute, Sarah Bartlett, Jonathan B. Shute and Harriet Shute, the sum of Fifty dollars to be equally divided between them.

Second: I give and bequeath to my daughter Rebeckah Sargent One Hundred dollars, and one cow, and eight bushels of corn and rye, and one hundred pounds of Beef and Pork, and one half of all my household furniture.

Third: I give and bequeath to my sons Michael Shute, William B. Shute and Daniel Shute the sum of Fifty dollars apiece; and I also give and bequeath to the above-named William B. Shute, one half of my wearing apparel, and my chaise and Harness.

Fourth: I give and bequeath to Rev'd Daniel Goodwin the sum of Forty dollars, provided that I shall be in possession of money and good securities for money, to that amount at the time of my decease, but if not, then I give him whatever sum there may be of that description of property not exceding the sum of forty dollars. I also give and bequeath to my daughter Rebeckah Sargent one half of all the money and good securities for money of which I shall be in possession at the time of my decease, after the above-mentioned forty dollars shall have been deducted from the amount of the money and securities, above-mentioned.

Fifth: I give and devise to my son George Shute, his heirs and assigns all my real estate situated in Derry in the County of Rockingham and State of New Hampshire and also all my real estate situated in Londonderry in said county of Rockingham. To have and to hold the same to him the said George Shute, his heirs and assigns forever.

Lastly: As to all the rest, residue and remainder of my Personal estate, whatever, I give and bequeath the same to my son George Shute, his executors, administrators and assigns, to his and their own use and benefit forever.

Also, my will is that from the property above devised and bequeathed to my son George Shute which is hereby made chargable with the payment of the same; he the said George Shute, who is hereby constituted and appointed to be the Executor of this my last will and testament; shall pay the aforesaid several legacies which are to be paid in money, in one year from and after my decease; the cow bequeathed to my daughter Rebeckah Sargent is to be delivered to her at any time which she may choose within one year after my decease; the corn and rye and beef and pork bequeathed to her, to be delivered to her on demand after my decease, as also the furniture above bequeathed to her; and the chaise & harness and the half the wearing apparel bequeathed to my son William B. Shute is to be delivered to him on demand after my decease. I also order and direct that my son

George Shute, shall pay all the just debts which I may owe at the time of my decease, and also the charges and expenses of my funeral, and also that within one year after my decease, he shall purchase and erect at my grave a suitable set of Grave Stones, whereon shall be inscribed my name, age, and the time of my decease, and also the name, age and time of the decease of my first wife Rebeckah Shute and likewise the name, age and time of the decease of my second wife Lucy Shute. And I hereby revoke all former wills by me made.

In witness whereof I have hereunto set my hand and seal this ninth day of January in the year of our Lord One thousand eight hundred and forty six. [signed] Benjamin Shute.

Signed, sealed and declared by the above mentioned Benjamin Shute to be his last will and testament in the presence of us, who at his request, in his presence, have subscribed our names as witnesses thereto -- [signed] John Upton, Samuel Clark, William Anderson.

Bibliography

The following is but a partial list of published works utilized in preparing this work. Additional sources may be found in reviewing the annotated footnotes after each register report.

Babson's History of the Town of Gloucester, Cape Ann
Banks' The Planters of the Commonwealth
Bell's History of Exeter, NH
Bradford's The History of Plymouth Colony
Bridgman's Memorials of the Dead in Boston (1852)
Brighton's Port of Portsmouth Ships and the Cotton Trade 1783-1829 (1986)
Chamberlain's Genealogical Records of Early Settlers of Malden, MA
Clemen's American Marriage Records Before 1699
Coffin's A Sketch of the History of Newbury, Newburyport and West Newbury
Corey's History of Malden, MA, 1633-1785 (1899)
Currier's History of Newbury, MA, 1635-1902
Currier's History of Newburyport, MA 1764-1905 (2 vols.)
Davis' Genealogical Register of Plymouth Families
Farmer's Genealogical Register of the First Settlers of New England
Fitts' History of Newfields, NH 1638-1911
Gage's History of Rowley, MA
Gray's Maine Families in 1790 (3 vols.)
Greene's History of Boothbay, Southport and Boothbay Harbor, ME, 1623-1905
Hammatt's The Hammatt Papers: Early Inhabitants of Ipswich, MA 1633-1700
Holbrook's Boston Beginnings 1630-1699
Holmes' Dictionary of Ancestral Heads of New England Families 1620-1700
Hoyt's Old Families of Salisbury and Amesbury
Lincoln's History of Hingham, MA
Metcalf's One Thousand New Hampshire Notables
Munsell's Index to American Genealogies
New Hampshire Genealogical Record (6 vols.)
Noyes, Libby and Davis' Genealogical Dictionary of Maine and New Hampshire
Parker's History of Londonderry
Poore's Memoir and Genealogy of John Poore (1881)
Pope's Pioneers of Massachusetts
Rose-Troup's The Massachusetts Bay Company and its Predecessors
Runnels' History of Sanbornton, NH (1881)
Savage's Genealogical Dictionary of the First Settlers of New England
Scales' Colonial Era History of Dover, NH
Sewall's The Diary of Samuel Sewall (2 vols.)
Sibley's Harvard Graduates

Spencer's <u>Pioneers on Maine Rivers</u>
Stearns' <u>History of Littleton, NH</u> (1905)
Stearns' <u>History of Plymouth, NH</u> (1906)
Thwing's <u>Inhabitants and Estates of the Town of Boston, 1630-1800</u>
Thwing's <u>The Crooked and Narrow Streets of Boston</u>
Watkins' <u>Old Boston Taverns and Tavern Clubs</u>
Willey's <u>Book of Nutfield</u>
Wyman's <u>Charlestown Genealogies and Estates</u>